P9-DOB-156

the
POLITICS
of
CONGRESS

DAVID J. VOGLER

Wheaton College

Allyn and Bacon, Inc.
Boston • London • Sydney

To all the Voglers and Marshalls,
and to Alice, who is both.

Library of Congress Catalog Card Number: 73–88851

Printed in the United States of America

ISBN: 0-205-04247-3
Third printing . . . May, 1975

Acknowledgements

From *Waiting for Godot* by Samuel Beckett, copyright 1954 by Grove
Press. Reprinted by permission of Grove Press, Inc.

Robert Coover, "The Cat in the Hat for President." From *New American
Review, No. 4*, p. 26.

Lewis Carroll, *Alice's Adventures in Wonderland and Through the Looking
Glass.* From Lancer Books, 1968, page 177.

Donald Barthelme, *City Life*, page 155. Copyright © 1970 by Farrar,
Straus & Giroux. Reprinted by permission.

Joseph Heller, *Catch 22*, pages 47 and 418. © Copyright 1955 by Joseph Heller.
Reprinted by permission of Simon and Schuster, Inc.

Contents

Preface

Two central questions guided the research and writing of this book: How do we evaluate Congress?; and "So what?" By providing some different perspectives for judging congressional performance, and by relating these to reform proposals, I hope to show that a person's judgement of Congress and his support or opposition to specific reform proposals depend on a broad evaluation of the entire political system and not just of short-term legislative goals such as "efficiency" or "standing up to the president." Judging Congress does require some information about the way things are, however, and I have sought to provide this without imposing my own interpretations about the way things ought to be. Political scientists in the past decade have gathered a great deal of information about Congress, and this book brings some of that to you. Unless these "facts" about Congress are viewed within a framework of alternative ways in which the system should operate, though, they do little toward expanding our critical understanding of the politics of Congress. That is why the first chapter is more concerned with alternative views on the way things ought to be than with the way things are.

Even if one understands the legislative process, however, he or she might ask "So what?" Politics, after all, determines who gets what, and detailed explanations about congressional seniority and influence on a particular committee might seem irrelevant to people concerned about their childrens' education, a tax bill, food prices, a war in Indochina, or medical costs. Political scientists are lately coming to understand that policy is the be-all and end-all of politics. In the final chapter I have sought to provide some answers to the question of "So what?" by showing how the politics of Congress is related to the policies which emerge from that body. In providing this policy focus the book gives readers more information on which to base evaluations of congressional performance and proposals for reform.

Nobody, of course, writes a book by himself, and many people helped me. For their criticism, editing, encouragement, reading, teaching, and typing, I thank the following: Ann Shapero Adler, Helen Durant, Dan Friedman, Jay Goodman, Sharon Halpin, Candy Nelson Jacobson, Nancy Perry Klaffky, David Kovenock, Alice Marshall, Donald Matthews, Melinda Murray, Robert Patterson, Harriett Posner, Kathleen Rogers, Carole Williams Segal, Nancy Shepardson, Joan Silva, David Snook, Paulette Sullivan, Anita Teixeira, and Alice Vogler. I also wish to acknowledge the help of the anonymous reviewers selected by the publisher.

CHAPTER 1

Judging Congress

Vladimir: *"Well, Shall we go?"*
Estragon: *"Yes; let's go."*
(They do not move.) (Curtain)

Samuel Beckett
Waiting for Godot

After serving for nine years in what many call "the greatest deliberative body on earth," Eugene McCarthy tagged it "the last primitive society left on earth" and described how senators resembled the savages of New Guinea in their obsession with seniority, taboo, and precedent. In another speech, he referred to the upper chamber as "the leper colony."[1]

Few institutions in America are subject to such widely varying evaluations as Congress. Another former senator, Joseph Clark of Pennsylvania, has expressed his belief "that the legislatures of America, local, state and national, are presently the greatest menace in our country to the successful operation of the democratic process."[2] Stephen K. Bailey, after long study of the institution, comes to a different conclusion: "As one of the great institutional forces in the life of modern man dedicated to the perpetuation of freedom, Congress in the last analysis deserves our respect and our reverence."[3] Consumer advocate Ralph Nader disagrees: "Congress, the anthropologists would say, is a severely acculturating institution. With rigid procedures, seniority rules, pervasive

1

committee secrecy, and a system of petty rewards and giant punishments, the federal legislature faithfully reflects the power alignments in the society. Power goes to those senior legislators who serve powerful interests, while isolation goes to those who merely represent powerless people."[4]

Whenever people judge Congress and congressmen they are acting in terms of some notion of what Congress should be like. Sometimes this takes the form of voting for a candidate who can "straighten out the mess" in Washington, or supporting the incumbent because he has done "a good job." Students who put in long hours working for candidates supported by the Movement for a New Congress or the Universities National Anti-War Fund, or who helped to end the careers of nine of the twelve men listed by the Friends of the Earth as "The Dirty Dozen," might have a more clearly articulated conception of the role Congress should play in the political system. Editorial cartoonists, those who put a bomb in a Senate washroom, political scientists, incumbents pushing for congressional reform, and even the guy who cannot remember his congressman's name but can trace the career of each member of the Oakland Raiders' defense—all have opinions on Congress.

To really understand the "facts" about Congress, one must first realize that these "facts" are never objective statements of reality, that they will vary greatly from one observer to the next. This is true, not only for muckraking journalists and Fourth of July orators, but also for political scientists who employ functional analysis rather than elitist theory, or whose research utilizes statistical manipulation of a large number of cases rather than in-depth analysis of a single case. Any of the "facts" discovered by political scientists or asserted by proponents of a particular ideology take on meaning only when they are considered in terms of the theoretical framework from which they emanate. If a political scientist says that the seniority system is functional for Congress because it precludes hot intraparty battles over who will be chairman of a particular committee, this "fact" can be fully understood only when one takes into account the political scientist's implicit value premise that controlling the level of conflict is a prerequisite for the institution's performing its decision-making functions. Similarly, reformers' efforts to have committee chairmen chosen by open voting in the party caucus, rather than automatically selected on the basis of seniority, can be fully comprehended only when one understands the reformers' choosing the value of faithful representation of public opinion over the value of low-conflict decision-making. In evaluating both proposed reforms and objective "facts," we should heed Edmund Burke's advice of 1782: "In every political proposal we must not leave out of the question the political views and object of the proposer; and these we discover, not by what he says, but by the principles he lays down."[5]

This chapter will outline some of the different ideas people have about what Congress is supposed to do. By looking at these various notions about what Congress is and should be, I hope to provide not only a framework for evaluating the various reforms and proposed changes in the system, but also a means for interpreting the "facts" about how the present system operates.

THE FUNCTIONS OF CONGRESS

Almost everybody will agree that there are certain functions which Congress should perform for the political system as a whole. Voters have expectations about what their congressman should be doing for them. Politicians, political scientists, and the general public all have standards for evaluating the performance of Congress as a whole. Reformers seek to change certain parts of the system to make it better able to perform some functions. All will agree that Congress should be the representative branch and that the many activities a congressman is expected to perform together make up his acting as representative for his district. In a moment we will have a closer look at the different ways in which people think of representation and how that affects their expectations and evaluation of Congress and congressmen. But first, I think it would be helpful to consider the many functions which Congress is expected to perform.

A general list of such expectations would include: representation through the articulation of constituency interests; lawmaking, or representation of constituency interests and/or national interest by reaching decisions; administrative oversight; public education by gathering and disseminating information; and constituent service or casework.[6] All of these specific functions may be considered part of the process of representation, and there is considerable overlap among these different functions. A congressman's helping a constituent to solve a minor problem with a federal agency, for instance, might lead to the congressman's obtaining information useful in drafting legislation and passing a law or to his beginning public hearings on that agency. But it is worth considering these functions at a specific level because, as we shall see, the relative importance one attaches to different activities will lead to quite different conceptions of the proper legislative role.

Representation through Interest Articulation

The common notion of Congress is that of a forum where the interests and demands of all of the many groups in society are expressed. A congressman is expected to act as a spokesman for the different ethnic, economic, religious, political, and professional groups within his geographic district. The idea of Congress as a slow-moving deliberative body is closely associated with representation in this sense. Political scientists often talk of Congress's maintaining the stability of the political system by its acting as a "safety valve" which partially disarms potentially disruptive groups by permitting expression of grievances and demands. Similarly, the agonizingly slow movement toward decision on matters such as civil rights is regarded by some observers as important because the consensus produced by such deliberation means that the decision, when it comes, is regarded as legitimate by almost all groups in the society.

Many of the points made in current debates over the role of Congress are directly related to expectations stemming from this conception of representation. If the overwhelming presidential victory in 1964 gives Lyndon Johnson a secure position for implementing his policies on Vietnam, how is the citizen who disagrees with these policies in 1965 able to have his views represented? If blacks constitute 20 percent of a particular congressman's district, should he devote all of his efforts to implementing the position on a civil rights measure favored by the white majority in his district or should he at least articulate the demands of his black constituents? If certain interest groups in a district supported the losing candidate in the last congressional election, must they suffer lack of representation in the national forum for two years? All of these questions center not so much on implementing majority decisions through the voting behavior of congressmen as they do on expressing the interests of electoral minorities by a congressman's participation in debate, casework, and other activities. Associated with this conception of representation we find the ideas of decentralization, access for a vast number of groups to the government, the predominance of local interests over some national interest expressed through presidential elections and national parties, and, generally, the idea that Congress should be an avenue for providing inputs into the political system independent of those which come through the executive branch.

Lawmaking

The term representation is used in another sense when people talk about the need for Congress to be responsive to policy mandates, however unclear, expressed in the last election. To be representative in this sense requires that Congress at some point call a halt to the articulation of interests and debate; that it arrive at a policy decision. When the Senate considers a tax bill, for example, a lot of time is given to the representation of groups, individuals, and industries seeking tax benefits. Most senators feel that they should articulate the demands made by any significant group in their states. If depletion allowances for Florida's phosphate industry are proposed by that state's senators, then surely no final action on the bill should be taken until Louisiana's senators are able to suggest depletion allowances for industries in that state. But, at some point, the Senate must call a halt to this sort of interest representation. For it also has a responsibility to decide on a final bill; it must end its deliberations and vote. If it does not do this then it is failing to represent all those voters who supported one or the other party's candidates in the last election because of that party's pledge on tax policy.

There are a number of questions associated with this sort of representation by lawmaking. When should a congressman vote against constituency interests in favor of his perception of the national interest? If a majority of his constituents takes a position that the legislator regards as harmful to them, should he vote in line with the expressed will of his constituents or in favor of his perception of their real interests? How much time should the congressman devote to acquiring expertise in areas so that he can cast a well-informed, rational vote, and how much should he spend talking with constituent groups so that he can vote the way they want him to? All of these considerations clearly relate to representation, but there is an important difference between the two ways in which the term is used.

Representation through interest articulation includes the representation of a broad array of minority interests. The congressman is expected to introduce into legislative deliberations not just the positions of the electoral majority in his district, but also the positions of significant minorities. He should, in other words, bring the policy debate from his constituency into the legislative process. But when it comes to actual voting, normal expectations of representation seem quite different. A congressman's vote is expected to be in accordance with some electoral majority relevant to him. This may be his district's majority, an electoral decision in the past presidential election, or what he regards as a policy mandate given his political party. A congressman from a district which is 20 percent black, for instance, might feel that he should represent his black constituents in policy debates over school busing, but that he should represent the white majority's position in voting on the matter.

We have touched on a number of complex questions about the nature of representation which will be discussed more fully later. For now, though, it should be enough to mention the fact that some of the concepts associated with representation as interest articulation are not associated with representation as lawmaking. A decentralized legislative system with many access points, for instance, makes it harder for Congress to arrive at policy decisions within a limited period of time. Congressional emphasis on local matters makes it more difficult to achieve consensus on policies designed to deal with a national or international problem. And transforming party or presidential mandates into policies requires the cutting off of debate and deliberation at some point, a limiting of minorities' expression in order to enact the majority's decision. These differences will be more thoroughly discussed below. Let us first quickly run through the other functions mentioned earlier.

Administrative Oversight

If Congress is to perform effectively its lawmaking function, it must also see that the laws it has passed are administered so as to produce the results intended. Congress seeks to achieve this through the process of administrative oversight. Committee hearings provide a means for congressmen to hear the testimony of those who administer the law and to review the bureaucracy's implementation of its policies. Effectively used, administrative oversight can be a powerful tool for maintaining the integrity of legislation already passed, for gathering information which can serve as the basis for future legislation, and for reducing the amount of discretion, and thus political power, granted to the executive bureaucracy.

Questions of representation also enter into evaluations of congressional performance in overseeing the bureaucracy. It has been suggested, for instance, that the decentralized structure of Congress makes it well suited to performing representation through articulation by its giving vent to the myriad individual dissatisfactions with bureaucratic operations. These sort of challenges to official testimony in hearings are an important avenue of access to the system for groups outside of the administration.

How well Congress fulfills expectations about its oversight functions is one of the considerations of Chapter 6. Some people argue that most of the oversight through hearings is relatively worthless because it does not really change the way bureaucracy behaves, and because it is cursory and ill informed. Others contend that Congress has abdicated much of its lawmaking power by avoiding tough questions through a process of increasing the discretionary power of bureaucracy. If Congress lets administrators decide the meaning of a bill's phrase, how then can it later criticize the administrators for not following the "dictates" of the legislation?

While how well Congress performs this oversight function is subject to debate, it is clear that most people accept such oversight as a legitimate function of Congress and an integral part of its being the representative branch.

Education

The importance of Congress's raising issues and providing forums for educating the public on political matters has long been recognized. Woodrow Wilson, writing in 1885, emphasized this function: "Quite as important as legislation is vigilant oversight of administration; and even more important than legislation is the instruction and guidance in political affairs which the people might receive from a body which kept all national concerns suffused in a broad daylight of discussion."[7]

Much of Congress's information gathering and dissemination is a by-product of its other functions. Public hearings can be convenient forums for articulating interests, a good system for gathering information useful to lawmaking, and an effective vehicle for administrative oversight. But sometimes a legislator or group of legislators will seek to raise issues and disseminate information even when this activity is not directly related to these other functions. Some recent examples: Representative Joseph Reznick's ad hoc hearings on the American Farm Bureau held in the Midwest during 1967–1968; the hearings on air pollution conducted by Representative Leonard Farbstein and other New York congressmen in New York City in November 1969; Senator George McGovern's itinerant hearings on the problems of hunger in the United States; and California Representative Ron Dellum's media-oriented hearings on the Vietnam War.

One can think of many reasons for engaging in such activities. By publicizing the extent of problems in an area a congressman might hope that constituent demands, which are presently nonexistent, will be generated and lead to new legislation. Or, while writing off the likelihood of new programs, a legislator might feel that the general education of the public is one of the goals of any political system. Or, one might feel that such educational activities are important for developing public tolerance of minorities and a sense of community and for maintaining civil liberties.

Constituent Service

An important function of the individual congressman in the American system is acting as a "go-between" for the private citizen and the large, impersonal federal government. Much of the legislator's time and staff are occupied with "casework"—intervention on behalf of a constituent faced with a problem stemming from government activity (or inactivity). Individual representation means that a congressman not only is expected to articulate constituency interests in debate and vote in accordance with the electoral majority, but also to be available to constituents who have a problem.

Former Representative Luther Patrick captured the essence of this constituent service function in suggesting that:

> A Congressman has become an expanded messenger boy, an employment agency, getter-out of the Navy, Army, and Marines, a wardheeler, a wound healer, trouble shooter, law explainer, bill finder, issue translator, resolution interpreter, controversy-oil-pourer, glad hand extender, business promoter, veterans affairs adjuster, ex-servicemen's champion, watchdog for the underdog, sympathizer for the upperdog, kisser of babies, recoverer of lost baggage, soberer of delegates, adjuster for traffic violations and voters straying into the toils of the law, binderup of broken hearts, financial wet nurse, a good samaritan, contributor of good causes, cornerstone layer, public building and bridge dedicator and ship christener.[8]

CONFLICTING FUNCTIONS

So far we have had a brief look at some generally agreed-upon ideas about what functions Congress should be performing in the political system and what a congressman should be doing with his time. But the expectations people have about congressional performance are bound to vary with people's different conceptions of political goals and with their relative economic and political position within society. And any sort of list of universally accepted functions of Congress is bound to gloss over important conflicts about what the proper legislative role is. What we might do, then, is to look at a summary of congressional functions discussed so far and to consider some areas of potential conflict. In Table 1, I have summarized some of the points made earlier about different conceptions of representation and arranged them within a framework suggesting the inherent conflict between maximizing representation through interest articulation and maximizing representation through enactment of electoral mandates. For shorthand reasons, and to comply with common usage, I have used the term representation for the former and lawmaking for

TABLE 1   *Differing Views on the Primary Function of Congress*

Representation	Lawmaking
1. Congress as forum for articulating group interests.	1. Congress as decision-maker which translates popular mandates into law.
2. Emphasis on representation of minorities.	2. Emphasis on majority rule.
3. Favor decentralized legislative structure.	3. Favor centralized legislative system under party presidential leadership.
4. Legislative coalitions formed after elections—likely to be shifting pattern of dissimilar groups brought together through logrolling.	4. Legislative coalitions formed at elections. Congressmen expected to follow party and presidential mandates reflected in elections.
5. "Public interest" defined as the sum of the many constituency interests.	5. "Public interest" defined in national terms as being more than just sum of constituency interests.
6. Constituency casework considered an important part of individual legislator's role.	6. Casework should be largely relegated to staff to free individual congressman for important work.
7. Administrative oversight regarded as a process for advancing ideas and information and for representing interests of constituent groups.	7. Administrative oversight regarded as a process of insuring that mandates of earlier legislation are being carried out.
8. Chief values for evaluating legislative performance center on maximizing the number of groups and interests considered in the legislative process.	8. Chief criterion for evaluating legislative performance is the efficiency with which electoral mandates are translated into policies.

the latter. While I do not want to suggest that these categories are mutually exclusive, I do think that they lead to quite different conceptions of the legislative process and thus to reforms which pull against one another, which cannot increase the potential for achieving one goal without decreasing the chances of satisfying another.

It should be emphasized that this list is not presented with the idea of suggesting two completely distinct and logically incompatible schools of thought as to congressional functions. A particular reformer, for instance, might feel that Congress should strengthen its lawmaking ability so as to become a source of policy independent of the president and national party leadership. The difference between this person and one who wants efficient legislative ratification of presidential programs has more to do with defining representation in terms of legislative constituencies or in national terms than with a question of maximizing lawmaking or representation. Yet I do think that many of the differences in evaluating Congress and the debates over reform reflect an underlying conflict between representation and lawmaking. We might look, then, at instances where people have to make choices and see what the dimensions of conflict are in these cases. The conflict between maximizing representation or lawmaking can be seen both in the choices an individual congressman must make and in the debate at an institutional level over certain reforms.

At the level of an individual congressman's decision-making, this conflict is reflected in the twin demands that he devote considerable time to the study and reflection needed for responsible lawmaking, yet be ever ready to respond to the unending flow of small favors sought by constituents. "I thought I was going to be Daniel Webster," remarked one congressman, "but I found that most of my work consisted of personal work for constituents." Says another: "The least appealing aspect of my job is the service we have to perform for constituents. . . . Too much of our time and energy is diverted in that direction with the result that the opportunity for creative thinking in a legislative way is greatly lessened."[9]

The inconsistency between representational and lawmaking functions is also seen in the choice that a representative must make between pursuing a "House career" with its demands of specializing in some area of policy and making the slow climb up the committee and seniority ladder until reaching some pinnacle, such as Ways and Means Committee, where full time can be devoted to lawmaking functions, or deciding that he prefers to emphasize the representative function of articulating a broad array of constituent interests over many policy areas. Those who choose the latter course often find that maximizing the representational function requires giving up hopes of advancement through the House decision-making hierarchy and seeking instead a Senate seat.

The inconsistency between representational and lawmaking functions is even more pronounced at the institutional level. This is seen both in general evaluations of Congress and in proposals for reform. If a particular Congress maximizes the lawmaking function of efficiently passing legislation, some will denounce it as a "rubber stamp" or "me too" Congress; if it maximizes representation, and delays legislation so that all interests can have a say, it runs the risk of being tagged a "do nothing" Congress. Specific reform proposals highlight the inherent conflict between representation and lawmaking. Debate over reform will generally produce one side arguing for measures to increase the efficiency with which Congress may perform its lawmaking function and the other contending that inefficiency is the price which the legislature must pay if it is to maximize its representational potential.

A 1971 attempt to reform the Senate filibuster rule illustrates this underlying disagreement over functions. Under the present rule, two-thirds of the senators present and voting must agree to invoke cloture cutting off debate on a matter. Otherwise, any senator may speak as long as he wishes. In February 1971 an amendment to Rule 22 was offered which would permit three-fifths of the senators present and voting to cut off debate. Those senators who emphasize the representational function of that body opposed any attempts to reduce the number of senators needed to invoke cloture. Senator William Fulbright suggested that the debate over changing the cloture rule raised the larger question of whether the Senate would "remain an element in the American constitutional process." Stressing the importance of representation over lawmaking, he went on: "Some issues, such as civil rights and war-making power, arise in our kind of governmental community that need time for delay and consideration so that a compromise can be worked out. A simple majority—and that's what it would be if this rule is changed—should not have the right to impose a decision on a significant minority."[10]

Senators in favor of the rules change tended to emphasize the lawmaking function. Senator James Pearson of Kansas was one of these, and he predicted that "eventually the right of the Senate to vote will win out over the right of the Senate to debate." President Nixon also invoked the lawmaking value of efficiency in saying that he endorsed any Senate move "to reform or to adjust its work procedures and schedules in a way that would allow them to deal with business more promptly and expeditiously."[11]

Another reform proposal which required legislators to weigh the relative importance of decision-making and representation was the successful effort to change House rules governing teller votes. The House has three ways of taking nonrecord votes: a voice vote in which the ayes and nays are yelled out; a division vote in which members stand and are counted; and a teller vote in which the members file past tellers who count those favoring and those opposing a measure. Most House votes are taken while the chamber is sitting as a Committee of the Whole House. The Committee of the Whole procedure, which has been used since the First Congress, is intended to maximize the lawmaking function of Congress. Instead of needing a majority of the membership to conduct business (218 members), the Committee of the Whole needs a quorum of only 100. Acting on measures by voice, division, or teller votes, the Committee of the Whole is able rapidly and efficiently to dispose of legislative matters. A teller vote, the longest of the Committee of the Whole procedures, takes only ten minutes to complete as compared to the thirty minutes which must be alloted for each roll call vote.[12]

In terms of decision-making, the teller vote procedure of the Committee of the Whole was seen as an efficient way for the House to meet its responsibilities. But in terms of representation, the nonrecord voting in the Committee of the Whole was regarded as an obstacle to the House's effectively fulfilling its functions. One reason for this is the small turnout produced by non-record votes. On January 29, 1970, for instance, only fifty members took part in a standing vote which rejected an amendment requiring court review before the right of cross examination could be denied to persons whose security clearance was challenged.[13] Teller votes also permitted congressmen to abrogate their representational duties by voting both ways on a measure and by keeping their voting positions a secret from constituents.

The Legislative Reorganization Act of 1970 contained a provision which sought to redress the balance between lawmaking efficiency and representational accountability. Under the new procedures, the House must record teller votes whenever twenty members so request. As in the case of Senate filibuster reform, legislators had to choose between procedures which maximized lawmaking functions and those which maximized representation.

Washington journalist Louis Kohlmeier, Jr. points out that "Congress is the least efficient, and most democratic, of the three branches."[14] The measure of democracy in this case is the representativeness of Congress as compared to the executive or judicial branches. Implicit in such an evaluation is the idea that efficiency and representativeness, while not mutually exclusive, pull in different directions. To maximize efficiency, Congress would have to sacrifice some procedures which assure fuller representation. The basic conflict between the lawmaking and the representation functions is perhaps best demonstrated by looking at two evaluations of Congress which start from these opposing points of view.

The lawmaking function was stressed in a study conducted by the Cambridge, Massachusetts, management consulting firm of Arthur D. Little. "Congressional decision-making," say these management consultants, "is the heart of all Congressional action and effectiveness. Congress does contribute to the process of government not only by its formal decisions; merely its investigation and discussion of public issues assist public understanding, help develop consensus, and thereby facilitate Congressional decisions. But important as they are, neither investigation nor public discussion can justify Congress in the public eye if it does not decide, for when as a body it makes no decisions, it fails to perform its great constitutional function of setting national policy."[15] Starting from such a point of view, the Arthur D. Little people came up with a number of reform proposals designed to improve the efficiency of Congress by reducing the existing points of delay, and points of representation, produced by such procedures as those requiring a full hearing in both Senate and House committee before acting on legislation.

If one emphasizes the legislative function of representation, however, the reforms proposed to streamline the "creaking machinery of the U.S. Congress"—as the Arthur D. Little consultants call it—would do more harm than good. For while the present system may be inefficient, it does provide for fuller representation of all interests than would be achieved in a more streamlined legislative system. A quite different view of what Congress is, and should be, is offered by a leading student of the Senate, Ralph K. Huitt, who starts from a value premise emphasizing the representational function of the legislature:

> Congress has the strength of the free enterprise system; it multiplies the decision makers, the points of access to influence and power, and the creative moving agents. It is hard to believe that a small group of leaders could do better. What would be gained in orderliness might well be lost in vitality and in sensitiveness to the pressures for change.
>
> Moreover, Congress resembles the social system it serves; it reflects the diversity of the country. There is much to be said for a system in which almost every interest can find some spokesman, in which every cause can strike a blow, however feeble, in its own behalf.[16]

The relative emphasis given to the lawmaking and to the representation functions of Congress serves to structure how one evaluates the legislature and to determine the nature of proposed reforms. In the rest of this chapter we will be looking at various models of Congress used to evaluate the legislature and at reform proposals related to these models. While doing so, one should keep in mind the inherent conflict between representation and lawmaking. For "a *perfectly representative* government," Theodore Lowi reminds us, "would be virtually incapable of making a decision!"[17]

MODELS OF CONGRESS

Alexander Hamilton talked for five hours one day at the constitutional convention of 1787 in order to "give my sentiments of the best form of government—not as a thing attainable by us, but as a model which we ought to approach as near as possible."[18] In

1964, political scientist Ralph K. Huitt noted that "there is no 'model' of a proper legislature to which men of good intentions can repair."[19]

Both men use the term "model" to refer to a set of inter-related assumptions and statements about the proper role of the legislature in the American political system. In constructing a model of Congress, the political theorist creates a simplified view of reality by choosing to emphasize certain legislative functions. Evaluations of Congress and reform proposals arise when people compare the existing system with the idealized legislative model. Three different models of Congress will be outlined in this chapter. Two of them focus on the lawmaking function of Congress and one emphasizes the representation function. While both representation and lawmaking are deemed appropriate legislative functions in all three models, it will be seen that the relative value assigned one of these functions over the other leads to quite different conclusions about the proper role of Congress and about the type of reforms needed to improve that institution.

MODELS EMPHASIZING THE LAWMAKING FUNCTION

The Hamiltonian, or Strong President, Model[20]

"A feeble Executive," wrote Hamilton, "implies a feeble execution of the government. A feeble execution is but another phrase for a bad execution; and a government ill executed, whatever it may be in theory, must be, in practice, a bad government."[21] So it was that Hamilton and the early Federalists developed a model of executive-legislative relations which emphasized the need for a president who would dominate the national government. The Congress would have a modifying and ratifying role, but the real initiation and implementation of policy was to lie with the executive. Leonard White has described the Federalist concept of government as one in which "decisions on programs thought out by national leaders might be subject to the vote of popular assemblies, but the latter . . . had neither the capacity, nor the unity, to work out the plans themselves."[22]

The Hamiltonian model was developed in conjunction with a desire to enact a comprehensive Federalist program and a distrust of the people and their representatives. Over a century later, Woodrow Wilson outlined a conception of executive-legislative relations similar to Hamilton's. "Leadership in government," said Wilson, "naturally belongs to its executive officers, who are daily in contact with practical conditions and exigencies and whose reputations alike for good judgement and for fidelity are at stake much more than are those of the members of the legislative body."[23] But the justification for a strong presidency was now made in terms of its more accurately reflecting the wishes of the people. The president should initiate and implement policy because "the nation as a whole has chosen him, and is conscious that it has no other political spokesman. His is the only national voice in affairs."[24]

More recent advocates of the Hamiltonian model have included most political scientists and journalists writing about the president and Congress during the 1950s and early 1960s. This model has been most clearly outlined by leading scholars of the presidency. Clinton Rossiter, writing in 1956, observed that "the strength of the Presidency is a measure of the strength of the America in which we now live. Those who accept this America and do not fear the one that is coming accept the strong Presidency soberly."[25] In one of the most influential books of the 1960s, Professor Richard Neustadt explicated the central role which the president must play:

> Our Constitution, our traditions, and our politics provide no better source for the initiatives a President can take. Executive officials need decisions, and political protection, and a referee for fights. Where are these to come from but the White House? Congressmen need an agenda from outside, something with high status to respond to or to react against. What provides it better than the program of the President?[26]

The Hamiltonian model, as it was advanced by politicians, political scientists, and journalists, was not disconnected from partisan and policy preferences. Neustadt formulated his concept of the strong presidency during the placid years of the Eisenhower administration. It is inextricably combined with a desire not only for vigorous executive action, but for activity along policy lines of a liberal Democratic nature. As in the Federalist case, the strong president model had a programmatic content. When the 1968 election brought a conservative Republican into the White House, many of the earlier advocates of the Hamiltonian model began to look to the Congress, particularly the Senate, for leadership. After President Nixon ordered troops into Cambodia in 1970, the corridors of Congress were flooded with political scientists (including Professor Neustadt) seeking to reassert senatorial power in the making of foreign policy.

The strong president model commands widespread support among the public. Socialization studies have shown that children acquire knowledge about the president before they do about Congress.[27] The president, as a single individual, more easily becomes a symbol of the government. All of our "great" presidents tended to fit into the activist, Hamiltonian mold, and the American public expects the president to exert active leadership. As George Gallup has observed: "I would say that any sharp drop in popularity is likely to come from the President's inaction in the face of an important event. Inaction hurts a President more than anything else. A President can take some action, even a wrong one, and not lose his popularity."[28]

The Hamiltonian model may be summarized as one which advocates a strong vigorous president acting within a somewhat unbalanced system of checks and balances. The Congress is not ignored, but its chief function becomes one of modifying and providing legitimacy for programs and policies emanating from the executive branch. The lawmaking function is deemed the most important legislative function by advocates of the Hamiltonian model. In order to create a Congress capable of acting with dispatch on programs submitted by the president, proponents of the Hamiltonian model suggest reforms which would centralize leadership in the legislature and make it more responsive to the executive's programs. Some specific reform proposals illustrate this.[29]

One reform put forward is that Congress be required to act on all executive proposals within a specified time period. By creating a deadline for legislative action, Congress would be forced to change its work patterns in order to deal more rapidly and efficiently with presidential proposals. This, of course, would require giving up the present system of slow deliberation which maximizes representation. Because the seniority system often produces committee chairmen who disagree with their party's programs and hinder the passage of legislation, many adherents of the Hamiltonian model propose that committee chairmen be chosen by the party caucus rather than automatically selected on the basis of seniority. The reasoning behind such a proposal is that the lawmaking function is better served when committee chairmen are in tune with the national party and presidential programs. Reforms which would reduce the individual legislator's work load and allow him to concentrate on passing legislation also fit into the Hamiltonian framework. Legislation giving broad mandates and long-term authorization to executive agencies would greatly reduce the time a congressman has to devote to reviewing annually programs established the previous year. He would have more time to devote to performing his lawmaking function. Another reform proposal designed to achieve the same end is to create a congressional bureaucracy which would handle legislators' constituent casework.

All of these proposals share the basic assumption which is the defining characteristic of the Hamilton model: that the preferred political system is one in which the lawmaking function of Congress is maximized. All of these reforms would make Congress less able to carry out its representational function by reducing the points of access of interests to the legislature and by speeding up the deliberative process. Some representation would be sacrificed in order to improve legislative efficiency.

The Jeffersonian, or Party Government, Model

The Hamiltonian model emerged at a time when most political leaders in the country agreed that political parties, or "factions," were evil institutions which could imperil the existence of the new government. Opposition to the Federalist economic programs and pro-British foreign policy, however, soon led to the organization of state parties to combat those policies through elections. Unlike most of the early American political thinkers, Thomas Jefferson regarded parties as an integral part of politics. "In every free and deliberating society," he said, "there must, from the nature of man, be opposite parties, and violent dissensions and discords; and one of these, for the most part must prevail over the other for a longer or a shorter time."[30]

After winning the election of 1800, Jefferson instituted an extensive system of party organization in the legislature. By joining the executive and legislative branches, the party was a vehicle for translating the majority will into policy. The president and his advisors would propose policy and Republican legislators, working through party caucuses, would transmute these proposals into law. Republican legislators who acted independently of the party were called "wayward freaks" by the president and were sometimes the targets of electoral purges.[31] An extensive intelligence system and selective dispersal of patronage were also important instruments in the implementation of the Jeffersonian system of party government.

Woodrow Wilson, we have already seen, thought the American system worked best when the executive was dominant. Like Jefferson, he regarded the political party as the most likely vehicle for achieving that dominance. Openly admiring the British parliamentary system, Wilson saw the political party as a vital link between the executive and legislative branches. By bringing together the two branches separated in the constitutional system, the political party could produce an effective government, responsive to the majority. Emphasizing the role of party in uniting the two branches of government, Wilson laid down the political maxim that:

> When the several Chief organs of government are separated by organic law and offset against each other in jealous seclusion, no common legal authority set over them, no necessary community of interest subsisting amongst them, no common origin or purpose dominating them, they must of necessity, if united at all, be united by pressure from without; and they must be united if government is to proceed. They cannot remain checked and balanced against one another; they must act and act together. They must, therefore, of their own will or of mere necessity obey an outside master.[32]

Elected as a minority president in 1912, Wilson set about to build a strong national Democratic party by providing patronage rewards to party legislators in return for policy support. Two times during his presidency Wilson considered resigning from office and seeking reelection in a party referendum similar to British practice.

In 1950, a group of people on the American Political Science Association's Committee on Political Parties came up with a critique of the existing party system and a set of reform proposals which run along the lines of the Jeffersonian model. The political scientists shared Jefferson's and Wilson's view of political parties as an essential link between public mandates voiced in elections and policies emanating from Congress. The populist "responsible two-party system" favored by the committee was one in which: (1) both presidential and congressional candidates campaign on a platform of consistent party policy proposals; (2) there is a significant difference between the two parties' policies; (3) voters make their choice between parties on the basis of these consistent platforms; and (4) if elected, both the president and his congressional colleagues from the same party seek to implement the party platform by passing laws.[33]

Reforms suggested by party government advocates are aimed not just at Congress and the president, but at restructuring the entire political system. Changes would be effected not only in legislative organization, but also in grassroots party organizations. Voters must perceive the policy differences between the two parties and act in terms of these differences. Central to all of these changes is the notion of providing party leaders with sanctions to employ against "wayward freak" legislators who do not support party programs. Rather than gaining the party label simply by winning a primary, a congressional candidate would have to demonstrate his support of the national party's program. Party government advocates seek to eliminate the present system which leads to situations, such as occured in the Ninetieth Congress, where 75 Democrats (including 42 committee and subcommittee chairmen) voted against, more often than in support of, the national Democratic position.[34]

Specific reforms advocated by party government spokesmen are similar to those put forward by Hamiltonians. Both seek to centralize leadership in order to maximize the lawmaking functions of Congress. Some of the reforms proposed by those who want a party government include:[35] (1) nationalizing the party organizations by requiring that congressional candidates bearing the party label be approved by the national party headquarters, and that national party leaders have a voice in selecting the party's legislative leaders; (2) using party caucus votes to bind all members to supporting the party position on important issues; (3) creating strong party policy committees in Congress to make committee assignments on the basis of demonstrated party loyalty, and to handle matters of legislative scheduling; (4) expanding committee staff assistance so that both minority and majority members have the resources for developing meaningful party positions on committee matters.

The Jeffersonian model is like the Hamiltonian in that both seek to overcome the dangers of inaction implicit in the Madisonian system of checks and balances. They both advocate a central role for presidential leadership. The differences lie in the nature of that leadership and its resources. In the Hamiltonian model, the president relies on his personal sources of power. Legislative majorities must be put together with each new issue. In the Jeffersonian model, the president has a continuing base of support on all issues in his party's legislative coalition. Because these legislators have been elected on the basis of support for the party program, the president can expect their support without having to employ tactics to build a majority coalition on each issue. The party government model also gives the legislators a more central role in the formulation of party policy. Because they have been elected on the same party platform as the president, legislators may be expected to initiate programs designed to implement that policy. They do not need to wait for executive initiatives and, because of their joint election on the same platform, can count on White House support for programs in line with that platform.

DECISION-MAKING EMPHASIS OF BOTH MODELS

Both the strong president and party government models deal with the question of representation. The "public interest" is defined in terms of electoral mandates, and the people are "represented" by passing laws which reflect that mandate. By increasing the ability of Congress to perform its lawmaking function, advocates of both models contend that Congress is being representative because it is enacting the programs desired by a majority.

The definition of representation in both models is one emphasizing the importance of electoral mandates and the ability of elected officials to transform that mandate into policy through a process of virtual representation. Both assumptions, about mandates and about virtual representation, are subject to criticism and alternative interpretations. If a voter, given a choice between two parties' candidates, votes for a Democratic candidate because of his position on economic matters while disagreeing with that party's position on foreign policy and civil rights; and if a successful Democratic candidate interprets his winning as a mandate for all Democratic programs; then the process of representing that voter's opinions becomes distorted as a result of the party's considering electoral success a measure of voters' policy preferences. By making Congress more able to transform quickly such electoral mandates into policy, the chances of representing that constituent's dissenting opinions on civil rights and foreign policy are greatly reduced. Similarly, an emphasis on virtual representation, such as that afforded in a system which stresses the party label, can lead to representation being defined in wholly different terms from that which would come about in a system emphasizing geographic representation. Simply put, the question is this: Is a Democratic congressman from Alabama being more "representative" by voting consistently with his party, or is he being more "representative" by speaking for the economic and social interests of his district in Alabama even when these run counter to the Democratic party's programs?

By defining representation solely in terms of electoral mandates and the legislator's transforming that mandate into policy, advocates of the Hamiltonian and Jeffersonian models tend to favor any reforms which would increase Congress's ability to perform its lawmaking function. But making Congress more efficient in this way necessarily leads to there being fewer points of access for electoral minorities to state their case and a shorter time period in which all interests are given a hearing in the deliberative process. If representation is thought of primarily as interest articulation rather than as policy-making in accordance with an electoral majority, then the reforms suggested by these two models can be regarded as sacrificing the representational function of Congress to the lawmaking function. By looking at a model which emphasizes this meaning of the representational functions of Congress, we can see how such an emphasis leads to quite different notions about the optimal political system.

A MODEL EMPHASIZING THE REPRESENTATION FUNCTION: THE MADISONIAN SYSTEM

Although both Hamilton and Madison envisioned a government structured in a form of checks and balances, there is a distinct difference of emphasis between the two. Where Hamilton sought a government capable of vigorous action, Madison feared that such action might endanger individual liberties. Seeking to establish a state where "the private interest of every individual may be a sentinel over the public rights," Madisonian theory proposes an executive and legislative branch not only with equal powers, but with means for each effectively to check the actions of the other. Rather than fearing an undemocratic minority, Madison felt that the real threat to a republic would come from a majority "faction" able to execute policies detrimental to minority groups by gaining control of the government. To prevent such majority control of the whole government, Madison proposed a solution "by so contriving the interior structure of the government as that its several constituent parts may, by their mutual relations, be the means of keeping each other in their proper places."[36] Instead of there being separate institutions with separate powers, the president and Congress were to be separate institutions sharing powers. "I am part of the legislative process," President Eisenhower often remarked, and the Madisonian system made it so.[37] The presidential veto, Senate role in the making of foreign policy and approving presidential appointments, shared control of the military, and congressional control of the purse strings were all checks on precipitous government action in response to majority demands.

The Madisonian model of Congress is an essentially negative one. Rather than focusing on joint executive-legislative actions, it emphasizes a system of mutual distrust of legislative and executive action. As one recent scholar has noted: "In the system that Madison envisages, the danger is action and the safeguard is stalemate, or, as he would have it, balance. Factious interests are to be 'broken,' 'controlled,' and 'balanced' against each other to produce 'stability.' "[38]

Twentieth century variations of the Madisonian model are generally called the "constitutional" or "literary" models of Congress because they find their support in a strict reading of the Constitution.[39] They generally advocate greatly increasing congressional strength vis-à-vis the executive simply to restore a balance which most feel has been seriously upset. Emphasis is generally placed, not on streamlining Congress so that it might more readily respond to presidential initiatives, but on strengthening the congressional role of blocking legislation and checking the executive. In *Obstacle Course on Capitol Hill*, Robert Bendiner discusses this role:

> A United States Congressman has two principal functions: to make laws and to keep laws from being made. The first of these he and his colleagues perform only with sweat, patience, and a remarkable skill in the handling of creaking machinery; but the second they perform daily, with ease and infinite variety. Indeed, if that government is best that governs least, then Congress is one of the most perfect instruments of government ever devised.[40]

Some of the strongest advocates of the Madisonian model are, not surprisingly, congressmen themselves. A study by Davidson, Kovenock, and O'Leary found that 55 percent of congressmen they interviewed agreed with the statement, "Congress and the executive should be equal partners in the making of public policy."[41] As part of the American political culture, the system of checks and balances also receives support by the public. A Louis Harris survey of March 1970 showed that 54 percent of the American public gave an overall negative rating to the Democratic Ninety-first Congress while giving President Nixon a favorable rating for his relations with Congress. Yet at the same time, 46 percent of the respondents indicated that they would vote for Democratic congressmen in 1972. Harris suggests the public had come to the conclusion "that perhaps a Congress controlled by the opposition party is not undesirable after all. Scarcely more than one in three voters can see any merit in having a Congress of the same party as the president. Fundamentally, the current mood is to endorse a system of checks and balances rather than to reject it."[42]

Prior to 1968, it would have been accurate to say that conservatives tended to favor a Madisonian model of Congress. This was certainly true during the Kennedy and Johnson administrations when those who opposed the Democratic programs sought to have these programs blocked by Congress. With the election of Richard Nixon, however, these same conservatives looked to the executive branch for leadership. The presidency rather than the Congress became the target of those who sought a reduction in funds for domestic programs. Many of those who had earlier advocated a strong presidency became ardent Madisonians in their seeking to make Congress an effective force for blocking presidential programs and for appropriating more money for education, poverty, and medical programs than that requested in the president's budget.

The Madisonian model may be termed conservative if we define it in broader terms than its American political connotations. The system of checks and balances is conservative in the sense that it minimizes government activity and is greatly weighted toward maintenance of the status quo. Madison's system is founded on the premise that government action constitutes the greatest threat to individual liberties. To protect these liberties it is necessary to devise a government which can perform its lawmaking function only with great difficulty. Given a choice between emphasizing representation or lawmaking, supporters of the Madisonian model will always choose the former.

This emphasis on representation rather than lawmaking generally takes two forms when it is used to evaluate the present system and applied to reform proposals. On the one hand, followers of Madison want to increase legislative representation in the decision-making process. Senate doves in the late 1960s and early 1970s were not advocating that the Senate make foreign policy decisions, but rather that the president should include the representation of Senate opinions in policy-making. This fear of secret and overly hasty executive policy-making, on the other hand, is also turned against legislative decision-making, and generally leads to Madisonians upholding the same decentralized structure which makes it difficult for Congress to play an active representational role in executive decision-making.

"Congressional acts, like the common law, ought to move carefully from precedent to precedent" is the way one congressman puts it.[43] To insure that legislation is not passed without a thorough airing of all interests, adherents of this model generally support reform proposals which would maintain and extend a congressional system giving minorities greater access and control over the legislative process. While supporters of a checks and balances model are many times opposed to reform proposals which would change the existing system, and at other times in favor of reforms, consistency in their views is provided by their always supporting procedures which seek to maximize the representational function. Madisonians thus oppose changes in the filibuster rule which would dilute minority representation, while they support the 1970 change which provided for recorded teller votes.

The Legislative Reorganization Act of 1970 contained many reforms which adherents of this model support because they increase the legislature's representational capabilities. Included are: (1) the requirement that committees make public all roll call votes taken in committee meetings; (2) a provision giving committee members three days within which they may file minority views to a committee report on a bill; (3) a rule which divides debate on a conference report between majority and minority positions; (4) a stipulation that committee meetings and hearings be open to the public unless the committee votes to close them; (5) a provision that open committee hearings be broadcast over radio or television as long as a majority of the committee agrees; and (6) a requirement that committees announce hearings at least one week in advance unless there is an obvious reason for starting hearings at once.

Other reforms favored by adherents of this model show the same concern for representation. Expanding congressional sources of information independent of the executive by increasing the size of legislator's and committee staffs is such a proposal. Madisonians also oppose any efforts to increase the individual legislator's lawmaking function by turning over his constituent casework to a central legislative bureau. Instead of streamlining the legislative process by cutting down on the time spent on administrative oversight, adherents of this model suggest expanding that function by providing only limited grants of authority to executive agencies and by giving Congress an active oversight role through hearings and investigations, review of appointments, and tight budgetary controls.

We find many of the values associated with the Madisonian

system in contemporary pluralist descriptions of Congress. Without getting too deeply involved in the debate over the merits of pluralism, we should at least have a quick look at the representative aspects of the pluralist model and its similarity to Madison's.

In *The End of Liberalism,* Theodore Lowi has outlined the basic assumptions of the pluralist model as articulated in its ideological form, "interest group liberalism." These are: (1) that organized interests are homogeneous and easy to define, and that any "duly elected" spokesman for an interest accurately reflects the opinions of the members of that group; (2) that organized interests represent almost all sectors of our lives, so that there is always an organized group to check effectively the demands made by another organized group; and (3) that government's role is to provide access to organized groups and to ratify the agreement and adjustments reached by competing group leaders.[44]

It is clear that the first two assumptions deal directly with the question of representation. The validity of the pluralist model as an empirical description of reality and as a normative model for evaluating other political systems and institutions hinges on the correctness of its assumptions about group leaders accurately representing membership opinions and about organized interest groups providing a truly representative picture of the total society. Studies of political, corporate, and labor leadership and policy-making in such diverse areas as taxes and agriculture cast doubt on both assumptions.[45] These matters will be dealt with at greater length in Chapters 2 and 6. For the present, it is enough to note the representational base on which the pluralist model rests, and to observe that assumptions or hypotheses about the nature of this representation are often treated as observed facts rather than hypotheses.

This emphasis on group interaction as the basic process of politics is closely tied to the way pluralists define "the public interest." In the Hamiltonian and Jeffersonian models the public interest is defined in terms of policy goals favored by an electoral majority. For Madison, the public interest is achieved by protecting individual liberties from incursions by the state. Pluralists, on the other hand, tend to deny that there is some substantive definition of the public interest apart from that which emerges by balancing group interests, and by defining the public interest solely in terms of this group process.[46] The differences I am talking about can be seen in the contrasting notions of the public interest, and the resulting differences about the role of government, provided in the observations of Edmund Burke in 1774 and David Truman in 1951:[47]

> *Burke:* "Parliament is not a congress of ambassadors from different and hostile interests, which interests each must maintain, as an agent and advocate against other agents and advocates; but Parliament is a deliberative assembly of one nation, with one interest, that of the whole—where not local purposes, not local prejudices, ought to guide, but the general good, resulting from the general reason of the whole."
>
> *Truman:* "Assertion of an inclusive "national" or "public interest" is an effective device. . . . In themselves these claims are a part of the data of politics. However, they do not describe any actual or possible political situation within a complex modern nation. In developing a group interpretation of politics, therefore, we do not need to account for a totally inclusive interest, because one does not exist."

Whereas Madison was articulating a normative model of politics, an attempt to achieve the good society, political scientists such as Truman have generally presented the pluralist model as an empirical one, a description of "the way things are." By eliminating such considerations as the "public good" or the "public interest," group theorists sought to skirt problems of definition associated with models which try to avoid "tyranny" or to achieve "democracy." They attempted to provide a model which would permit objective study of the American political system, study not tainted by their own political predilections.

At the beginning of this chapter, it was suggested that the framework one employs for observing reality greatly affects the picture of reality one obtains. "It is the theory," Einstein once said, "which decides what we can observe."[48] By viewing American politics through the lenses of an empirical pluralist model, political scientists found a system which seemed to maximize representational values. Most pluralists would agree with Ralph Huitt's favorable view of a Congress which has "the strength of the free enterprise system" because it seemed to provide for the representation of all societal interests. In considering the findings of studies which employ a pluralist framework, then, we should look for ways in which the theoretical framework might affect the results.

Since most congressional research is carried on within a pluralist framework emphasizing interest articulation and policy-making through long-term bargaining, we often find political scientists tacitly defending aspects of the legislative process which many would consider to be a silly way to go about making laws.

One of the criticisms leveled at pluralists who offer a "balancing" definition of the "public interest," or other value questions, is that they avoid basic value conflicts and judge political questions on the basis of how many people favor which position, rather than weighing the merits of opposing arguments.[49] The same thing, I think, can be said about most people who judge Congress and offer reforms. The basic conflict between representation and lawmaking is ignored, and reformers generally offer some "mix" of reforms designed to partially satisfy all interests while actually avoiding the basic conflict between these values. Look, for instance, at the final report of the 1965 Joint Committee on the Organization of Congress:

> Fundamental differences of opinion exist as to the proper role of Congress. Generally, the members of the joint committee agree that Congress should be maintained as a study and deliberative body, that the machinery of Congress must be modernized in order to provide for efficient handling of the Nation's affairs and that rule by majority must be preserved with adequate protection for the rights of the minority.
>
> Our aim has been to search for a practical means to make Congress a more effective institution for carrying out its basic modern functions: the legislative function, the oversight function, and the representative function.[50]

Such platitudes obscure the very real conflicts which occur whenever congressional reforms are considered. They hide the basic value conflict which is the core of this chapter's discussion. The five chapters which follow attempt to present a picture of what goes on in Congress: Chapter 2 deals with the question of representation; Chapter 3 with the political party as an instrument for transforming electoral mandates into policies; Chapter 4 with the committee system in the House and Senate; Chapter 5 with rules and norms; and Chapter 6 with the impact of interest groups and executive lobbying on legislative policies. Hopefully, this chapter has sensitized you to the important value questions involved in evaluating the present system and in judging various proposals for reform. Now we must disregard Bismarck's advice "that to appreciate both sausage and legislation, one should see neither being made," and have a close look.

NOTES

1. Quoted in Lewis Chester, Godfrey Hodgson, and Bruce Page, *An American Melodrama* (Viking, 1969), p. 68.

2. Joseph S. Clark, *Congress: The Sapless Branch* (Harper & Row, 1964), p. 23.

3. Stephen K. Bailey, *Congress in the Seventies* (St. Martins, 1970), p. 109.

4. Ralph Nader, "Making Congress Work," *The New Republic*, Vol. 165, nos. 8 and 9, August 21 and 28, 1971, p. 19.

5. Edmund Burke, "Speech on the Representation of the Commons in Parliament" (1782), in Peter Stanlis, ed., *Edmund Burke: Selected Writings and Speeches* (Anchor, 1963), p. 333.

6. Discussions of the various functions of Congress may be found in: Roger Davidson, David Kovenock, and Michael O'Leary, *Congress in Crisis: Politics and Congressional Reform* (Wadsworth, 1969), pp. 34ff.; Malcolm Jewell and Samuel Patterson, *The Legislative Process in the United States* (Random House, 1966), pp. 8–15, 23–25; William Keefe and Morris Ogul, *The American Legislative Process* (Prentice-Hall, 1964), pp. 8–26; and John Saloma, *Congress and the New Politics* (Little, Brown, 1969), pp. 22ff.

7. Woodrow Wilson, *Congressional Government* (World Publishing Company, 1967 edition), p. 195.

8. Luther Patrick, "What Is a Congressman?" *Congressional Record*, May 13, 1963, daily edition, p. A2978. Quoted in Clark, *Congress: The Sapless Branch*, p. 62.

9. Quoted in Charles Clapp, *The Congressman: His Work as He Sees It* (Anchor, 1964), p. 57 and pp. 61–62. There is some disagreement about how much time a legislator devotes to such constituency service. Samuel P. Huntington accepts the generally high estimate made by most congressmen (in "Congressional Responses to the Twentieth Century," in David Truman, ed., *The Congress and America's Future* (Prentice-Hall, 1965), p. 25. But studies by David Kovenock and John Saloma suggest that most legislators spend more time on legislative tasks than on constituency service. See David Kovenock, "Communications and Influence on Con-

gressional Decision Making" and "Influence in the U.S. House of Representatives," papers delivered at the annual meetings of the American Political Science Association, 1964 and 1967, and Saloma, *Congress and the New Politics*, pp. 178ff.

10. *Congressional Quarterly Weekly Report*, Vol. 29, no. 8, February 19, 1971, p. 416.

11. *Ibid.*

12. *Congressional Quarterly Weekly Report*, Vol. 28, no. 26, June 26, 1970, p. 1651. The House spent a total of 176 hours, or seven full days, on roll calls and quorum calls in 1969.

13. *Ibid.*

14. Louis M. Kohlmeier, Jr., *The Regulators* (Harper & Row, 1969), p. 291.

15. Philip Donham and Robert Fahey, *Congress Needs Help* (Random House, 1966), p, 148.

16. Ralph K. Huitt, "Congressional Organization in the Field of Money and Credit," in Commission on Money and Credit, *Fiscal and Debt Management Policies* (Prentice-Hall, 1963), p. 494.

17. Theodore Lowi, *Legislative Politics, U.S.A.* (Little, Brown, 1962), p. x.

18. James MacGregor Burns, *Presidential Government* (Avon Books, 1965), p. 24.

19. Ralph K. Huitt, "What Can We Do about Congress?" *Milwaukee Journal*, December 13, 1964, Part 5, p. 1. Quoted in Davidson et al., *Congress in Crisis*, p. 16.

20. The term for this and the Madisonian and Jeffersonian models are taken from James MacGregor Burns discussion in *Presidential Government*, pp. 43–47 *passim*.

21. Alexander Hamilton, Federalist paper #70, in *The Federalist Papers* (Modern Library edition, n.d.), p. 455.

22. Leonard White, *The Federalists* (Macmillan, 1948), p. 510.

23. Woodrow Wilson, *Constitutional Government in the United States* (first published 1908; Columbia University Press, 1964), p. 72.

24. *Ibid.*

25. Clinton Rossiter, *The American Presidency* (Mentor Books, 1956), p. 151.

26. Richard Neustadt, *Presidential Power* (John Wiley, 1960), pp. 6–7.

27. Fred Greenstein, *Children and Politics* (Yale University Press, 1965), pp. 61–63.

28. *Opinion Polls: Interviews by Donald McDonald with Elmo Roper and George Gallup* (Santa Barbara, Calif., Center for the Study of Democratic Institutions, 1962), pp. 34–35. Cited in Murray Edelman, *The Symbolic Uses of Politics* (University of Illinois Press, 1967), p. 78.

29. Davidson et al., *Congress in Crisis*, p. 31. See also Rossiter, *The American Presidency*, p. 148.

30. Saul K. Padover, *Jefferson* (Mentor Books, 1955), p. 107.

31. Quoted in Louis Koenig, *The Chief Executive* (Harcourt, Brace & World, 1964), p. 102. James Young's incisive study of legislative-executive interaction under Jefferson suggests that the president's legislative coalitions were more a result of personal interaction and skillful lobbying by Jefferson than they were a result of party control. See his *The Washington Community: 1800–1828* (Harcourt, Brace & World, 1966).

32. Woodrow Wilson, *Constitutional Government in the United States*, p. 211.

33. American Political Science Association Committee on Political Parties, *Toward a More Responsible Two Party System* (Holt, Rinehart & Winston, 1950).

34. Based on a study by the staff of the Democratic Study Group of 30 key votes in the Ninetieth Congress; reported in the *Congressional Record*, March 18, 1969.

35. Davidson et al., *Congress in Crisis*, p. 34, outlines these reforms. Other discussions of party government reform proposals can be found in Richard Bolling, *House Out of Order* (E. P. Dutton, 1966); James MacGregor Burns, *The Deadlock of Democracy* (Prentice-Hall, 1963); Joseph Clark, *Congressional Reform* (Thomas Y. Crowell, 1965); and the APSA Committee on Political Parties, *Toward a More Responsible Two Party System*.

36. Federalist paper #51, *The Federalist Papers*, p. 336.

37. Richard Neustadt, *Presidential Power* (John Wiley, 1960), p. 33.

38. Hannah Fenichel Pitkin, *The Concept of Representation* (University of California Press, 1967), p. 195.

39. See, for instance, Saloma, *Congress and the New Politics*, pp. 44–45; and Davidson et al., *Congress in Crisis*, p. 17–25.

40. Robert Bendiner, *Obstacle Course on Capitol Hill* (McGraw-Hill, 1964), p. 15.

41. Davidson et al., *Congress in Crisis*, p. 69.

42. "The Harris Survey," *Boston Globe*, March 23, 1970, p. 9.

43. Edwin M. Yoder, Jr., "Washington Report: Eckhardt of Texas," *Harpers*, June 1970, p. 36.

44. Theodore Lowi, *The End of Liberalism* (W. W. Norton, 1969).

45. See, for example, Theodore Lowi's *The End of Liberalism* and *The Politics of Disorder;* Murray Edelman, *The Symbolic Uses of Politics* (University of Illinois Press, 1964); Philip Green and Sanford Levinson, eds., *Power and Community* (Vintage, 1970). Grant McConnell, *Private Power and American Democracy* (Vintage, 1966) and E. E. Schattschneider, *The Semi-Sovereign People* (Holt, Rinehart, & Winston, 1961). For agriculture and tax policies see the notes to Chapter 6.

46. For a good discussion of the conservative effects of this "balancing definition" of the public interest in administrative law, see Charles Reich, "The New Property," *Yale Law Journal*, Vol. 73, no. 5, April 1964, pp. 733–787; and Reich, "The Law of the Planned Society," *Yale Law Journal*, Vol. 75, no. 8, July 1966, pp. 1227–1270.

47. Edmund Burke, "Speech to the Electors of Bristol," *Writings and Speeches of Edmund Burke* (Little, Brown, 1901), pp. 93–98; reprinted in Neal Riemer, *The Representative* (D. C. Heath, 1967), p. 11; and David Truman, *The Governmental Process* (Alfred A. Knopf, 1962), p. 51.

48. Norwood Hanson, *Patterns of Discovery* (Cambridge University Press, 1958).

49. Charles Reich, "The New Property."

50. "Organization of Congress," *Final Report of the Joint Committee on the Organization of Congress,* (U.S. Government Printing Office, 1966), pp. 1–2.

CHAPTER 2

Representation

Now you see/What I can do!
I can give you/Something new!
Something true/And Impromptu!
I can give you/A new view!

Robert Coover
"The Cat in the Hat for President"
New American Review, No. 4

On the night of January 12, 1966, President Lyndon Johnson rode up Pennsylvania Avenue to address a joint session of Congress. While there, he surprised many people by proposing that House members serve for terms of four, rather than two, years.[1] Calling for swift congressional action on a constitutional amendment to this effect, the president said:

> The present two year term requires most members to divert enormous energies to an almost constant process of campaigning, depriving this nation of the fullest measure of both their skill and their wisdom. Today, too, the work of government is far more complex than in our early years, requiring more time to master the technical tasks of legislating. And a longer term

will serve to attract more men of the highest quality to political life. The nation, the principle of democracy, and I think each congressional district, will all be better served by a four year term.[2]

The sustained congressional applause which greated this proposal suggested easy passage. The four-year term proposal, while it was nothing really new, seemed to elicit broad support both on Capitol Hill and throughout the country.[3] Representative Frank Chelf of Kentucky had polled 362 of his colleagues and found that 70 percent (254) of them favored his proposal for staggered four-year terms.[4] Three political scientists found that 68 percent of the congressmen they interviewed in 1963 supported such an increase in House terms.[5] The Gallup Poll has shown a steady increase in public support for a four-year term, going from 40 percent in 1946 to 61 percent in 1964.[6] Two months after the president's speech, over twenty different resolutions calling for four-year House terms had been introduced in Congress.[7] Observers reported that a majority on the House Judiciary Committee, the committee which would be responsible for such a measure, favored the four-year term proposal.

Yet during the next few months it became evident that the proposed reform of House terms was a dead issue. As the House Judiciary Committee began hearings on the proposal, members of Congress began to consider the possible consequences of such reform and to re-evaluate their earlier support. At one point in the hearings Attorney General Nicholas Katzenbach remarked that four-year terms coinciding with the president's would greatly promote legislative-executive party solidarity. Representative Richard Poff of Virginia, himself a supporter of staggered four-year terms, indicated the dissension in the reformers' ranks by his reaction to the Katzenbach statement. "I cannot imagine a better argument for the opposite of what you are trying to uphold. The function of Congress is to defy the executive when necessary—to resist conformity and standardization."[8]

By this time, the prospects of Congress passing the reform proposal had dimmed to the point where it seemed unlikely that the House Judiciary Committee would even report it out favorably for a floor vote. The plight of those favoring a four-year term is suggested by the following exchange between two supporters of the reform measure, Representatives Poff and Chelf:[9]

Poff: I want to be a helpful ally. Which version are you trying to promote?

Chelf: I'm going to promote any version that can get out of the committee.

It never got out. And the reasons why the proposal for a four-year House term failed to obtain congressional approval provide an interesting demonstration not only of the differing normative models of Congress adhered to by reformers and their opponents, but also of more general questions about the representative function of the House. Defenders of the four-year term generally phrased their arguments in terms of making Congress more efficient. They focused on the decision-making functions of the legislature. Opponents of the four-year term tended to emphasize the representative function of Congress. They thought it a good thing that House members be subject to continuous contact with the folks back home. Such a procedure might hinder the smooth movement of government policy-making, but it provided a short-term barometer of the public mood and assured the representation of all interests in the policy-making process. The arguments for and against the four-year House term may be summarized as follows.

Proponents of the reform argued that a four-year term would:

1. *Make Congress a more responsible and efficient policy-maker.* The House would be more responsible because it would be elected in conjunction with the president and would thus govern with a program mandate. Central to this idea of responsibility is the belief that the presidential election is a mandate calling for particular programs and that the role of Congress is to transform this mandate into law. Attorney General Katzenbach articulated this viewpoint: "The Presidential election is the only truly national election, when all the people have the opportunity to install a new administration. Their choice should include the right to elect as Representatives men who they believe will help the President they have selected."[10] In order to maximize such policy-making functions, the legislator must be able to devote himself to activities related to decision-making rather than activities related to constant representation of constituent wishes. By extending House terms to four years the congressman would be relieved of some of the demands which many members feel preclude effective law-making:[11]

It seems to me that the drains on a congressman's energy for administrative and 'representative' duties are very considerable, even assuming he has a fine staff and is able to delegate intelligently. Most people in comparable positions in business and executive life would not put up with the interruptions of their thought processes that are a necessary price of entry to this arena.

This life consists of preoccupation with the unimportant at the expense of the more important. My committee has been relatively active this year, but my committee responsibilities are not what occupy my time. It is taken up with the row over which of three good party members is going to get the nomination for postmaster in a town and what is going to happen to a party committeewoman if I can't get her a job as a part time postal employee.

A four-year term would free a legislator of such pressures and permit him to concentrate his full efforts on making laws which reflect the policy mandates of the last election. It would produce a Congress committed to passing the president's program.

2. *A four-year term would greatly improve the nature of elections in American politics.* By reducing the number of elections, the costs of staying in Congress would be diminished. The costs of campaigning for a House seat often exceed $50,000. With such an expense coming every two years, some congressmen are driven to a position of having to retire from the House for financial reasons. Representative Chelf was one of those. Before leaving, he observed: "I have had to make four hard, brutal, costly races in the past three years, and I cannot stand this. Really and truly I cannot stand it financially to remain on in Congress much longer with such a financial drain."[12] A four-year House term would also reduce the states' costs in administering elections. In addition, it is suggested that House members running for election concurrently with the president would tend to emphasize national rather than local issues in the campaign. Such an emphasis would reduce the parochialism of Congress and would enhance the prospects for cohesive party programs supported by the president and Congress.

3. *Four-year terms would lead to more qualified candidates for House seats.* In the words of President Johnson, it would "attract the best men in private and public life into competition for this high public office." The definition of "qualified" members is highly subjective

and measured by crude indicators such as education level, occupation, and previous political experience. Senators are generally regarded as more qualified by such measures, and proponents of the four-year House term attribute this, in part, to the senators' longer term. The stability provided by a four-year House term, it is argued, would increase the number of qualified candidates willing to leave the security of their private occupation for politics.

Opponents of the four-year term contend that extending the term of office would greatly reduce the representative function of the House. They agree with Madison in believing that the House "should have an immediate dependence on, and an intimate sympathy with, the people" and that "frequent elections are unquestionably the only policy by which this dependence and sympathy can be effectually secured."[13]

Those who oppose longer House terms argue that a four-year term would:

1. *Make Congress overly dependent on the executive and destroy the system of checks and balances.* Defenders of the two-year term suggest that the major function of Congress is not one of efficiently passing the president's program, but rather of maintaining an effective check on that branch. A representative comments:

> Checks and balances, I think, are the great obstacles that prevent any department or branch of government from running wild. . . . And when you take away this 2-year term and lodge the legislative responsibilities of the House in Members who have 4-year terms, I think you are removing this very important constitutional concept and contribution to government.[14]

As in the Madisonian model, no legislation is seen as better than bad legislation. The representative function of Congress is regarded as more important than the policy-making function. Midterm elections are an important instrument in this representation. They permit voters to express preferences more often, and they tend to be more issue-oriented than elections in presidential years.

2. *A four-year term, in changing the nature of elections, would greatly reduce congressmen's sensitivity to constituent needs.* Proponents of the short term suggest that the constant campaigning which results from a two-year term is a vital part of the process of representation. By forcing the legislator to make frequent trips home,

it keeps him aware of issues of concern to his constituents and gives him a chance to educate the public on matters of public policy. A defender of the short term observes:

> I find that it is very useful to have to run every two years, because this compels a legislator to go home, to do what I do, which is to bend my ear as much as I can, to ring door bells, to find out what people are thinking about Viet Nam, about the war against poverty. They want to expand it or cut it back. They have their reasons about the draft, about inflation, about economic policy, about a million other things, and I doubt very much, considering the clay I am made of, that I would be quite as assiduous in going back and making those rounds if I had to run only once every four years.[15]

Supporters of a two-year term also argue that national issues are already the major ones in congressional campaigns and that the increased competitiveness produced by four-year terms would make campaigns even more expensive than they are presently.

3. *A four-year term would not guarantee more qualified legislators.* A willingness to submit one's actions to the voter's judgement is seen as one of the most important ingredients of being a qualified legislator. A potential candidate not willing to endure these pressures would not be effective within Congress regardless of how "qualified" he is in terms of education or professional background. The pressures of frequent campaigning are regarded as one of the qualifications for Congress. In addition, say defenders of the two-year term, there is no proof that qualified candidates decline to run because of the length of term. "I have never heard," says one congressman, "any candidate, actual or potential, for the House of Representatives, of either party, give as a reason for not running or as an ingredient in his decision, the fact that it was a two year term."[16]

Whether or not one supports a four-year House term depends on the relative emphasis one gives to the representational and decision-making functions of Congress. Adherents of the Hamiltonian or Jeffersonian models tend to favor a four-year term because it unites Congress and the president into an efficient decision-making team. The public interest is "represented" by policy decisions responding to the earlier electoral mandate. But the major emphasis is on action rather than deliberation. A four-year term, by removing the distractions of perpetual campaigning and by increasing the level of technical expertise, is regarded as a positive factor for increasing the decision-making ability of the Congress. Supporters of the Madisonian model oppose the four-year term because it would eliminate the conflict produced by the president and Congress representing different constituencies. Such conflict is recognized as a hindrance to decision-making but it is seen as an integral part of the system of checks and balances. Pluralists also support the decentralized representational system produced by two-year terms, and maintain that such short terms help to maximize the points of access for all interests in the policy process. A four-year term would perhaps increase congressional ability to perform the major decision-making functions in the government. It would, however, weaken the representational justification for the legislature's having this central role of policy-maker.

The four-year term proposal, while it cannot be presently considered a live issue, is instructive for many of the reasons discussed in the preceding chapter. While much of the debate is centered on whether the quadrennial elections would be held in presidential election years or in between, the two sides essentially are seeking to maximize either the representational or the lawmaking functions of Congress. Those who feel that a House member should devote most of his time to the study and deliberation needed for developing sound legislation see the four-year term as a way of freeing congressmen from the distractions of constant campaigning. On the other side are those who feel that short House terms assure that congressmen will listen to constituent demands and articulate those interests in the legislative process.

A key element in the debate surrounding this reform proposal, and indeed in any evaluation of Congress, is the meaning of the term *representation*. People may be referring to quite different things when they say that Congress is, or is not, the representative body it was intended to be. In this chapter we will have a closer look at some of the meanings of the term and apply these measures to the modern Congress. A useful starting point for this discussion is Hannah Pitkin's analysis in *The Concept of Representation*. She talks about four different dimensions of representation: formal, descriptive, symbolic, and substantive.[17] These four aspects of representation provide a framework for our investigation of how representative Congress is.

I. FORMAL REPRESENTATION: ONE MAN, ONE VOTE

Formal representation is the transfer of authority to act in one's behalf, brought about through an institutional arrangement such as elections. The essence of representation is that the representatives are authorized in advance to act in behalf of their constituents and to bind them by their collective decisions.[18] The emphasis is on the formal arrangements which precede the actual representative behavior. This notion of representation as a formal transfer of authority from any people to one delegate was a central part of Thomas Hobbes's conception of the state. In *Leviathan* (1651), Hobbes observed: "A multitude of men are made *one* person, when they are by one man, or one person, represented; so that it be done with the consent of every one of that multitude in particular."[19] It is the covenant between the people and the person selected to act in their behalf which establishes the latter as a representative. The formal arrangements of selection, not the behavior of the representative, define representation.

More recent political analysts have adopted the Hobbesian concept of formal representation. The remarks of a political scientist, Joseph Tussman, illustrate this:

> The essence of representation is the delegation or granting of authority. To authorize a representative is to grant another the right to act for oneself. Within the limits of the grant of authority one is, in fact, submitting himself in advance to the decision or will of another. . . .
>
> The fact that our rulers are elected does not make them any less our rulers. . . . To say that we send our representatives to Congress is not to say that we have sent our servants to market. We have simply designated the person or persons to whose judgement or will we have subordinated ourselves. Nor does the fact that at a later date we must redesignate a representative alter the fact that an act of subordination has occured.[20]

Defining representation this way leads us to focus on the procedures for selecting representatives rather than to the representatives behavior once in office. We can measure representation, in this sense, only by reference to the institutional procedures for selecting legislators. When the Seventeenth Amendment provided for direct election of senators, it made the Senate a more representative body than it had been when state legislatures were the electors. It is more representative simply because it provides a more direct method for the people to select senators. Another example of the use of formal representation as a criterion for evaluating Congress is found in discussions of reapportionment. Here again, the question of how representative Congress is is phrased in terms of the formal procedures of elections.

Critics of the Congress have long maintained that the House was not a representative body because of the great disparity in populations of congressional districts. In 1964, one observer pointed out that the nearly 1,000,000 constituents of Texas's 5th congressional district had to be content with a single representative, although the 177,000 residents of Michigan's 12th district also were entitled to a congressman.[21] In the 1962 election, the largest congressional district in Texas had 951,527 residents while the smallest had 216,371. The same was true of Michigan which had 802,994 in its largest district and 177,431 in its smallest.[22] Because of this great variation in size of constituencies, critics of the Congress maintained that a majority in Congress did not necessarily reflect a majority in the country. In particular, there was overrepresentation of rural areas at the expense of those living in cities and the suburbs.

The Supreme Court, in a series of cases beginning in 1962, leaped into the political thicket of reapportionment. Chief Justice Warren outlined the Court's notion of representation:

> Legislators represent people, not trees or acres. Legislators are elected by voters, not farms or cities or economic interest. As long as ours is a representative form of government and our legislatures are those instruments of government elected directly by and directly representative of the people, the right to elect legislators in a free and unimpaired fashion is a bedrock of our political system.[23]

In *Wesberry v. Sanders* (1964), the Court ruled that Article I's statement that "Representatives shall be apportioned among the states according to their respective numbers" and "chosen by the people of the several states" meant that "as nearly as is practicable one man's vote in a Congressional election is to be worth as much as another's." The impact of *Wesberry v. Sanders* is shown in Table I which compares the pre-*Wesberry* variation in congressional districts populations with the post-*Wesberry* variation in the ten states with the greatest malapportionment.

What Table 1 shows us, basically, is that the grossest discrepancies in the population of House districts were quite impressively corrected by state legislatures in compliance with Supreme Court dictates. But more important questions are left unanswered. Who is to gain by reapportioning districts to reflect population: Republicans or Democrats; liberals or conservatives; cities or suburbs; the North, the South, or the West? Or would it make any difference?

The conventional wisdom of the 1960s was that *Wesberry* would produce a more liberal House and one more attuned to the problems of the cities. But two studies by political scientists in the early 1960s suggested otherwise. Andrew Hacker and William Goss looked at a few representative bills of the Kennedy and Johnson administrations which divided the House along liberal/conservative lines (the 1961 expansion of the House Rules Committee, the 1962 proposal to create a Department of Urban Affairs, the 1964 Civil Rights Act, and the Economic Opportunity Act of 1964). They then compared the actual votes in the House

TABLE 1   *The Impact of* Wesberry v. Sanders

State	Before *Wesberry* (February 1964) Maximum Variation[a]	After *Wesberry* (September 1966) New Maximum Variation
Arizona	− 54.3%	− 7.8%
Colorado	− 55.4	+12.6
Florida	+ 60.3	+13.2
Georgia	+108.9	+16.4
Indiana	+ 64.6	−12.8
Maryland	+ 83.5	−14.9
Michigan	+ 84.8	− 2.1
Ohio	+ 72.1	−20.9
Tennessee	+ 58.2	+14.4
Texas	+118.5	+10.2

[a]The maximum variation is expressed in terms of the largest or smallest congressional district's population as a percentage of the average district's population.

SOURCE: *Congressional Quarterly*, Weekly Report No. 37, September 16, 1966, p. 2006.

on these measures with a weighted vote for each member which adjusted the value of his vote to reflect the actual population of his district.

What this procedure did was to estimate the impact which perfect apportionment on the basis of population would have on vote outcomes in the House. The results were surprising. The weighted votes (those based on actual population of districts) produced the same or even less support for these measures than that which the bills actually gained in the malapportioned house.[24] The policy changes brought about by reapportionment are difficult to assess in broad "liberal" or "conservative" terms. But an underlying difference between rural constituencies and urban or suburban ones is that the former tend to be producers of primary goods, especially agricultural products, while the latter tend to be consumers of goods and services. The sort of issues, therefore, which have gained support in a reapportioned house are consumer issues such as mass transit, antipollution measures, and education.

While it is difficult to assess the impact of reapportionment on policies emerging from the House, the differences in terms of population characteristics of House constituencies and in terms of party benefits can be more easily determined. Table 2 shows the relative gains for cities and suburbs from reapportionment taking place between 1964 and 1970. Reapportionment in the 1960s benefited the central cities as well as suburbs. But the 1970 census showed a decline in the population of core cities and an increase in the population of surrounding suburbs. As congressional districts are redrawn to reflect these population changes, then, the major beneficiaries of reapportionment in the 1970s will be voters living in the suburbs.[25]

A final question to be answered about the changes brought about by reapportionment is this: Does it favor Republicans or Democrats? We have only one election on which to base some sort of answer. The 1972 election was the first to occur after the redistricting founded on the 1970 census. The changes, reflecting the increasing suburban population, generally helped Republicans. A post-election study by *Congressional Quarterly* "showed that 17 of the 24 seats that moved into Republican hands did so largely because of redistricting or reapportionment; . . . with redistrict-

TABLE 2 *Population Composition of House Districts Before and After Redistricting, 1964–1970*

Population Composition	Before Redistricting		After Redistricting		Net Change
	N	%	N	%	N
Urban*	86	22	95	24	+9
Suburban	61	15	66	17	+5
Midurban	186	47	185	47	−1
Rural	59	15	15	12	−8
At large	5	1	0	0	−5
	397	100	397	100	0

*An urban district is defined as one with 60 percent or more of its people living in a central city of one of the 213 urbanized areas of the nation; a suburban district has 50 percent or more of its inhabitants living on the fringes of an urbanized area; a rural district has 90 percent of its population living outside the urban areas; a midurban district typically includes a medium sized city (50,000–250,000) which does not dominate the district.

SOURCE: Jack L. Noragon, "Congressional Redistricting and Population Composition, 1964–1970," *Midwest Journal of Political Science*, Vol. XVI, no. 2, May 1972, p. 298.

ing and reapportionment eliminated, the 1972 House elections would have been a virtual standoff."[26]

So we can conclude this section on formal representation by observing that population changes reflected in congressional districts redrawn under the dictates of the *Wesberry* decision work to the benefit of those living in the suburbs and the Republican party. But this does not really tell us much about how representative Congress is. What it suggests is that formal representation is an inadequate measure of how representative Congress is because it really does not tell us much about how legislators behave. To say that the House is more representative because of equal district populations assumes a great deal about linkages between constituent demands and congressmen's behavior. It tells us that congressman X "represents" the people in constituency Y because they elected him. That is all. In order to provide a more complete picture of representation in Congress we must look at additional meanings of the term. Another such dimension is that of descriptive representation.

II. DESCRIPTIVE REPRESENTATION: MAINSTREET, MIDDLETOWN, U.S.A.?

Descriptive representation is the extent to which representatives reflect the characteristics of those they formally represent. Such characteristics as ethnic background, social class, age, place of residence, and occupation are considered important. According to this measure, a representative legislature "should be an exact portrait, in miniature, of the people at large."[27] Representative Jim Wright of Texas illustrates the descriptive dimension of representation in remarking:

> Congress is the mirror of the people, and it reflects the aggregate strengths and weaknesses of the electorate. Its membership might include just about the same percentage of saints and sinners, fools and geniuses, rogues and heroes as does the general populace. Congress is a highly concentrated essence of the virtues and faults of the nation as a whole.[28]

Descriptive representation rests on a belief that a legislator acts in terms of his own social-economic background. A suburban district with a high percentage of professional people in it will be automatically represented by selecting a congressman who is typical of those living in that district. There will be no need to seek continually to influence the congressman's vote because he will be predisposed to vote the way most people in his district would wish him to. A state legislator articulates this idea of descriptive representation:

> Basically you represent the thinking of the people who have gone through what you have gone through and who are what you are. You vote according to that. In other words, if you come from a suburb you reflect the thinking of people in the suburbs; if you are depressed people, you reflect that. You represent the sum total of your background.[29]

To determine how representative Congress is according to this definition we can compare congressmen with the general population and with other political leaders in terms of such characteristics as family background, place of residence, education, and age.

Family Background   Studies of legislators' family backgrounds show that the middle and upper classes are overrepresented in the Congress. Donald Matthews's study of postwar senators led him to conclude that "Senators were sons, with only a handful of exceptions, of men possessing upper- and middle-class occupations. The children of low-salaried workers, wage earners, servants, and farm laborers, which together comprised 66 percent of the gainfully employed in 1900, contributed only 7 percent of the postwar Senators."[30]

Residence   Place of birth or residence has often been cited as a factor contributing to the unrepresentativeness of the Congress. Congressmen are seen as "small town boys." The typical postwar senator, according to Matthews, was the product of "Mainstreet, Middletown, U.S.A." Andrew Hacker's comparative study of senators and corporation presidents showed that senators were more likely to live in small towns or rural areas, to have attended nearby colleges, and to have returned home after college.[31] A study in 1963 comparing geographic mobility of congressional leaders and administration leaders reinforced this notion of the legislature being insulated from an increasingly urban society. Thirty-seven percent of the congressional leaders were still living in their places of birth, as compared to 11 percent of the administration leaders. Seventy-seven percent of the congressional leaders still lived in their states of birth as compared to 30 percent of the administration leaders. Sixty-one percent of the administration leaders had moved from one region of the country to another; only 19 percent of congressional leaders had done so.[32]

There is some evidence to indicate that the notion of a congressman as small town boy is no longer an accurate description. Thirty-two percent of the representatives in the Ninetieth Congress (1967–1968) were born in cities with a population of 50,000 or more as compared with 15 percent of the Senators in Matthews's study (1947–1957). People born in cities constituted a greater percentage of the House than their proportion of the population; only those born in rural areas were underrepresented.[33]

Education   Congressmen are not typical of the whole population in terms of education. Matthews found that 84 percent of the senators had attended college as contrasted with 14 percent of the general population during this period. In addition, 53 percent of the senators had attended law school or done other postgraduate work.[34] The high education level of congressmen is, of course, directly related to their relatively high class origins.

Occupation The occupational background of congressmen tends to overrepresent high prestige professional and business jobs. Matthews's study of the Senate showed the "log cabin-to-Capitol Hill" myth to be grossly inaccurate. Not only did senators come from high prestige occupations immediately before entering the Senate, but 81 percent of them entered the highest occupational classes as their first job after completing school.[35] Occupational groups such as factory and farm workers, and those in service occupations have always been underrepresented or not represented at all. The most striking aspect of legislators' backgrounds, however, is the number of lawyers among them. Over half of the members of the Ninety-first Congress were lawyers, while lawyers in the general population constituted only about .1 percent of the work force. This overrepresentation of the legal profession in Congress is not new. Thirty-seven percent of the membership of the House were lawyers in 1790, 70 percent in 1840, and 54 percent in 1957.[36] The lawyer's affinity for politics is explained not only in terms of the expertise which he brings to the job, but also by the fact that lawyers are more able to combine politics with their professional careers. While most professionals, such as doctors, educators, architects, scientists, and engineers, would find that running for office or serving in Congress hampered their professional knowledge, lawyers are able to take such a leave of absence and return with contacts and new information helpful for their law careers.

Age The average age for representatives in the Ninety-third Congress (1973–1974) was 51 and the average age of senators 55. Matthews's study of the Senate found that a far smaller proportion of senators were in their thirties than was true for the general population, and that about the same proportion of senators as the general public were over 65.[37] A study of the 1958 elections showing winning House candidates to be older than their defeated opponents lends support to a belief that the public's image of a congressman includes his being a middle-aged man.[38] The average age of congressional leaders, rather than the whole membership, is perhaps a better measure of how representative the Congress is. While the average age of members has not changed drastically in the past century (the average age of representatives was 46 in 1870), the average leadership age has. In 1870, the average age of a committee chairman was 49; in 1970, it was 70. When Representative William Colmer of Mississippi became chairman of the Rules Committee in 1967, he was 77 years old and had served in Congress for 35 years.

Leadership in the executive branch tends to be younger than that of Congress. The average age of cabinet members under Kennedy was 48, under Johnson, 50, and under Nixon, 55.[39] The effect of aged leadership in distorting the representativness of the House was noted by a freshman congressman:

> We promote disequal representation. The rural district of a southern state has much greater control over national affairs than the urban district of a northern, western, or eastern state. The 435 Congressmen who will be elected next November will be elected by equal numbers of constituents. But gentlemen those Congressmen will not arrive in Washington next January with equal capacity to serve their constituents. They will arrive ranked. One district will be represented by a private, and another district will be represented by a general.[40]

Minorities   These measures of descriptive representation in Congress suggest that the "typical" congressman is quite unlike the "typical" constituent. Representation in Congress is biased in favor of the middle- and upper-middle classes, the more highly educated, those with professional occupations, and especially lawyers. Minority religious groups and minority ethnic groups also tend to be underrepresented in Congress. Legislators belonging to Protestant denominations made up 76 percent of the membership in the Ninetieth Congress (1967–1968), yet Protestants constituted only 55 percent of the national church membership. Catholics and Jews, with 41 percent of the church membership in 1967, held only 24 percent of the seats in Congress.[41]

In the Ninety-third Congress, elected in 1972, there were fifteen black representatives and one black senator. Although this figure includes the first black representatives from southern constituencies in this century (Representatives Barbara Jordan of Texas and Andrew Young of Georgia), and although it shows a sizeable increase over the five black congressmen sitting in the Eighty-eighth Congress (1963–1964), the number of blacks in Congress does not come close to reflecting their numbers in the general population. A representation of blacks equal to their proportion of the population would produce fifty black representatives and eleven black senators.[42]

The number of women in Congress reflects a similar pattern. There are fourteen in the Ninety-third Congress, the most since 1962, but again far fewer than would be the case if the make-up of Congress reflected the proportion of women in the general population.

All of these informal "requirements" of office and biases in legislative recruitment reflect a class structure in the political system. A man's class is sometimes defined by the ceiling he puts upon expectation. Matthews suggests that less than 5 percent of the population could reasonably expect to serve in the Senate. Political offices in the United States appear to be class ranked, with people of high social status holding the more important offices. Matthews observes: "As long as the system of stratification in a society is generally accepted, one must expect people to look for political leadership toward those who have met the current definition of success and hence are considered worthy individuals. Voters seem to prefer candidates who are not like themselves but what they would like to be."[43] Another meaning of representation, that of symbolic representation, deals with the legislator as an atypical American.

III. SYMBOLIC REPRESENTATION

Symbolic representation, unlike formal and descriptive representation, is not easily measured by looking at aggregate data such as population, ethnic background, occupation, education levels. For the essence of symbolic representation is not what the representative is, but what he is perceived to be by his constituents.

The real measure of symbolic representation is whether or not the constituents accept the officeholder as their representative. "The crucial test of political representation," according to this definition, "will be the existential one: Is the representative believed in? And the basis of such belief will seem irrational and affective because no rational justification of it is possible. Hence, political representation will be not an activity but a state of affairs, not an acting for others but a 'standing for'; so long as people accept or believe, the political leader represents them, by definition."[44] An effective symbolic representative is one demonstrating traits and qualities with which his constituents can identify. Rather than being "typical" of his constituency, he is regarded as being a "better" person because of his wealth, his success in business (or the space program, movies, or sports), his sincerity, his articulateness, or his being a "concerned citizen" rather than a politician.

William Tindall has referred to the act of symbolizing as "an exact reference to something indefinite."[45] The successful symbolic political leader is one generating enough ambiguity about himself to permit people of quite different political persuasions to identify with him. Marshall McLuhan has described how this process worked in the 1960 television debates: "Kennedy did not look like a rich man or like a politician. He could have been anything from a grocer or a professor to a football coach. He was not too precise or too ready of speech in such a way as to spoil his pleasantly tweedy blur of countenance and outline."[46] Such a television image permits the viewer to project his own political beliefs and character traits upon the candidate. In so doing, the citizen comes to think of the candidate as his representative regardless of how different the candidate's real background or political beliefs are from his own.

The importance of symbolic representation in a political campaign is well illustrated in the 1962 Massachusetts senatorial campaign. The president's brother, who would just barely meet the minimum legal age for senator and who had never been elected to a political office, was able to turn political liabilities into assets because of their symbolic meaning. Murray Levin has described how the symbolic importance of the candidate's background overrode questions of political experience and ability:

McCormack's advisors believed, on this occasion, what they wanted voters to believe. They assumed that Kennedy, at the age of twenty-nine, could be criticized as too young for the job. They assumed that, being a millionaire, he could be criticized as a playboy—a ne'er do well, who had never worked for a living. And they assumed that since he had never held elective office his candidacy could be portrayed as presumptuous, as violating the log cabin-to-White House value system held (they supposed) by the voters of Massachusetts.

But, as we have seen, his youth contributed to his image as a political innocent and non-politician, his wealth was interpreted as an indication that he would not steal from the public till, and his office holding inexperience reinforced his image as a non-politician, a non-member of the Boston political gang, *i.e.*, as a clean outsider.[47]

The Kennedy Senate campaign was able to play on existing traits in developing the candidate as a symbolic representative. Sometimes, however, negative precampaign opinions of a candidate require that a favorable image be created from whole cloth. The 1966 race in the 7th congressional district of Texas was such a case. Republican businessman George Bush had precampaign polls showing that he was not well known to voters and was regarded as being neither "warm" nor "sincere." To counteract this, a campaign theme of "Vote for Bush and Watch the Action" was developed. Billboards pictured Bush, jacket slung over his shoulder, peering intently into the future. Television ads showed him briskly walking through a middle-class suburb, his jacket again slung casually over the shoulder. Encountering a flock of small children, Bush would warmly sweep one into his arms.[48] As one of the most successful political campaign film-makers has observed: "The way a man handles a child may say more about him than a speech against Vietnam."[49]

Television is by far the most effective medium for a candidate wishing to project an image which voters can respond to in terms of particular symbols. Analysts suggest that the best strategy even in a televised debate is not to become involved in a discussion of issues, but rather to restate one's basic campaign themes and, most of all, to look and sound like a senator or representative. A spot political ad lasting fifteen seconds and projecting a particular image is much more effective than a longer ad which permits the candidate to fully explain his stands on issues, but which threatens to alienate the viewer whose ball game or situation comedy has been interrupted.

The dramtic impact which effective use of TV can have was demonstrated in the 1970 Democratic primary for senator in Ohio. A poll conducted just two months before the May primary showed that former astronaut John Glenn was a familiar name to 97 percent of the Ohio voters, while his opponent, Howard Metzenbaum, was known to only 15 percent. Metzenbaum hired film-maker Charles Guggenheim, a man whose successful clients include the late Senator Robert Kennedy, Senators George McGovern and Abraham Ribicoff, and Representatives John Brademas and James Symington. Guggenheim made fourteen film spots costing $85,000. Television air time cost another $300,000. Some typical ads:[50]

> The scene is an outdoor marketplace. The camera zooms to a mound of vegetables and a pudgy hand picking up some cucumbers. It then pans to a grocer's winsomely ugly face. The sound track picks him up in mid-sentence: ". . . he should stick to astronauting. I'm a salesman. You're a Senator."
>
> Voice of Howard M. Metzenbaum: "Well, I'm not yet. I hope to be." Confident smile wreathes grocer's face. "You will be. Believe me—you will be." Cut.
>
> In one scene, Mr. Metzenbaum is talking with a roomful of workers on a home construction site. "I like to talk with people even if they get mad at me," he says at one point with a disarming, boyish smile. "I'm not a politician, I'm a businessman."

The two candidates were remarkably similar on issues, with the only difference being Glenn's opposition to further reductions in space program appropriations. Metzenbaum outspent Glenn five to one, with most of the money going for television. In the city of Cleveland alone there were 63 Metzenbaum TV spots during the last week of campaign. "I couldn't have done it without the TV" was Metzenbaum's comment after defeating Glenn by over 12,000 votes.[51]

Television campaigns are successful not only because they provide what one Madison Avenue dweller has called "the personal patina of personality projection," but also because they reach the apathetic, undecided voter who often determines the outcomes of elections.[52] Voters are more susceptible to advertising campaigns stressing images in a primary election where there are no party labels to separate the good guys from the bad. Both Bush and Metzenbaum lost Senate races in the general election, where party labels can provide a cue for voters which may offset even the slickest advertising campaign. In both the 1970 and 1972 general elections, the superstars of political advertising achieved mixed results—with stable party voting sometimes counting for more than sophisticated television campaigns.

Spending a lot of money for professional television campaigns may not assure victory, but the importance of image making and symbolic representation has led to the emergence of the campaign management industry as an integral part of American politics. A survey of the 67 Senate candidates with opposition in 1970 showed that 62 of them hired advertising firms, 30 used professional media consultants, 24 used national polling firms, and 20 employed campaign management and public relations services. Over two hundred business enterprises were gainfully employed selling candidates that year. One such consultant estimated that it costs $80,000 to handle an average campaign for a House seat.[53]

Up to the 1972 election, the only regulation of campaign spending and financing was provided by the Corrupt Practices Act of 1925. This law, once characterized by Lyndon Johnson as "more loophole than law," said that no House candidate could spend more than $5,000 and that no Senate candidate could spend more than $25,000. Since it generally costs many times that to run for a congressional seat, this meant that almost everyone in Congress was guilty of violating the intent of the 1925 act. Three hundred million dollars was spent on political campaigns in 1968. And between 1968 and 1970, expenditures for television and radio political ads increased by 70 percent.[54]

In February 1972, Congress passed the Federal Election Campaign Act. This new law replaced the toothless 1925 act. Perhaps its most important provision was the requirement that the names, addresses, and business affiliations of campaign contributors giving more than $100 be disclosed. But there were still ways to maintain the old pattern of campaign financing: fund-raising dinners, "earmarking" funds sent to campaign committees to make sure they get to specific candidates, providing "soft money" (such as computer time, "legal services," and advertising expertise), and giving the enforcement responsibilities of the new law to the same groups who were charged with carrying out the old law (the House clerk, the Senate secretary, and the Justice Department). So what happened in 1972, the first election to come under the provisions of the new campaign finance law? A record $400 million was spent, up $100 million from that of four years earlier. Senate and House races accounted for $200 million of that, Senator John Tower of Texas leading the way with a campaign costing an estimated $2.5 million.

A look at the 1970 New York Senate race shows how high the costs of running for office via television can be. Richard Ottinger spent approximately $650,000, or about $50,000 a week, on television commercials just to win the Democratic primary. Charles Goodell, after flying to such distant places as the Bistro restaurant in Beverly Hills for fund-raising dinners, spent $1.25 million on his losing campaign. James Buckley was elected after spending an estimated $4 million.[55] The financing of these high cost campaigns is administered so as to get around the provisions of campaign finance laws. Dummy committees are set up in Washington to channel funds to the candidates. These committees permit individual contributors to exceed the $5,000 limit of the 1925 law, and to avoid the listing of expenses and contributors required of state committees. In 1970, committees such as the "League of Middle American Women," "Scientists for Sensible Solutions to Pollution," and "Americans for Honesty in Politics" funneled $400,000 into New York county committees for Buckley. After a campaign in which Buckley stressed his opposition to the supersonic transport program, the senator's first vote in that chamber was one in favor of the SST. "That's the first payoff" said former Senator Goodell upon hearing the news.[56]

"It would be my guess that about 95 percent of campaign funds at the congressional level are derived from businessmen." The speaker, Senator Russell Long of Louisiana, carries with him the authority gained from being in charge of distributing funds for Democratic senators' campaigns and one of the oil industry's key representatives on Capitol Hill. His estimate was reinforced by the *Washington Post*'s Don Oberdorfer, who had a close look at the campaign financing of former Representative George Fallon of Maryland, then chairman of the Public Works Committee. Over three-fourths of the out-of-state contributors to Fallon's campaign represented highway construction interests.[57]

In 1970 Congress passed a bill limiting the amount of money which candidates could spend on radio and television ads. President Nixon, on October 12, vetoed the bill saying that it discriminated against the broadcast media and favored incumbents. Because incumbent congressmen have privileges such as free mailing, news coverage, research facilities, and the symbolic trappings of office—all of which are estimated as being worth $150,000 at election time, any limit on campaign spending is bound to hurt challengers more than incumbents. But the present campaign financing system also greatly favors incumbents. In the eight elections from 1954 through 1968, 92 percent of all incumbent members of the House who sought office, and 85 percent of all sitting senators who ran, were returned to Congress. Ninety-five percent of the House incumbents who ran for reelection in 1970 were returned to Capitol Hill.[58]

In 1971, a bill was passed which allowed individuals to check off one dollar on their tax returns for use by the major parties for campaigns. Because Republican candidates generally benefit more than Democrats from the present business-oriented system of campaign financing, the Nixon administration and Republicans on the Hill accepted the plan only after a compromise was worked out which postponed implementation of the plan until after the 1972 election.

The greatest impact of symbolic representation on the make-up of Congress, then, is that candidates who are able to raise enough money to run a strong media campaign are more likely to be elected than those who cannot. Again, the bias in the representational system is one favoring the middle and upper classes. As we shall see in Chapter 6, where a candidate's money comes from affects whose point of view he listens to when deciding how to vote on a particular bill.

IV. SUBSTANTIVE REPRESENTATION: DELEGATE OR TRUSTEE?

The three types of representation we have looked at so far fail to provide a complete picture of what the term means. Neither formal, descriptive, nor symbolic representation tell us how the representative actually behaves, once in office. Substantive representation is an extension of the term into the realm of action.

It deals with how a representative must act rather than how he was elected, background characteristics, or how constituents accept him as a symbolic representative. Hannah Pitkin provides a thorough definition of the term:

> Representing here means acting in the interest of the represented, in a manner responsive to them. The representative must act independently; his action must involve discretion and judgement; he must be the one who acts. The represented must also be (conceived as) capable of independent action and judgement, not merely being taken care of. And, despite the resulting potential for conflict between representative and represented about what is to be done, that conflict must not normally take place. The representative must act in such a way that there is no conflict, or if it occurs an explanation is called for. He must not be found persistently at odds with the wishes of the represented without good reason in terms of their interest, without a good explanation of why their wishes are not in accord with their interest.[59]

We may delineate two aspects of substantive representation: the representative's influence and the representative's orientation. A committee chairman may argue that his position and influence make him a more effective representative for his district or state than a less senior member would be. A representative's orientation refers both to how he perceives his legislative role and to his position on specific issues.

The influence which a legislator has within the Congress may determine his success at representing the interests of constituents. A committee chairman is able to influence members on other committees because they know they will need a return favor from the chairman's committee in the future. Thus it is argued that a district's representation is maximized by having a congressman with great seniority. "And the worst thing a district can do for itself," observed the late Speaker Sam Rayburn, "if it's got someone here doing the job right, is to keep changing its congressman."[60]

Voters, however, are often unimpressed with this argument. In 1966, Harold Cooley of North Carolina was defeated in spite of slick TV ads emphasizing the importance of his position as chairman of the House Agriculture Committee. Pictures showed the impressive committee meeting room and lingered on the chairman's gavel while a soft voice explained how being chairman enabled Harold Cooley to better represent his constituents in Washington. Senator Yarborough of Texas was defeated in the 1970 primary despite his campaign which stressed the importance of his position on the Senate Appropriations Committee ("The third Texan ever to serve there") and his being chairman of the Senate Labor and Public Welfare Committee.[61] The idea that constituents do not generally understand a legislator's influence as it affects his representative ability is suggested by a congressman's comment:

> If there is one thing I have found my people care nothing about it is my attainments in Congress. I could say I was chairman of four standing committees. I think they relate that to being chairman of a PTA committee or a Lions committee. I defeated a good man who made much of the fact that he was chairman of a congressional committee, and people laughed about it. I had hundreds tell me, "Why you will be a committee chairman before you have been up there three months."[62]

The congressman's orientation is often perceived as a choice between the trustee or delegate role of representation. A trustee votes for what he considers to be in the best interests of his constituents, regardless of their expressed preferences. A delegate reflects what he knows is the preference of a majority in his district or state. Edmund Burke captured the essence of the trustee role in observing: "Your representative owes you, not his industry only, but his judgement; and he betrays, instead of serving you, if he sacrifices it to your opinion."[63] As a trustee, the legislator is expected to vote in accord with his own judgement after studying the legislation carefully and determining that his vote will be in the interest of his constituents and the country as a whole. Underlying this role is a belief that constituents' preferences and their interests are often quite different. It is pointed out that preferences fluctuate, even when interests do not. The true representative, it is argued, should consistently represent those interests and not change his position in accord with changes in public opinion. Supporters of the trustee role say that constituents do not have the information that the legislator does, and therefore cannot really evaluate the legislation at hand. "I figure if they knew what I know, they would understand my vote," is the way one legislator put it. Another says:

I am sent here as a representative of 600,000 people. They are supposed to be voting on all the legislation. I try to follow my constituents—to ignore them would be a breach of trust—but I use my judgement often because they are misinformed. I know that they would vote as I do if they had the facts that I have.[64]

The delegate role is the complete opposite of a trustee orientation. Instead of relying on the judgement and conscience of the legislator, a delegate is expected to vote in accordance with majority opinion in his constituency. Parke Godwin expressed a rather extreme conception of the delegate role in his *Political Essays:* "A representative is but the mouthpiece and organ of his constituents. What we want in legislation as in other trusts, are honest fiduciaries, men who will perform their duties according to our wishes."[65]

One of the differences between the trustee and delegate roles is in their definition of the national interest. A trustee rejects the notion that he best serves the country's interests by always reflecting the wishes of his district. He will argue that by voting in accordance with his own evaluation of the national interest and by considering the cues given by the party or by the president he is being a more responsible representative. For the trustee, what is good for his district is not necessarily what is good for the nation. Since the welfare of the district is greatly dependent on the national welfare, the trustee feels he serves the former by voting for policies which help the country as a whole. A delegate, on the other hand, defines the national interest as being that which is best for a majority of the districts. The national welfare is seen as the sum of the individual districts' welfare:

I'm here to represent my district. This is part of my actual belief as to the function of a congressman. What is good for the majority of districts is good for the country. What snarls up the system is these so-called statesman—congressmen who vote for what they think is the country's best interest.[66]

Adoption of a particular representational role is related to a person's conception of the proper functions of the Congress. Those who emphasize an active, programmatic legislature which responds to national mandates see the trustee role as an integral part of the institution. Those holding to the Jeffersonian model suggest that Congressmen are being representative when they vote in terms of the national party program even when this runs counter to constituency opinion. The Hamiltonian model emphasizes the national interest over that of particular districts or states. The president is seen as a more important cue-giver for congressmen's votes than is the legislator's constituency.

A delegate role is more suitable to those models of Congress which emphasize representation rather than rapid decision-making. The Madisonian model requires that Congress represent a different constituency than that of the president. To achieve this, legislators are expected to be delegates reflecting district opinion in order to provide a check against the president representing a national constituency. Such delegate representation supports the Madisonian system both by providing viable checks and balances and by assuring that interests not held by a national majority will be nevertheless represented by particular congressmen. Both the pluralist and the Whig model also emphasize a delegate role as the desired representational role. For pluralists, a delegate role maximizes the number of interests which have access to the lawmaking process. Legislators as trustees would not provide this variety of interest representation because of their focus on national interests. The Whig model proposes legislative supremacy in decision-making, but bases its claim for such supremacy on the representational nature of Congress. If legislators were acting as trustees they would be representing pretty much the same constituency as the president. This, of course, would greatly weaken claims for legislative supremacy. A delegate role, however, assures representation of different constituencies than those of the president, and lends support to arguments for legislative supremacy based on the nature of legislative representation.

A major problem with discussing the congressman's role as a choice between that of delegate or trustee is the fact that it oversimplifies reality. One reason for this is that such a choice is based on the assumption that the legislator knows what a majority of his constituents want. As V. O. Key once observed, "The question of whether a legislator should be a man and vote his mature convictions in the national interest or be a mouse and bow abjectly to the parochial demands of his constituents is irrelevant," because "generally, a legislator may hear from a few people on a few issues. He must always, as he votes, assume the risk of antagonizing some constituents, but he is rarely faced by the difficult choice of rejecting or accepting the mandate of his constituency, for he does not know what it is. And, indeed, there may be none."[67]

A solution to this problem is provided by a third representational role, that of politico. The politico role is simply a combination of the trustee and delegate roles. One reason for adopting this role is the realization that the legislator often does not have information as to constituency opinion on many issues. Though essentially a delegate, he may feel that this lack of information requires him to adopt a trustee orientation on some issues. Abraham Lincoln, when running for reelection to the Illinois General Assembly, outlined this politico role based on limited information: "If elected, I shall be governed by their will on all such subjects upon which I have the means of knowing what their will is, and upon all others I shall do what my own judgement teaches me will best advance their interests."[68]

Another reason for adopting the politico role is provided by ranking issues in terms of importance. A legislator may feel that some issues are so important that he must vote against his constituents wishes when he thinks they are wrong. On other issues, those he feels are not very important, he will go along with constituency opinion. This occurs regardless of the amount of information about constituency opinion that the legislator has. Senator William Fulbright of Arkansas reflected this type of politico role when he said:

> The average legislator early in his career discovers that there are certain interests, or prejudices, of his constituents which are dangerous to trifle with. Some of these prejudices may not be of fundamental importance to the welfare of the nation, in which case he is justified in humoring them, even though he may disapprove. The difficult case is where the prejudice concerns fundamental policy affecting the national welfare. . . .
>
> As an example of what I mean, let us take the poll-tax issue and isolationism. Regardless of how persuasive my colleagues or the national press may be about the evils of the poll-tax, I do not see its fundamental importance, and I shall follow the views of the people of my state. . . . On the other hand, regardless of how strongly opposed my constituents may prove to be to the creation of, and participation in, an ever stronger United Nations Organization, I could not follow such a policy in that field unless it becomes clearly hopeless.[69]

The politico role suggests that rather than saying a particular congressman is a delegate or a trustee, it is more accurate to say that on particular issues he acts as a trustee and on others as a delegate. Because of the flexibility which the politico role provides, it is the role most often chosen by congressmen. A study of 87 House members in the Eighty-eighth Congress (1963–1964) found that 46 percent of the sample chose the politico role, 28 percent the trustee, and 23 percent the delegate.[70]

Because the politico role is a compromise which permits legislators to act sometimes as a delegate and sometimes as a trustee, it is worth considering factors determining selection of one role over another. The question here is: Under what conditions and on which issues is the congressman likely to adopt a trustee or delegate role? Roger Davidson's study of House members in the Eighty-eighth Congress showed that representational role choices were related to the margin of victory in the previous election. Table 3 shows this relationship.

Table 3 suggests that members from marginal districts are more likely to adopt a delegate orientation and those from safe districts are better able to be trustees. This same pattern was found in another study which focused on the sources of information, or voting cues, for congressmen who won by large margins

TABLE 3 *Margin of Victory and Choice of Representational Role*

| Role | District Type[a] | |
	Marginal	Safe
Trustee	19%	35%
Politico	37	54
Delegate	44	11
Total	100%	100%
(n)	(32)	(52)

[a]Marginal districts are those in which the incumbent won by less than 60 percent of the vote in the 1962 election. Safe districts are those in which the congressman won by 60 percent or more of the vote.

SOURCE: Roger Davidson, *The Role of the Congressman* (Pegasus, 1969), p. 128. Reprinted by permission of Bobbs-Merrill Co.

and for those who came from marginal districts. The more vulnerable a member was at the polls, the more likely he was to listen to a wide range of opinions and suggestions.[71] One reason for legislators from marginal districts tending to be delegates is the fact that they are afraid to alienate any voters who might have supported them in the last election. The small margin of victory in the last election must be maintained or improved upon. Because of the small margin, however, it is difficult to discriminate among supporters and nonsupporters and the congressman must try to represent a broad range of interests from within the constituency. "That margin was sufficiently narrow that anybody in the state can come into this office and claim credit for my winning" was John Kennedy's observation after his close election to the Senate in 1952.[72] The typical trustee may be characterized as a member who comes from a safe district and thus has achieved leadership status as a result of his seniority. A delegate, on the other hand, is more likely to come from a competitive district and thus have low seniority and no leadership status.

Thus far, we have looked at substantive representation as reflected in congressmen's adopting a delegate, trustee, or politico role. Such analysis is limited, however, because it tells us how the congressman says he behaves or how he feels he should behave, but not necessarily how he really does behave. Role analysis, in short, studies attitudes rather than actual behavior. In order to move beyond this level in studying representation we must look at actual voting behavior and relate this to constituency opinion. The Survey Research Center of the University of Michigan conducted an extensive study of this sort after the election of 1958. Incumbent congressmen, their opponents, and a sample of constituents in 116 congressional districts were interviewed. In addition, roll call votes of these congressmen and the social and political characteristics of their districts were studied. The results of this study are presented in an article by Warren Miller and Donald Stokes called "Constituency Influence in Congress."[73]

Miller and Stokes found that the extent of policy agreement between congressmen and their constituents varied a great deal from issue to issue. On the question of American involvement in foreign affairs there was no connection between the views of constituents and their congressmen (a correlation coefficient of −.09). There was more agreement on matters of social and economic welfare (correlation of .3), and a high level of correspondence between constituencies and their representatives on the question of civil rights (correlation of .6).

The existence of such correlations between constituency opinion and the congressman's attitude does not really tell us how this linkage is achieved. In order to do this, Miller and Stokes look at three requirements which must be met before we can say that the constituency influences or controls the behavior of its representative: (1) The legislator's votes in the House must agree substantially with his own policy views or his perceptions of the district's views, and not be determined entirely by other influences. (2) The attitudes or perceptions governing the congressman's voting behavior must correspond, to some degree, to the district's actual opinions. (3) The constituency must consider the policy views of candidates when it votes.

The first condition was satisfied in the congressional districts studied. The congressman's attitude and his perception of constituency views can together serve to accurately predict his voting behavior. This study and a later one using the same data both suggest that the legislator's perception of constituency opinion is more important than his own attitude in determining how he votes.[74] That is to say that when there is a difference between the legislator's attitude and his perception of constituency views, he is more likely to vote in terms of his perception of constituency views or to change his attitude to fit this perception than he is to distort his perception of constituency opinion so that it fits with his attitudes. The importance of perception also suggests that constituencies do not influence voting behavior by selecting legislators whose attitudes jibe with theirs. Rather, the control is achieved because of accurate perceptions by congressmen who want to keep their job.

The second condition, that perceptions of constituency views correspond with their actual views, is not met as well as the first condition. The highest correlation between congressmen's perceptions and actual constituency opinion was found on the issue of civil rights. On the issue of foreign involvement there was almost no relationship between the legislator's perception of constituency opinion and actual constituency opinion. The legislator's perceptions and attitudes on welfare issues were found to correspond more strongly with the views of his electoral majority in the district than they did with the opinions of the constituency as a whole.

The third condition of constituency control, that voters consider the policy positions of the candidates, is not satisfied. The low level of information which voters bring to the polls is one of the most widely documented findings of political science. In the 1958 election sample, 46 percent of those *who voted* said they had neither read nor heard anything about either of the congressional candidates. Even those who knew something about one or both candidates tended to express what they knew in broad evaluative terms ("He's a good guy"). "Only about three comments in every hundred had to do with legislative issues of any description."[75] A 1965 Gallup survey found the same low level of political information among the general public: "Of the nationwide sample of adults, 57% did not know the name of their own Congressman; 41% did not know his party affiliation; 70% did not know when he next stood for reelection; 81% did not know how he voted on any major legislation during the year; and 86% could not name anything he had accomplished for the district."[76]

The low level of information among the public suggests that legislators do not need to fear defeat at the polls due to constituent rejection of their position on specific legislative issues. On most issues, the legislator is free to play a trustee role without having to fear rejection by the voters. When an issue is highly visible and seen as important by most constituents (such as civil rights in the 1958 study), a congressman is more likely to behave as a delegate.

Increased visibility of a particular issue is likely to change legislators' behavior from a trustee orientation to a delegate orientation. While most congressmen in 1958 could be classified as trustees on the issue of foreign involvement, the increased visibility of this issue area brought about by the war in Indochina suggests that most legislators in the early 1970s were acting in terms of the delegate role in this area. In studying the actual behavior of legislators, we are led to conclude that they are all politicos, tending to be trustees in some areas and delegates in others.

Given the low information level of the public, we may ask: How important are issues in congressional elections? We may examine this in terms of an issue which many analysts consider to be a most important one in congressional elections: unemployment. An MIT economist, Duncan Foley, has found a close relationship between Republican congressional fortunes and unemployment rates. "Foley's Law," as it is modestly called, suggests that every 1 percent rise in the unemployment rate threatens the Republicans with a loss of fifteen congressional seats.[77] James Sundquist, in *Politics and Policy,* has also shown the importance of unemployment as a factor in the Democratic gains in the 1958 congressional elections.[78] In both of these studies, however, the association of the issue is with political parties and not with individual legislators.

The Gallup polls on which Sundquist bases his analysis ask the questions: "What do you think is the most important problem facing this country today?" and "Which political party do you think can do a better job of handling the problem you have just mentioned—the Republican party or the Democratic party?" The importance of unemployment as an issue in 1958 and the greater number of respondents feeling that Democrats could do a better job of handling it meant that many Republican congressmen were threatened with defeat regardless of their legislative record. The effect of this issue, then, is one which helped Democrats even if they had voted against programs for reducing unemployment and hurt Republicans even if they had consistently supported such measures. It is the party image associated with this issue which affected voting behavior more than an evaluation of the legislator's voting record in terms of the issue.

Another way in which the congressman's behavior on particular issues is translated into an image which voters react to is through the activities of intermediary agencies such as the local party, the news media, and interest groups. Miller and Stokes discuss how these agencies tend to reduce the issue content in the congressman's image:

> Very often the Representative reaches the mass public through these mediating agencies, and the information about himself and his record may be considerably transformed as it diffuses out to the electorate in two or more stages. As a result, the public or parts of it—may get simple positive or negative cues about the Congressman which were provoked by his legislative actions but which no longer have a recognizable issue content.[79]

This brief and incomplete review of the role issues play in congressional elections suggests that voters tend to react to vague images of the candidates rather than to their specific issue positions. A voter may have absolutely no idea how often a legislator supports his party's programs, but he will probably know whether he is a Democrat or a Republican. Though of decreasing importance in elections, this party association may be all a voter needs to know in order to choose a candidate. Other images which may serve as cues for the voter are "pro-labor," "dove," "liberal," "fighter for the little people," "friend of big business," "watchdog for his constituency." But the function of all these images is to provide the voter with some cues for selecting one candidate over another without requiring him to know the candidate's actual position on specific issues.

Although most congressmen tend to overestimate their visibility to the public, many of them are aware of how little the public actually knows about their positions on issues. Consider these comments made by representatives:[80]

The people back home don't know what's going on. Issues are not most important so far as the average voter is concerned. The image of the candidate plays a much greater role.

In my campaign last year I had ten or twelve joint appearances with my opponent and in not a one of them did he criticize a vote I cast. Most of the time he talked about state issues. And the people didn't seem to know which was the state issue and which was the federal issue.

I got myself on both sides of a critical and important issue: I voted for a bill that passed Congress and then voted to sustain the veto. I thought it would defeat me because I was in a ridiculous position. It was my first campaign for re-election and that is all my opponent talked about. Finally, though, I made hay out of it. I bought some radio time and said, I want to talk about a very serious issue. This is one I am expert on because I am one of the few people who have been on both sides of it."

You know I am sure you'll find out a Congressman can do pretty much what he decides to do and he doesn't have to bother too much about criticism. I've seen plenty of cases since I've been up here where a guy will hold one economic or political position and get along all right; and then he'll die or resign and a guy comes in who holds quite a different economic or political position and he gets along all right too. That's the fact of the matter.

Voting is not the only way in which a congressman is expected to represent his constituents. Regardless of how the legislator votes, he is expected to perform personal services for constituents who request them. A great deal of the congressman's work load consists of this casework for constituents. "The most pressing day-to-day demands for the time of Senators and Congressmen," noted Senator Hubert Humphrey, "are not directly linked to legislative tasks. They come from constituents."[81] Servicemen who want to get out, farmers who fear the proposed construction of a federal highway, students who want information on government scholarships, in short anyone wanting information or aid in dealing with the federal bureaucracy is told to "write your congressman." For it is the representative, more than anyone else, who is expected to provide a link between the citizen and the vast bureaucracy of the federal government.

Providing these services to his constituents can often be more important than how he votes. A representative who fails to maintain contact by frequent visits to his constituency and a quick response to constituent's requests subjects himself to campaign attacks on these grounds. For example, Senator Prouty of Vermont had gained a reputation among some political circles in the state as being more a citizen of Washington than of Vermont. His reluctance to visit the state since his election as representative in 1950, led his opponent in 1970 to remark: "President Nixon may come to Vermont, Agnew may come. Perhaps even Senator Prouty will come to the state."[82] Because voters know so little about the issue positions of legislators, their performance in maintaining contact with constituents and performing these errands may often be more important in a campaign than anything else. In the words of one representative:

> Unless you can keep constantly in contact with your people, serving them and letting them know what you are doing, you are in a bad way. My experience is that people don't care how I vote on foreign aid, federal aid to education, and all those big issues, but they are very much interested in whether I answer their letter and who is going to be the next rural mail carrier or the next postmaster. Those are the things that really count.[83]

Again, it is the image which the congressman projects to his constituents which is most important. A legislator who is more concerned with being a good legislator and devoting his time to committee work faces the threat of being isolated from his district. As we noted earlier, voters are not as much impressed with the position of influence which the congressman holds as they are with his being accessible and constantly in touch with his constituency. Even a former Speaker of the House, John McCormack, was aware of how important casework is to the congressman. Being Speaker was seen as less important to his constituents than his being ready to help them on personal matters. A contemporary Boston politician observed: "He's the only politician I ever met who, if he was talking to the President and the Pope at the same time and someone said, 'John, they're pinching Tommy Sullivan over there. He's a friend of ours and it's a bum rap,' He'd leave right away and see what he could do for Tommy."[84]

Substantive representation through casework and constituency errands not only helps the congressman's reelection chances, but it provides him with information he might not otherwise have. If there are a number of requests concerning a particular tax provision or clarification of a particular statute, this could lead to a congressman's seeking a change in those laws. By bringing the matter to the attention of the legislator, the constituents are aiding him to better perform his lawmaking function. Although such requests generally concern only a small portion of the constituency, constant attention to such matters can gain a congressman a large following of people who he has personally helped.

SOME CONCLUDING OBSERVATIONS

In this chapter we have looked at four different ways of evaluating how representative Congress is. Measures of formal representation suggest that House districts come much closer to equal representation for an equal number of people than they did prior to 1964. Congress was found to be not representative in descriptive terms. Legislators tend to come from upper- and upper-middle class families, from business and professional occupation groups, and to be more educated than the general public. Symbolic representation is often achieved through extensive use of the media, allowing the congressman to project an image psychologically pleasing to most constituents. Substantive representation is achieved to a degree, but it is not accomplished by issue-oriented voters responding to a legislator's voting record. Rather, the congressman is relatively free from constant signals from constituents as to how to vote. Casework activity helping individual constituents seems to be as important a part of substantive representation as is the congressman's voting record.

If one were to try to assess the cumulative effect of these patterns of representation, it seems that the most accurate conclusion would be that they heavily weight the system in favor of the status quo. They contribute to making the Congress a conservative institution in the American system. Formal representation, as reflected in reapportionment of districts to fit population shifts, tends to help the suburbs more than central cities. Because these suburbs tend to be white, middle-class, and Republican, they tend to select representatives who are not subject to the demands of urban minority groups. Instead of reapportionment leading to a more liberal House, as many observers thought it would, the trend seems to be in the other direction. Measures of descriptive representation indicate that members of Congress are not like the average American. Those from the upper strata of society are greatly overrepresented on Capitol Hill. Because those from upper-income groups, educational groups, and occupational groups have more of a stake in the existing system, it is again suggested that there will be a tendency among such people to maintain that system. Minority groups and those with less money, education, and a poor job are much more willing to change a system from which they benefit little. They are also less likely ever to serve in the Congress.

The impact of symbolic representation is seen chiefly in the great amount of money required to run a successful campaign. Unless a candidate is personally wealthy, he has to depend on many large contributors for campaign funds. This reliance on businesses and corporations who have political money again tends to predispose a congressman to support those interests once elected. And those interests have more stake in maintaining a stable economic and political system than they do in attempting major innovations and experiments in government programs. The fact that voters respond to cues rather than specific issues in campaigns has the same effect. The attentive public, those interests and organizations that have the most contact with congressmen and who provide voting cues to both the public and the legislator, is likely to consist of groups which have been successful in having their interests protected in existing laws. Other than marginal adjustments to further their interests, they generally favor a congressman who is not likely to propose drastic changes to existing statutes.

To suggest that the cumulative effect of these patterns of representation is one favoring the status quo is not to suggest that Congress is a part of a monolithic power elite. The representational system of Congress is a relatively open one which grants access to a wide range of interests. Generally speaking, however, those interests which are best able to use these points of access and to influence legislative behavior are those which favor maintenance of, or marginal changes in, the existing system.

NOTES

1. Rowland Evans and Robert Novak, *Lyndon B. Johnson: The Exercise of Power* (New American Library, 1966), p. 557.

2. *Congressional Record*, 89th Congress, 2nd Session, January 12, 1966 (daily edition), p. 131.

3. Since 1885, 91 resolutions calling for four-year terms have been introduced in Congress. See Charles O. Jones, *Every Second Year: Congressional Behavior and the Two Year Term*, (The Brookings Institution, 1967), pp. 14–19.

4. U.S. Congress, House, Committee of the Judiciary, Subcommittee No. 5, "Congressional Tenure of Office," 89th Congress, 1st and 2nd Sessions (1965–1966), p. 19; cited in Jones, *Every Second Year*, p. 22.

5. Roger Davidson, David Kovenock, and Michael O'Leary, *Congress in Crisis: Politics and Congressional Reform*, Appendix B, Table B–1 (Wadsworth, 1966), p. 192.

6. "Congressional Reform," *Congressional Quarterly Special Report*, April 1, 1964, p. 49. See also Jones, *Every Second Year*, p. 24; Davidson et al., *Congress in Crisis*, p. 65n; John Saloma, *Congress and the New Politics*, (Little, Brown, 1969), p. 62n.

7. Representative Laurence J. Burton, "The Cost of Getting There and the Length of Stay," in Mary McInnis, ed., *We Propose: A Modern Congress*, (McGraw-Hill, 1966), p. 237.

8. Quoted in Davidson, et al., *Congress in Crisis*, p. 108.

9. *Ibid.* Taken from accounts of the hearings in the *New York Times*, February 16, 1966, p. 18 and the *National Observer*, February 21, 1966, p. 2.

10. Quoted in Jones, *Every Second Year*, p. 27.

11. Quoted in Charles Clapp, *The Congressman: His Work as He Sees It* (Anchor Books, 1964), pp. 57 and 58.

12. Quoted in Jones, *Every Second Year*, p. 27.

13. Federalist paper no. 52, *The Federalist* (Modern Library, n.d.), p. 343.

14. Jones, *Every Second Year*, p. 38.

15. *Ibid.*, p. 36.

16. *Ibid.*, p. 48.

17. Hannah Fenichel Pitkin, *The Concept of Representation* (University of California Press, 1967). For another discussion of the different dimensions of representation see Malcolm Jewell and Samuel Patterson, *The Legislative Process in the United States* (Random House, 1966), pp. 29–34.

18. Pitkin, *The Concept of Representation*, p. 43.

19. Thomas Hobbes, *Leviathan*, Chapter 16 (Collier Books Edition, 1962), p. 127.

20. Joseph Tussman, "The Political Theory of Thomas Hobbes" (unpublished Ph.D. dissertation, 1947), quoted in Pitkin, *The Concept of Representation*, p. 43.

21. Daniel Berman, *In Congress Assembled* (Macmillan, 1964), p. 387.

22. Congressional Quarterly Service, *Politics in America*, (1969), p. 103.

23. *Reynolds v. Simms*, 377 U.S. 533 (1964).

24. Andrew Hacker, *Congressional Districting: The Issue of Equal Representation* (The Brookings Institution, 1964) and William Goss, "Measuring the Impact of Congressional Representation," cited in Nelson Polsby, ed., *Reapportionment in the 1970s* (University of California Press, 1971), p. 233.

25. Milton C. Cummings, "Reapportionment in the 1970s: Its Effect on Congress," in Nelson Polsby, ed., *Reapportionment in the 1970s*, pp. 209–241.

26. *Congressional Quarterly Weekly Report*, Vol. 3, no. 46 (November 11, 1972), p. 2955.

27. John Adams, "Letter to John Penn," quoted in Pitkin, *The Concept of Representation*, p. 60.

28. Representative Jim Wright, *You and Your Congressman* (Coward-McCann, 1965), p. 15.

29. Quoted in John Wahlke, Heinz Eulau, William Buchanan, and Leroy Ferguson, *The Legislative System: Explorations in Legislative Behavior* (John Wiley, 1962), p. 253.

30. Donald R. Matthews, *U.S. Senators and Their World* (Vintage, 1960), p. 19.

31. Andrew Hacker, "The Elected and the Anointed: Two American Elites," *American Political Science Review,* September 1961, pp. 539–549.

32. Samuel P. Huntington, "Congressional Responses to the Twentieth Century," in David B. Truman, ed., *The Congress and America's Future* (Prentice-Hall, 1965), p. 13.

33. Leroy N. Rieselbach, "Congressmen as 'Small Town Boys': A Research Note," *Midwest Journal of Political Science,* May 1970, pp. 321–330.

34. Matthews, *U.S. Senators and Their World,* p. 26.

35. *Ibid.,* p. 31.

36. George B. Galloway, *History of the House of Representatives* (Thomas Y. Crowell, 1968), p. 35.

37. Matthews, *U.S. Senators and Their World,* p. 13.

38. David B. Walker, "The Age Factor in the 1958 Congressional Elections," *Midwest Journal of Political Science,* February 1960, pp. 1–26.

39. Representative Michael Harrington (D.-Mass.) has noted these age differences in his efforts to reform the seniority system. See his remarks in *Congressional Record,* March 11, 1970 and June 23, 1970.

40. Representative Michael Harrington, "Congressional Reform Comes First," statement before the Democratic Committee on National Priorities, April 30, 1970.

41. William Keefe and Morris Ogul, *The American Legislative Process* (Prentice-Hall, 1968), p. 128.

42. *Ibid.,* p. 129.

43. Matthews, *U.S. Senators and Their World,* p. 45.

44. Pitkin, *The Concept of Representation,* p. 102.

45. William Tindall, *The Literary Symbol* (1955), quoted in Pitkin, *The Concept of Representation,* p. 97.

46. Marshall McLuhan, *Understanding Media: The Extensions of Man* (McGraw-Hill, 1965), p. 331.

47. Murray B. Levin, *Kennedy Campaigning* (Beacon Press, 1966), p. 120.

48. Dan Nimmo, *The Political Persuaders* (Prentice-Hall, 1970), pp. 90–91.

49. Charles Guggenheim, quoted in *New York Times,* May 9, 1970, p. 27.

50. Nan Robertson, "TV Helped a Winner in Ohio," *New York Times,* May 9, 1970, p. 27.

51. *Ibid.*

52. *New York Times,* April 17, 1970, p. 62.

53. "Professional Managers, Consultants Play Major Roles in 1970 Political Races," *National Journal,* II (September 26, 1970), pp. 2084–2085; cited in Robert Agranoff's comprehensive introductory essay in *The New Style in Election Campaigns* (Holbrook Press, 1972), pp. 3–50. The discussion of professional campaign management firms comes from *Congressional Quarterly Weekly Report,* May 1, 1970, p. 3.

54. Richard Harris, "Annals of Politics (Campaign Expenses)," *The New Yorker,* August 7, 1971, p. 60. Other useful sources on campaign financing include Herbert Alexander, *Political Financing* (Burgess, 1972) and his earlier *Financing the 1968 Election* (Heath Lexington Books, 1971) and Robert Peabody et al., *To Enact a Law: Congress and Campaign Financing* (Praeger, 1972).

55. *New York Times,* April 27, 1970, p. 26; and Richard Harris, "Annals of Politics," p. 56.

56. Harris, "Annals of Politics," p. 56.

57. *Ibid.,* pp. 53 and 50.

58. *New York Times,* April 5, 1970, sec. 4, p. 12; *Boston Globe,* May 19, 1970, p. 11; Harris, "Annals of Politics," p. 48. For an attempt to determine whether incumbents are reelected with such frequency because of the advantages of incumbency or because they better reflect the views of their constituency, see Robert S. Erikson, "The Advantage of Incumbency in Congressional Elections," *Polity,* Vol. 3, no. 3 (spring 1971), pp. 395–405 and the comments of Charles Tidmarch in *Polity,* Vol. 4, no. 4 (summer 1972), pp. 523–526. Barbara Hinckley's "Incumbency and the Presidential Vote in State Elections," *American Political Science Review,* Vol. 64, no. 3 (September 1970), pp. 836–842 is also worth looking at.

59. Pitkin, *The Concept of Representation,* pp. 209–210.

60. Booth Mooney, *Mr. Speaker* (Follett, 1964), p. 166.

61. *New York Times,* April 26, 1970, p. 58.

62. Quoted in Charles Clapp, *The Congressman: His Work as He Sees It,* pp. 121–122.

63. Edmund Burke, "Speech to the Electors of Bristol," *Writings and Speeches of Edmund Burke* (Little, Brown, 1901), Vol. 2, pp. 93–98. Reprinted in Neal Riemer, ed., *The Representative* (D. C. Heath, 1967), p. 11.

64. Both quotes are from Charles O. Jones, "The Agriculture Committee and the Problem of Representation," in Robert Peabody and Nelson Polsby, *New Perspectives on the House of Representatives* (Rand McNally, 1969), p. 168.

65. Quoted in Alfred de Grazia, "The Representative Ought to Consult the Majority," in Neal Riemer, ed., *The Representative,* p. 38.

66. Quoted in Lewis Anthony Dexter, "The Representative and His District," in Peabody and Polsby, *New Perspectives on the House of Representatives,* p. 6.

67. V.O. Key, Jr., *Public Opinion and American Democracy* (Alfred A. Knopf, 1964), pp. 482–483.

68. Quoted in T. V. Smith, "Congress Must Follow the Popular Will," in Neal Riemer, ed., *The Representative,* p. 44.

69. Center for the Study of Democratic Institutions, *The Elite and the Electorate* (1963), p. 6.

70. Roger Davidson, *The Role of the Congressman* (Pegasus, 1969), p. 117.

71. David Kovenock, "Influence in the U.S. House of Representatives: Some Preliminary Statistical Snapshots," paper delivered at American Political Science Association Annual Meeting, New York City, 1967, p. 17.

72. Theodore Sorenson, *Kennedy* (Harper & Row, 1965), p. 74.

73. Warren Miller and Donald Stokes, "Constituency Influence in Congress," *American Political Science Review,* March 1963, pp. 45–56.

74. Miller and Stokes, "Constituency Influence in Congress," in Peabody and Polsby, *New Perspectives on the House of Representatives,* p. 44; and Charles Cnudde and Donald McCrone, "Constituency Attitudes and Congressional Voting A Causal Model," in Edward Dryer and Walter Rosenbaum, eds. *Political Opinion and Electoral Behavior* (Wadsworth, 1967), pp. 407–411.

75. Miller and Stokes, "Constituency Influence in Congress," in Peabody and Polsby, *New Perspectives on the House of Representatives,* p. 48.

76. AIPO Survey, November 7, 1965. Cited in Davidson et al., *Crisis in Congress,* p. 49.

77. *Boston Globe,* May 31, 1970, p. 42.

78. James L. Sundquist, *Politics and Policy* (The Brookings Institution, 1968), pp. 456 ff.

79. Miller and Stokes, "Constituency Influence in Congress," in Peabody and Polsby, *New Perspectives on the House of Representatives,* p. 49.

80. The first three quotes are from Clapp, *The Congressman: His Work as He Sees It,* pp. 421, 423, 426. The fourth is from Dexter, in Peabody and Polsby, *New Perspectives on the House of Representatives,* pp. 4–5.

81. Hubert Humphrey, "To Move Congress Out of Its Ruts," *New York Times Magazine,* April 7, 1963, p. 39.

82. *Christian Science Monitor,* April 18, 1970, p. 4.

83. Clapp, *The Congressman: His Work as He Sees It,* p. 58.

84. *New York Times,* May 21, 1970, p. 28.

CHAPTER 3

Parties

"Of course, they answer to their names?" the Gnat remarked carelessly.
"I never knew them do it."
"What's the use of their having names," the Gnat said, "if they
won't answer to them?"
"No use to them," said Alice; "but it's useful to the people that
name them, I suppose. If not, why do things have names at all?"

Lewis Carroll, *Alice's Adventures in Wonderland and*
Through the Looking Glass (Lancer Books, 1968)

In the Ninety-first Congress (1969–1970) there were 57 Democratic and 43 Republican senators. The House held 244 Democrats and 188 Republicans. Long before the 1970 campaigns really got rolling, President Nixon and Republican strategists began making plans for returning Congress to their party. Forty-three House members were selected as "Democratic target representatives" because of their electoral vulnerability. By unseating 29 of these 43 representatives and by losing no seats themselves, the Republican party would hold a majority in the House for the first time in 16 years. The target seats were scattered throughout New York, Wisconsin, California, Colorado, Illinois, Indiana, Missouri, New Jersey, and North Carolina. But even the Republicans realized that such a party coup was unlikely. With the exception of 1934, the president's party had always lost seats in modern off-year elections. Because of the difficulty of winning a House majority, the president focused his attention on the Senate.

Twenty-five of the thirty-five Senate seats involved in the 1970 elections were held by Democrats. A net gain of only seven seats would give Spiro Agnew the tie-breaking vote in the Senate. Target seats were again selected, and the president went to work recruiting strong Republican candidates. Nevada's Senator Howard Cannon, who had won by only 84 votes in 1964, was one of the targets. In late April, Vice President Agnew called District Attorney William Raggio of Reno and convinced him to give up his race for governor, place personal considerations aside, and go after Cannon's seat.

President Nixon was credited with personally influencing many Republicans to give up safe House seats in order to make Senate races in target states. Wyoming's John Wold was persuaded to challenge Senator Gale McGee. George Bush, reelected to his House seat without opposition in 1968, gave it up for the greater glory of becoming the second Republican senator from Texas. Clark MacGregor, who had carried his district in the Minneapolis suburbs by wide margins in five elections, went after the seat being vacated by Senator Eugene McCarthy. Senator Frank Moss of Utah, a benefitter of the Democratic landslides of 1958 and 1964, was being challenged by Nixon-encouraged Representative Laurence Burton. When Air Force One thundered into Knoxville, Tennessee, in late May it brought with it Representative W. E. Brock, challenger of Senator Albert Gore, for a presidential blessing at a Billy Graham rally. Representative J. Glenn Beall of Maryland, following the advice of former Governor Spiro Angew, gave up his safe House seat to make the race against Senator Joseph Tydings. North Dakota Representative Tom Kleppe said he was running against Senator Quentin Burdick for one reason: President Nixon asked him to.[1]

In attempting to give his party a majority in the Senate, Nixon was acting in a way that most presidents before him had. These earlier attempts to give the president's party a majority had been colossal failures. President Truman, in 1946, claimed that a Republican victory would be a "return to reaction." The voters disagreed, Republicans gained 13 seats in the Senate, and the famous "Class of '46," which included such conservative leaders as Bricker of Ohio, Jenner of Indiana, McCarthy of Wisconsin,

Knowland of California, and Williams of Delaware, came into **being**. The effects of the 1946 election were long lasting in the Senate because of the seniority advantage it gave to southern Democrats. Twelve years later, President Eisenhower sought a party victory in Senate races and suggested that a Democratic win would send the country "down the left lane which leads inescapably to socialism."[2] Again voters ignored presidential pleas and the Democrats gained 15 seats. The Class of '58, including such senators as Cannon of Nevada, Dodd of Connecticut, Hart of Michigan, Hartke of Indiana, McCarthy of Minnesota, McGee of Wyoming, Moss of Utah, Muskie of Maine, Proxmire of Wisconsin, and Yarborough of Texas, provided the backbone of a liberal Senate bloc which had great influence during the 1960s. Many of the Republican's target seats of 1970 were occupied by members of the Class of '58.

After all the hoopla of the 1970 campaign, the party makeup of Congress was pretty much the same. When the Ninety-second Congress began its work there were 254 Democrats and 180 Republicans in the House; 54 Democrats and 45 Republicans in the Senate. Nationwide, the Democrats got 54 percent of the vote, as compared to 51 percent in the last midterm election. While the 1970 elections did not result in catastrophic defeat for the Republican administration, they did serve to show, once again, the problems which an incumbent president faces if he tries to turn an off-year election into a mandate for his party.

The difficulties which a president faces in attempting to produce a party victory in off-year congressional elections are the results of many factors. The lack of presidential coattails and the advantages of incumbency are two such factors. Election analyst Richard Scammon suggests that an incumbent who does even a reasonable job is all but guaranteed a vote 5 to 10 percent above his party's strength in his district.[3] A president often finds, therefore, that even though he heavily carried a particular district or state in the last election, the voters return an incumbent of the other party in the next election. But what is perhaps most instructive about these attempts to produce party majorities in Congress is their demonstration of the local orientation of parties in the American system.

While a president seeks a mandate in congressional elections for his party's candidates and programs, most people running for Congress are more concerned with immediate factors and local issues which will assure their victory. These are often completely unrelated to the search for a congressional mandate on a nation-wide scale. Because of these differences, a president may find that attempts to influence the selection of candidates are either resented by state or district politicians or pull the president into the quagmire of local party conflicts.

An episode in the 1970 campaign illustrates these dangers: Florida's Democratic Senator Spessard Holland had decided to retire at the age of 78. His seat was up in 1970 and Florida Republicans saw a good opportunity for capturing a second Republican Senate seat in Florida. The most likely candidate was Representative William Cramer of St. Petersburg, the first Republican representative from Florida since Reconstruction. President Nixon saw the Florida seat as an important one in the 1970 races, and personally urged Cramer to give up his House seat and run for the Senate. In July 1969, Nixon called Representative Cramer to the White House and told him "Bill, the Senate needs you, the country needs you, the people need you—now run." Cramer decided that he would, and had reason to be optimistic about his chances of winning. The Republican party in Florida had shown consistently increasing strength in recent elections, having elected a Republican governor in 1966 and a Republican senator in 1968. A poll taken in April 1970 showed Cramer defeating his only Republican primary challenger by 65 to 21 percent.

Then, suddenly, on April 21, the recently defeated Nixon candidate for the Supreme Court, G. Harrold Carswell, announced that he would run as a Republican candidate for the Senate. Carswell's announcement came as quite a shock to the Cramer forces, for it seemed that Carswell not only had the backing of Florida Governor Claude Kirk and Senator Edward Gurney, but also had cleared his candidacy with White House political aide Harry Dent. The involvement of Dent seemed to suggest that Carswell had White House approval for his Senate campaign. A great deal of confusion thus descended on the Florida Senate race in the spring of 1970 for it seemed that both candidates for the Republican Senate nomination could claim the support of President Nixon and his crack Republican campaign staff. As the clouds began to lift, it became clear that Dent, in responding to an early morning phone call by Kirk and Gurney, did not know that he was bringing the White House into a long-standing party feud by terming the Carswell candidacy an "ideal solution" to the vagaries of Florida politics.

The backers of Carswell, Governor Kirk and Senator Gurney, represented a wing of the Florida Republican party which was attempting to grasp the reins of state party leadership from the faction led by Representative Cramer. Caught in the middle, the Nixon administration could only proclaim its neutrality in the primary and leave the Florida Republicans to fight their own battles. The effect of the abortive White House intervention, however, was one which left the eventual Republican senatorial candidate, William Cramer, in a weaker position for his unsuccessful race in the general election. Attempting to recruit the strongest possible Republican candidate for the Florida Senate seat, the president and his political advisors had become involved in a state party conflict and had weakened the chances of the already endorsed party candidate for the office.

The 1972 election was quite a different show from that of two years earlier. President Nixon and Senator McGovern were heading the lists of the two parties' congressional candidates, and the president had learned something from his relatively unsuccessful attempt to pull in Republican legislators in 1968. Voters were asked to "reelect the president" with little emphasis put on who that was or which party he represented. In accordance with this low-profile approach, President Nixon made only a handful of campaign appearances in behalf of Republican candidates for the House or Senate. This was in sharp contrast to the active recruitment of and campaigning for party candidates carried on by the president in 1968.

President Nixon's landslide victory ranked only with those of Warren G. Harding in 1920, Franklin Roosevelt in 1936, and Lyndon Johnson in 1964. The congressional results, however, were another story. The 1972 election was the first time in American history that a president had won 60 percent or more of the popular vote yet failed to increase his party's seats in both the House and the Senate; and the first time that such an overwhelming party victory at the presidential level failed to give that party control of both chambers of Congress. Democrats picked up two additional seats in the Senate, the same number they added in the Democratic landslide in 1964. To win control of the House in 1972, the Republicans needed to win 41 new seats. They gained only 13. The party composition of the Ninety-third Congress was not much different from that of the Ninety-second: the Senate held 57 Democrats and 43 Republicans; the House, 242 Democrats and 192 Republicans. After the 1972 returns were in, the Republican national chairman described it as "a personal triumph for Mr. Nixon, but not a party triumph."[5]

Whenever an incumbent president tries to bring in enough candidates to give his party a legislative majority he is acting in terms of a model of Congress which highly values decision-making. The argument for his party's having a majority is that this is the best way for voters to make sure that Congress rapidly enacts legislation reflecting the electoral mandate. What this assumes, however, is the existence of a legislative party organization capable of producing majorities in line with the policy mandates of elections. In order to evaluate the impact of political parties on congressional behavior, we have to look at three different aspects of the political process: the role which parties play in congressional elections, the role parties play in legislative voting, and party organization in Congress.

What we find, in the present system, is that there are a number of factors working against the fulfillment of a genuine party government model. To begin with, there is the fact that a number of people hold the representational function of Congress to be more important than the lawmaking function. Reforms which would tighten national party control over legislators' voting would necessarily weaken the strong geographic representation which the present system favors. When such changes reach the point where many members of Congress feel that following the national party in their voting threatens reelection from their districts, then the idea of party voting to reflect national electoral mandates becomes unsatisfactory. This emphasis on geographic representation permeates all discussions of the possibility of achieving a party government system in Congress. It really sets the limits within which American parties may attempt to influence legislative voting.

The essential irony of political parties in the American legislative system is this: while party identification is perhaps the most important determinant of voting behavior in elections as well as legislative voting, the sort of unified, efficient party organization which would seem to be a necessary part of such a system is lacking both at the electoral and the legislative level. In order to explain this system we have to look at the way parties influence electoral and legislative voting in spite of this lack of a strong organization, and at the way the legislative party organization is able to exert influence within the limits set by the system's emphasis on geographic representation.

PARTIES AND VOTERS

Anthony Downs, in *An Economic Theory of Democracy,* outlined the way in which a perfectly rational human being would go about voting.[6] A rational voter is defined here only in terms of means; he seeks efficiency by either maximizing output for a given input (casting his vote in such a way that it has the greatest impact in bringing about policies he favors) or by minimizing input for a given output (not spending scarce resources such as time and money on gathering information in order to cast an "informed" vote which really will not make any difference in the political system).

To cast a rational vote for every candidate, the individual citizen would have to spend most of his waking hours evaluating the policy positions of all candidates. Such behavior, while insuring an informed voting decision, would be grossly inefficient in terms of payoffs the voter would receive. The likelihood that his one vote will elect the chosen candidates and produce the desired policies is not great enough to justify the tremendous costs of gathering the information. A rational solution to this problem is to delegate the evaluation and analysis of political information to another person or agency.

If citizen A has a friend who is an economist, and if he knows that his friend's political goals are basically the same as his own, then it makes sense to rely on his friend's analysis of which candidate would be more likely to help achieve those goals in the economic sector. By relying on the superior information which his friend has in this area, citizen A greatly reduces his own costs of gaining information to cast a rational vote. Similarly, if the voter knows that one political party is committed to particular groups or segments of the electorate, he may cast a rational ballot by voting strictly in terms of party labels. Again, the voter is able to support candidates who share his policy goals without having to expend a great deal of time and energy on the information gathering process itself. The most important requirement of such delegation of analysis and evaluation is that the delegated agency share the policy goals of the delegating individual. It is irrational to delegate such analysis to a political party if that party is likely to change its base of group support or policy goals in order to broaden its political appeal.

We noted in Chapter 2 the low level of political information which voters bring to the polls. Because the average voter knows so little about the candidates and their issue positions, it is difficult to say that he casts a rational vote. By voting in terms of party, however, even an uninformed voter may cast a ballot in line with his own interests. In studying the American electorate, political scientists have found great consistency in citizen's identification with one party or the other.

Table 1 shows this pattern over an 18-year period. A person's identification with the Democratic or Republican party is not only a remarkably stable phenomenon; it also is an attitude which he acquires early in life. At the age of ten, most American children already think of themselves as Democrats or Republicans.[7] This early established party attitude tends to act as a perceptual screen through which all political stimuli are given meaning. Information about issues or candidates generally takes on meaning as it is related to party identification. Although one cannot accurately predict electoral outcomes solely on the basis of party identification, it is found to be the single most important variable in such prediction.

In recent years, many political observers have talked about the declining importance of party identification in determining electoral outcomes. The importance of a candidate's personality (Eisenhower in 1952 and 1956 and McGovern in 1972), or of a single overriding issue (Vietnam in 1968) may lead to many people voting against the party with which they identify. There has also been an increase in split-ticket voting, such as the great number of Democrats who voted for Nixon in 1972 and then pulled the Democratic lever for congressional races. The impact of "short-term forces" such as candidate personality and issues must certainly be considered along with party identification if we are fully to comprehend the role parties play in elections.[8] But the great stability in the distribution of party identification shown in Table 1 cannot be ignored. And this is most evident when we consider voting patterns in midterm elections.

Table 1 Distribution of Party Identification

Party Identification	Oct. '52	Oct. '54	Oct. '56	Oct. '58	Oct. '60	Oct. '62	Oct. '64	Nov. '66	Nov. '68	Nov. '70
Strong Republican	13%	13%	15%	13%	14%	12%	11%	10%	10%	10%
Weak Republican	14	14	14	16	13	16	13	15	14	15
Independent Republican	7	6	8	4	7	6	6	7	9	8
Independent	5	7	9	8	8	8	8	12	11	13
Independent Democrat	10	9	7	7	8	8	9	9	10	10
Weak Democrat	25	25	23	24	25	23	25	27	25	23
Strong Democrat	22	22	21	23	21	23	26	18	20	20
Apolitical, don't know	4	4	3	5	4	4	2	2	1	1
Total (N):	100% (1614)	100% (1139)	100% (1172)	100% (1269)	100% (3021)	100% (1289)	100% (1571)	100% (1291)	100% (1553)	100% (1802)

SOURCE: John P. Robinson et al., *Measures of Political Attitudes* (Ann Arbor: Survey Research Center-Institute for Social Research, 1968), p. 496, reprinted by permission. Reprinted in Fred Greenstein, *The American Party System and the American People* (Prentice-Hall, 1970), p. 37. The 1968 and 1970 data are from Walter DeVries and V. Lance Tarrance, *The Ticket-Splitter* (William Eerdmans, 1972), p. 143.

Voting turnout in off-year elections is consistently lower than it is in presidential years. About 25 percent of the people voting in presidential elections fail to show up at the polls two years later. Those who drop out are generally independents or weak party identifiers. The effects of a charismatic leader at the head of the ticket are absent, and volatile issues are seldom raised. The importance of party identification in Congressional elections is reflected in the fact that Democrats won a majority in 19 of the 21 congressional elections between 1932 and 1972. This Democratic edge is what we would expect if elections were determined by party identification and not influenced by candidate or issue factors which are so often pivotal ones in presidential elections.

Two other characteristics of party identification are worth mentioning here. First, this identification is with the national Democratic or Republican party and not with a state or regional variant. A 1960 survey showed that even southern Democrats responded to questions about the party in terms of the national party rather than its state or southern Democratic wing.[9] Second, party identification patterns in the population do suggest a relatively stable group basis of support for the parties. Indeed, the basic difference between the two parties is often expressed as a difference in the group represented by each rather than an ideological one.[10]

The Republican party can generally count on support from the college educated, business and professional groups, and those living in suburbs or rural areas. The Democrats main strength is found to lie with the less educated, skilled and unskilled laborers, and those living in central cities. Although a presidential election may find many members of these groups crossing over to the other party (blue-collar workers in the North who voted for Wallace or Nixon in 1968 on the basis of the "law and order" issue, for example), an off-year congressional election is more likely to produce voting patterns in keeping with the group basis of the two parties. Table 2 shows a pattern of group voting in a recent congressional election which is quite similar to the distribution of parties identification among these groups.

The affiliation of a group with a particular party would be quite meaningless unless members of that party consistently sought policies which would favor that group. In spite of the great slack in the American party system and the existence of "wayward

TABLE 2   *Group Voting in the 1966 Congressional Election*

Education			Religion		
	Dem.	*Rep.*		*Dem.*	*Rep.*
College	41%	59%	Protestant	45%	55%
High School	53	47	Catholic	65	35
Grade School	61	39	Jewish	75	25

Race			Community Size		
	Dem.	*Rep.*		*Dem.*	*Rep.*
White	50%	50%	500,000 and over	56%	44%
Nonwhite	81	19	50,000–499,999	57	43
			2,500–49,999	48	52
			Under 2,500	48	52

Occupation		
	Dem.	*Rep.*
Professional and Business	42%	58%
White Collar	48	52
Manual Workers	62	38
Farmers	50	50
Union Members	65	35

SOURCE: American Institute of Public Opinion release, December 14, 1966. Based on 9,000 interviews in selected sample of districts. Reprinted in C. Peter Magrath, Elmer Cornwell, Jr., and Jay S. Goodman, *The American Democracy* (Macmillan, 1969), p. 238. Courtesy American Institute of Public Opinion (The Gallup Poll).

freaks" who almost always vote against their party, it is possible to discern a consistent difference between Democratic and Republican policy emphases. More congressional Democrats favor policies providing benefits to the less educated, to the blue-collar worker, and to the city dweller. More congressional Republicans will favor policies benefiting those groups which provide the bulk of G.O.P. support.

The lack of a strong national party organization means that party labels are often misleading as indicators of policy preferences. A Republican, Javits of New York, will consistently support policies favorable to traditionally Democratic groups, more often than Democrats Stennis or Eastland of Mississippi will. Being a Republican senator from Connecticut is quite different from being a Republican senator from Florida or California. But if we are to speculate as to how a voter with little interest in or information about politics might cast a rational vote in terms of his own interests, the importance of party labels cannot be overlooked. Knowing the party of a congressional candidate requires the expenditure of little or no time or effort by the voter. It provides him with a cue which enables him to vote in his own general interests even though he may know nothing about the particular candidates running or their policy positions developed during the campaign. And it is in this sense of cue-giver, rather than in the sense of an organization controlling the selection and behavior of legislators, that the political party most directly affects congressional elections.

PARTIES AND LEGISLATORS

When we move from the setting in which a voter makes a decision to that in which a congressman acts we are struck by obvious differences. The average voter cares little about politics; a congressman's entire life centers around it. While most voters do not have much information on which to base a voting decision, legislators are flooded with information provided on every issue by the press, interest groups, executive agencies, and their own staffs. It would seem, therefore, that the process by which a congressman makes up his mind about a legislative vote would be quite different from that of the voter in elections. The party cue would not seem to be such a reliable basis for casting a rational vote. For the legislator not only has information available, he also has a great interest in using this information to cast a knowledgeable vote. In short, the costs of casting uninformed votes are great enough to the legislator to justify his assuming the costs of gathering information.

These differences between the citizen's voting decision and the legislator's voting decision seem not so great, however, when we consider the number and scope of decisions which the congressman must make. A voter makes a political decision every two years; a legislator is constantly called on to make such decisions. In the House alone, the number of roll call votes has increased from 93 in 1958 to 233 in 1968.[11] Added to this are the great number of voting decisions which the congressman makes unrecorded on the floor, in committee and subcommittee, and in his office.

The scope of these decisions is mind boggling. During the course of one day in June 1969, the House discussed the following subjects: financing of airport facilities, disposal of surplus lead, cigarette sales and advertising, congressional ethics, the use of Defense Department facilities in making movies, aid to the arts, treatment of laboratory animals, creation of a national wildlife refuge, textile imports, Post Office salaries, chemical and biological warfare research, and patents and copyrights.[12] Because of the number and variety of issues, legislators often find themselves in a low information decisional situation not unlike that of the voter. Two representatives' comment:[13]

> I have to vote on 150 different kinds of things every year—foreign aid, science, space, technical problems, and the Merchant Marine, and Lord knows what else. I can't possibly become an expert in all these fields.
>
> It's not uncommon for me to go the floor with the bells ringing, votes being taken, and it's on a bill or issue that I have never heard of before. I haven't the remotest idea of the issues involved. You've got to make up your mind; you can't vote "maybe" and you can't vote "present"—you don't want to. So you have to make a decision on the best basis you can.

Members of Congress seek to make rational decisions in voting on issues about which they know little. Because of the number and scope of decisions it is impossible for the legislator to avail himself of the technical information needed to cast an informed, independent vote on the merits of the issue. Two students of Congress, Donald Matthews and James Stimson, have suggested that the normal process of congressional decision-making follows a low information strategy of seeking cues from fellow members.[14] These cues serve the same function for the legislator as they do for the voter in elections; they permit the decision-maker to make rational voting decisions without having to incur great costs of gathering information. The sources of these cues will vary a great deal from member to member and issue to issue. These sources include state delegations, parties, subject matter experts, members of a similar ideological bent, those who come from similar districts, and other members with whom the legislator has apolitical, informal ties (such as playing squash or drinking bourbon).

By building a network of cue-givers for different issues, the legislator assures himself of fairly reliable information on how he should vote without having to expend a great deal of time and effort arriving at an independent decision. Instead of trying to determine the impact of his constituency of a proposed tax reform bill by extensive research on constituency opinion, the congressman may simply follow the advice of a Ways and Means Committee member whose district is similar to his own. Similarly, a legislator might find it more reasonable to vote with the other members of his state delegation than to run the risk of notoriety which comes with being "the only congressman from Illinois to vote against the interests of her citizens."

The political party occupies a central position in the cue-seeking network within Congress. This influence is achieved both through the party leadership's control over certain kinds of information (such as the number of pro and con voters on an issue before it comes to the floor) and through the attachment which the legislator has to the party label. The impact of party leadership and the party organization as an intelligence network will be discussed below. Here we are more interested in the way party acts as a cue for the legislator's vote much as it does for voters in the election.

Congressmen indicate a desire to support their party even when other pressures, such as constituency opinion or ideology, lead them often to oppose their party in floor votes. A survey by Randall Ripley in the Eighty-eighth Congress found 94 percent of the Democratic representatives interviewed and 96 percent of the Republicans responding affirmatively to the question: "Do you want to act in accord with your party's position?" Seventy-four percent of the Democrats and 72 percent of the Republicans indicated that this was generally their first consideration in determining their position.[15] Senator Mark Hatfield of Oregon, one of five Republicans in the Senate most often voting against their party in 1969, commented on the problems raised by such behavior: "How many times can I vote against an ABM and a Haynsworth and still be in the ball game as a Republican Senator with a Republican President."[16]

Numerous studies of roll call votes in Congress have suggested that party is the single most important predictor of roll call behavior.[17] A *Congressional Quarterly* study in 1969 showed that the average congressman supported his party on 62 percent of the votes in which a majority of his party was in disagreement with a majority of the other party.[18] What most of these studies indicate is that in the absence of strong pressures from constituency or from committee leadership, the average congressman is predisposed to support his party's position on issues. The party cue becomes less important, however, when the party position runs counter to the legislator's own electoral or ideological interests. A study of Democratic party leadership in the House by Lewis Froman and Randall Ripley outlines six conditions which help to create a situation in which most congressmen will follow their party's leadership:[19]

1. *Party leadership is committed and active.* By terming a particular issue a party vote, by disseminating information as to the importance of the vote through the interpersonal cue-giving networks, and by polling legislators so as to gain information and a commitment, the legislative party leaders can make it more difficult for a congressman to vote against his party.

2. *The issue is procedural rather than substantive.* Parties achieve their greatest cohesion on the most procedural measures such as the election of a Speaker and the greatest number of defections on narrowly substantive measures such as votes on conference committee reports and amendments to bills.

3. *The visibility of the issue is low.* The more complex an issue is and the less play it gets in the news media, the more likely is it to produce a vote along partisan lines. This is a direct result of the fact that congressmen are more likely to support their party position in the absence of strong conflicting pressures. The complexity and low visibility of an issue reduces these outside pressures.

4. *The visibility of the action is low.* The most visible type of activity, roll call votes on the floor, produces the greatest number of party defections. Voice votes, division votes, and unrecorded teller votes generally produce more cohesive partisan voting patterns. This again results from the fact that congressmen may support their party against conflicting pressures when it is unlikely that those agents urging a defection from party will be aware of how the congressmen voted.

5. *There is little counterpressure from constituencies.* While the average northern Democrat in the Senate supported his party on 71 percent of the party roll call votes in 1969, the average southern Democratic senator supported it on only 46 percent of these votes. The same pattern held in the House with northern Democrats supporting their party on 73 percent of the votes and southern Democrats supporting it on 40 percent of the votes.[20] The lower party support by southern congressmen is generally explained in terms of their coming from different types of constituencies than northern Democrats. Indeed, most deviations in party votes are explained in terms of constituency factors.

Lewis Froman suggests that differences between northern Democrats and northern Republicans are a function not just of party, but also of the fact that Democrats tend to come from different types of constituencies than Republicans. Looking at such variables as percentage owner-occupied dwellings, percentage non-white population, average population per square mile, and percentage urban, Froman found that Democrats tended to represent constituencies which were more urban, more racially mixed, had a lower percentage of owner-occupied dwellings, and had more people per square mile than Republican constituencies.[21] In supporting the programs of Democratic Presidents Kennedy and Johnson, these northern Democrats were able best to represent their constituents by supporting their party programs.

A congressman's party interests and constituency interests are not always the same and it is in these cases that much deviation in party voting occurs. When we look at Republican senators and representatives who in 1969 had the highest records of opposition to their party, we find that most of them come from constituencies which have characteristics associated with Democratic party affiliation. Senators Case of New Jersey, Schweiker of Pennsylvania, and Goodell and Javits of New York and Representatives Whalen of Ohio, Fulton and Biester of Pennsylvania, and Reid, Button, and Horton of New York are examples. To consistently support Republican party positions in Congress these legislators would have to go against what they consider the interests of their constituencies and would thus risk electoral defeat. The legislative party is more likely to receive support on issues in which there is no conflict between constituency interests and party interests.

6. *State delegations are not engaged in collective bargaining.* Members of Congress from the same party and the same state are an

important reference group for legislators. State delegations are the primary socializing agency for freshmen and continue to play an important cue-giving role throughout his tenure in the legislature. Voting in line with party colleagues from the same state provides a member with an automatic rationalization for his vote. He need only point out to those who challenge his position that every Democrat or every Republican from the state voted the same way. By acting in unison the state delegation can be an effective bargaining agent in winning concessions from the party leadership. The party leadership may be forced to meet the demands of a state delegation in return for needed votes. The North Carolina delegation demonstrated the effectiveness of this tactic in 1964 when it effectively bargained for a guarantee that Adam Yarmolinksy, disliked by southerners because of his leadership in integrating southern military bases, would not hold a position in the proposed Office of Economic Opportunity. Democratic leaders, needing the North Carolina votes, agreed.

In cases like this, when state party delegations are united in opposition to the national party, legislators may conceive of such "deviant" behavior as being, in fact, party loyalty. Because of the decentralized nature of American parties, congressmen may think more in terms of state than national parties. The North Carolina Democrats in the case mentioned could feel that real party loyalty demanded that they act in terms of the North Carolina Democratic party rather than the national party. They were being "good Democrats" by opposing congressional Democratic leadership on this one point. As a potent source of cues conflicting with the legislative party, then, the state delegations may weaken the effectiveness of the party in much the same way that constituencies do. About half of the state delegations in the House meet on a regular basis and seek unified issue positions. This represents about half of the total membership of the House. Roll call analyses show that state delegations are most influential on two quite different sorts of issues: "tough questions, controversial both within the party and within the House," and "matters of trivial or purely local importance."[22] The party's strength as a cue-giver is greatly enhanced when state delegations have either been co-opted to support the party leadership position or are not separated from the party position on the issue.

The congressional party, then, is most correctly conceived as an effective source of voting cues within a complex network of competing cue sources. At times, the constituency cue or state delegation cue will be more important in determining the legislator's vote. But over the great number and wide range of issues voted on, the party is one of the most consistent sources of legislative cues. And this helps to explain its importance in determining legislative outcomes in spite of its lack of a cohesive national and legislative organization.

PARTY ORGANIZATION

Basic changes in the existing structure of congressional party organization often have been put forward by reformers on and off Capitol Hill. In Chapter 1 we looked at some of those proposed reforms. Ralph K. Huitt has suggested that these proposals for creating party government in Congress have failed to gain widespread support because their enactment would too drastically alter the present political context in which legislators operate.[23] Congressmen highly value their role as representative of their district and they generally support the internal decision-making structure of the standing committee system. Creating a strong party organization would require legislators many times to subordinate representation of district interests to voting with party leadership. It would also establish a legislative power structure which threatened the existing one of standing committees. The congressional party has always been a decentralized entity seeking to keep its members in office. Its success rests on the continued reelection of legislative members and this goal precludes too close an identification with a president whose electoral base is quite different from that of most legislators. Because of this dependence on many heterogeneous constituencies the legislative party's loyalties are directed more toward maintaining the existing party structure and its congressional members than toward developing a unified national party organization. This appreciation for the decentralized, local nature of parties has a profound effect on the party organization in Congress.

A party leader is hesitant to ask a congressman to support the party position if he knows that such support might seriously endanger the chances of that man being returned to Congress. The fact that party leaders and followers share the same dependence on local constituencies and the fact that both have been socialized into a congressional system placing a premium on reelection and the virtues of decentralization makes it unlikely that party leaders will insist on party loyalty at the sacrifice of these other considerations. One reason, then, that the Jeffersonian model's requirement of both a unified national party and effective control over the behavior of legislators is not met is because party leaders necessary to effecting such a system are more committed to the needs of fellow legislators than they are to bringing such a model of party control into being.

Another reason for the legislative party's not meeting the organizational requirements of the Jeffersonian model is the party's lack of ultimate sanctions. To be able to control the behavior of legislators the party must be able to punish those who ignore leadership requests. And because party leadership has no control over the basic question of who shall be seated as a Democratic or Republican congressmen, its ultimate sanctions are limited. The party leadership, as Lyndon Johnson observed when he was Senate majority leader, has "no authority to discipline, no authority to fire Senators like a President can fire his members of Cabinet."[24]

In seeking to determine what sanctions party leaders do have, Randall Ripley asked a sample of representatives in the Eighty-eighth Congress what the leadership could do to them if they did not support the party position. Over a third from both parties responded "Nothing." Forty-three percent of the Democrats mentioned "isolation" as a leadership sanction and over half of the Republicans mentioned control over committee assignments.[25] The nature of these sanctions reflects both party leaders' and rank-and-file dependence on maintaining the legislative system as a highly integrated network of friendship and mutual respect. In such a system, isolation becomes a powerful sanction. Not only do you "feel lonesome when you are not in his [the Speaker's] good graces," as one congressman noted, but your effectiveness as a legislator is seriously impaired.[26]

To be an effective party leader a representative or senator must work within this legislative system which emphasizes electoral survival over party loyalty and denies party leaders ultimate sanctions. Lyndon Johnson's tenure as Senate Democratic leader from 1953 to 1960 is often cited as the textbook case of strong party leadership within the constraints of the existing system. The genius of Johnson's leadership, according to Huitt, was his recognition that individual senators "must play many different and often conflicting roles, and that one task of leadership is to structure a situation so that a member can select a role which will allow him to stand with the party."[27] Such a style of leadership seeks to avoid potential conflicts between the member's party role and his other roles of constituency representative, ideological spokesman, committee member, and substantive policy expert, or that of a career representative or senator. Some of the techniques of party leadership possible in the present legislative system, ones which were effectively employed by Johnson, include the following.[28]

1. *Personal contact.* The network of general friendships which develop in Congress is greatly affected by party. Responsibility for socializing a freshman belongs chiefly to state delegation members of the same party, and this tendency to develop friends among one's party colleagues continues throughout a member's tenure. Because of this, party leaders often attempt to influence voting behavior by making appeals through these friendship networks. This may be done directly by party leaders or indirectly by utilizing members who are recognized as cue-givers to particular congressmen in that issue area. Lyndon Johnson, it was said, saw every Democratic senator every day for a number of years.

When asked what kind of appeals party leaders made to them to achieve party unity, 86 percent of the Democrats and 48 percent of the Republicans in Randall Ripley's study of the House listed personal appeals.[29] Such personal appeals, phrased simply "we need you" were cited more often than appeals in party terms, on the merits of the issue, or appeals phrased in punishment-reward terms.

2. *Committee assignments.* Both parties in both chambers put people on committees by having a party committee on committees make recommendations which are ratified by the full party caucuses. Democrats on the House Ways and Means Committee serve *ex officio* as that chamber's Democratic Committee on Committees. Although a study of this committee found it to be regionally and ideologically representative, membership on Ways and Means does tend to be heavily weighted in favor of senior and safe-seat

congressmen.[30] The House Republican Committee on Committees is made up of one member for each state having a Republican representative. Since the number of votes a committee member has depends on the number of Republicans in his state delegation, the advantage goes to larger states and to heavily Republican states. The Senate Democratic Steering Committee and the Senate Republican Committee on Committees make committee assignments in that body. Democratic party leadership tends to be more centralized than the Republican's, and the Democrat's committee membership is generally more senior than its Republican counterpart.

Prior to the far-reaching changes made in House rules after the revolt against Speaker Joe Cannon in 1911, party leaders in the House had more direct control over committee assignments. "Committee assignments," said one of the leaders of that revolt, "were the rawhide used to promote party subserviency and to crush any spirit of independence."[31]

In recent times, party leaders have exerted a more indirect influence over committee assignments. When Lyndon Johnson was running the Senate and his fellow Texan Sam Rayburn was Speaker of the House, they were able to influence assignments to the Ways and Means and Senate Finance committees so as to block prospective members who might seek changes in tax policies favorable to the oil industry.

At times the importance of committee assignments in affecting policy is dramatized in the battle over a single seat. In 1962, pro-administration Democrats were successful in defeating Representative Landrum of Georgia for a seat on Ways and Means. Such a tactic was seen as crucial to passage of the president's tax program, the medicare bill, and his trade program.[32] As majority leader, Lyndon Johnson used his influence over committee assignments to reward the faithful and to consolidate his intricate network of debts owed for past favors. John Kennedy received, through the machinations of Johnson, a highly prized seat on Foreign Relations in 1957, a seat which by rights of seniority should have gone to Estes Kefauver of Tennessee. Here is the way that went:

> After the presidential election of 1956, Estes Kefauver of Tennessee and John F. Kennedy of Massachusetts, who had competed on the National Convention floor at Chicago for the vice

presidential nomination the previous summer, were competing again, this time for a single vacancy on Foreign Relations.

Johnson, who had backed Kennedy against Kefauver at Chicago, was now trying to bring Kennedy closer to his orbit. He was determined to have the vacancy go to Kennedy over Johnson's old foe, Kefauver. But how to get around Kefauver's four year seniority bulge over Kennedy? In December, 1956, long before Congress convened, Johnson telephoned (Sen. Clinton) Anderson (D-New Mexico) with a most curious question: "How are you getting along with your campaign for the Foreign Relations Committee?"

Anderson was puzzled. Could Johnson have forgotten that his "campaign" had ended two years earlier? But Johnson persisted.

"This may be your chance," he said.

Before Anderson could reply that he had his hands full as chairman of Atomic Energy, Johnson rushed on.

"You have seniority now over Jack Kennedy," Johnson explained. "But if you don't claim it, Estes Kefauver may get there first."

Johnson's ploy suddenly came through to Anderson. Both Anderson and Kefauver were members of the Class of '48, and therefore had equal seniority. If they both applied for one vacancy on the Foreign Relations Committee, Johnson could throw up his hands in the Steering Committee, declare a standoff, and give the vacancy to Kennedy. Anderson went along with this neat strategy, and Kennedy was given the seat.[33]

Party leaders' control over committee assignments is exercised within the constraints of the seniority system, the interests of members and their constituents, and the decision-making power of the committees on committees. Still, this is a weapon which party leaders may use to punish "wayward freaks" and reward the loyal. That most congressmen recognize this indirect power is suggested by a ditty popular in the late 1950s:

> I love Speaker Rayburn, his heart is so warm,
> And if I love him he'll do me no harm.
> So I shan't sass the Speaker one little bitty,
> And then I'll wind up on a major committee.[34]

3. *Party position in committee.* By developing a unanimous party position in committee, legislators improve the chances of holding together party support for the bill on the floor. To achieve this unanimity, Democratic or Republican committee members will sometimes hold caucuses which exclude all opposition party members of the committee. Such meetings often produce party unanim-

ity only by ignoring potentially divisive issues and by structuring the legislative debate along lines which permit all party members to support the party position without creating conflict between the party role and constituency role.

During the 1960s Republican members would often attempt to break Democratic ranks by playing on the North-South schism over civil rights. An example of this was a Republican amendment to the Food and Agriculture Bill of 1962 which would have provided that all recreational facilities established under the act be integrated. A Democratic leader commented on the real purpose of the amendment by noting that the Republican who offered the amendment "heard the fire alarm, so he comes running with a can of gasoline in each hand."[35] Democratic leaders were able to hold together party ranks in committee only by defeating the amendment and eliminating civil rights as an issue in considering the farm bill. The success of developing such party unanimity in committee depends to a great extent on the seriousness of intraparty differences and on the ability to compromise by excluding issues which generate this conflict.

4. *Making an issue a party issue.* This technique is used when party leaders feel that an official party position on the issue will convince some waverers to join party ranks. If a Democratic leadership coalition depends heavily on liberal Republican support, however, such behavior would serve only to weaken such support for the bill. Dissemination of an official party position may be by a floor speech, a letter to all party members, or by bringing the matter to a vote in the party caucus. To be most effective, party leaders make use of recognized experts on the subject and their position as cue-givers.

Democratic leaders employed this technique on the 1963 tax reduction bill by sending a short letter to all party members from the Speaker, majority leader, whip, and the highly respected chairman of Ways and Means. It simply said: "The passage of this bill is essential to our national well-being. A motion to recommit, which would be highly destructive of the bill, will be made. We urge that you be present for the debate, and that you vote to defeat the motion to recommit and for final passage of the bill."[36]

5. *Displacing conflict to new issue dimension.* Sometimes the House or Senate will be divided on an issue along lines which cannot be changed simply by making an appeal to party unity.

This comes about because of conflict between certain members' party roles and their other legislative roles related to constituency, region, ideology, committee membership, or their legislative career. The task of party leaders in such cases is to change the nature of the conflict, to restructure debate so that it takes place along different lines. By doing this, the leadership can often resolve individual legislators' role conflicts and bring in enough votes to win. Senate debate in 1954 over the nomination of Albert Beeson to the National Labor Relations Board illustrates how this tactic works:

> The Democratic minority on the Labor and Public Welfare Committee was strongly opposed to Beeson, whom organized labor accused of anti-labor bias, because they said his failure to sever his relations completely with a California corporate employer constituted a conflict of interests. This left conservative Democrats unmoved; they recalled many years when the NLRB had been frankly stacked in favor of labor. The Senate vote on Beeson seemed sure to provide yet another occasion for a sharp division between northern and southern Democrats.
>
> Then a careful reading of the committee testimony showed that Beeson's statements had shifted from one hearing to another. Immediately, Johnson saw the way: Beeson should be opposed not for conflict of interest, but for flouting the dignity of the Senate. . . .
>
> The Democratic Policy Committee decided to rally Democrats against Beeson, not on conflict of interest but for false statements to its committee. The minority report was written that way. Speeches were written for Democrats, stressing the theme that the Senate's dignity had been flouted. Lister Hill, a southern Democrat, dominated the presentation. A Republican senator detected the shift in emphasis; had the conflict of interest objection been dropped? The Democrats assured him it had not, but said no more about it."[37]

The Democrats lost the 1954 fight against Beeson, but displacing the conflict to the issue of false statements to a Senate committee did bring in many southern Democrats and shored up a minority coalition which had been sharply divided over the labor issue.

In putting together a coalition to defeat G. Harrold Carswell's nomination to the Supreme Court in 1970, Senate leaders were able to use the same tactic. At first the conflict over Carswell's nomination was strictly one of civil rights. Included in a list of past incidents showing racial bias on the part of the nominee was the allegation that he had been one of the incorporators of a segregated golf course established in 1955 in Tallahassee, Florida. The night before his appearance before the Senate Judiciary Committee, Carswell was shown his signature on the corporation papers for the club by members of an American Bar Association committee. In his testimony before the Senate committee the next day, however, the aspirant judge maintained that his recollection of the role he played in setting up the golf club was hazy.

A Kentucky senator who later voted against confirmation explains how displacement of the issue conflict from one of civil rights to one of honesty before a Senate committee affected his own position: "There are segregated golf courses all over the United States," he said, and added that many members of the Senate belonged to them. "However, what bothered me was his lack of memory about his role, and if he did remember it and denied it before the Judiciary Committee, this was even more of a strike against him."[38] There were many issues involved in the Carswell battle of 1970, but most senators credited with casting the key "no" votes mentioned the nominee's shaky testimony as one of the incidents which led to their rejecting the nomination. The importance of conflict displacement in this case was underscored by the comment of an anti-Carswell leader after the Florida judge had been turned down: "We couldn't win if we had to make it strictly a civil rights fight. We had to have a 'cover issue.' "[39]

6. *Co-opting important members into support.* If a party position fails to attract enough of the faithful, party leaders may seek to take advantage of the other chief sources of cues in the legislature such as the standing committee system or the prestige of certain senior members as regional spokesmen. By convincing a member respected for his expertise or role as regional spokesman, but not regarded as a party man, to support a particular measure party leaders can often pull in those members who respect both the expertise or prestige of that member and his independence. This technique seeks to supplement the party cue system with the other cue systems which exist in Congress.

Co-optation is usually effected by including the legislative leader in substantive and strategy meetings about the bill to which his formal position would not ordinarily admit him. By making him a part of the process which produces the final bill, party leaders increase the chances that he will support it, and that his support will affect those members who follow his cues.

Lyndon Johnson often used this technique during his reign as Democratic leader. By finding a prestigious senator to serve as an "umbrella" for wavering senators he was able to expand the base of support for a bill far beyond that which would have been possible on the basis of party loyalty or support for the issue alone. In 1958, Johnson worked out a compromise on two labor bills, and used the support of Senator John McClellan of Arkansas as an umbrella; southerners felt that they could safely support the legislation because they could point to McClellan's favorable vote to justify their own. Senator Walter George of Georgia also often was used by the majority leader as a means of gathering southern votes which he might otherwise not have.

Donald Matthews's classic study of the Senate in the 1950s uncovered another incident which shows Johnson's effective use of this technique of party leadership:

> In a recent Congress, for example, Senator Johnson was positive that an important bill would pass if a certain Southern senator would vote for it, but according to a careful canvass of the situation the senator was still undecided. Abruptly, in the middle of floor debate, Johnson approached the wavering senator, announced that he had to leave the chamber for an hour or so and casually asked the potential dissenter to take over as floor manager of the bill. The senator hesitated and then agreed as Johnson left the floor. The undecided senator voted for the bill.[40]

7. *Information about members' positions.* An important part of party leaders' authority is their legitimate right to obtain information as to how a member will vote on a measure not yet brought to the floor. Membership polls taken by the party whip organizations not only give the leadership a count of supporters, waverers, and opponents, but they indicate what compromises must be accepted to gain more supporters. This information is invaluable to the leadership in its building a majority coalition on the bill. For the leadership knows not only the expected division on the vote, but also which demands of particular individuals or blocs must be met in order to insure a favorable outcome.

This type of information is different from the technical information on which the committee cue system relies. It says nothing about the technical quality of the bill under consideration. Rather, it indicates how the members are divided and what demands must be met to change that division. Party leaders, because of their positions of authority, have access to this information, and their possessing it allows them to know which individuals, blocs, and interests must be wooed in order for the measure to pass.

8. *Technical and substantive information.* The source of the party leadership's ability to use this technique is similar to that outlined above. It is a power based on information to which the party leadership has access because of its formal position. But while the previously discussed information is basically that of the distribution of members' opinion, this technique depends on a second type of information, that pertaining to the technical and substantive parts of a bill.

Because of the low information base on which most members make decisions, the party leadership can influence this decision-making by providing reliable technical information on a bill. In becoming the source of such substantive cues, the leadership greatly expands the influence which formal position gives it. To effectively employ this technique, party leaders must work in conjunction with substantive experts in the committee system. By acquiring technical information from committee experts and by disseminating it through party channels, party leaders are able to establish themselves as a primary source of reliable cues on the technical nature of legislation.

9. *Tangible rewards.* The most direct way for party leaders to reward the loyal is to bestow patronage or projects for the member's constituency. The "everybody wins" nature of rivers and harbors legislation supports the legislative norm that reelection is an overriding concern for all members. Party leaders are able to affect marginally the amount of each member's reward, and by increasing that of regular party voters and decreasing that of mavericks, they are able to convey the message that party loyalty does not go unnoticed. Committee assignments, junkets, commission appointments, and office assignments are other tangible rewards which the leadership may dispense or withold.

In 1955, Senator Johnson demonstrated the use of tangible rewards when he commandeered for his use as a second office the spanking new office space previously assigned to Senator Paul Douglas of Illinois. By taking away Douglas's coveted suite Johnson dramatized his ability to punish those, such as Douglas, who failed to support the party leadership. Johnson's giving a highly valued corner suite in the New Senate Office Building to the loyal Mike Monroney of Oklahoma made the same point.

10. *Concessions to minority party.* This technique is the opposite of that outlined in point four. Instead of making an issue a party one, leaders often feel that they can maximize support by avoiding a partisan conflict and building a coalition on the basis of both parties. In order to do this it is usually necessary to grant minority party leaders certain demands.

The development of bipartisan support for the Civil Rights Act of 1964 provides an example of this technique. Because Republican objections threatened to doom the bill, Democratic leaders permitted major revisions in the bill to be made by Senate minority leader Everett Dirksen and his party colleagues. Meeting in Dirksen's office with representatives from the Justice Department, Republican leaders conducted what were in effect informal committee hearings on the bill. By granting the Republicans this leeway in changing the bill, the Democratic leaders picked up an awful lot of amendments to their original bill, but they also picked up enough Republican votes to get it passed.

Whether or not the party leadership will employ this technique depends primarily on how crucial minority support for the measure is. In a close partisan split the leadership runs the risk of losing some of its own members if it makes too many concessions to the other party. In such a case leaders are more likely to follow the tactic of taking an official party position than they are to try to attract minority votes by granting concessions on the bill.

11. *Floor control and scheduling.* As Senate majority leader, Johnson was a master at controlling the Senate's floor proceedings. By carefully obtaining precise figures as to probable voting patterns, Johnson almost always made sure that no measure was brought to the floor until he was certain of its success. The extent to which Johnson controlled floor proceedings, though, is perhaps best illustrated by an incident in 1959 when he made a counting mistake. In building support for an amendment to repeal tax advantages for dividend income, Johnson had miscalculated the voting split. When the roll call ended the measure had been defeated 41 to 40. Johnson looked across the Senate floor at J. Allen Frear of Delaware, a consistent Johnson supporter who, in this instance and with Johnson's okay, had voted against the amendment. "Change your vote!" Johnson shouted. Stunned by this blatant display of leadership control, Frear hesitated.

Johnson again yelled across the silent chamber: "Change your vote!" Frear complied and the amendment carried.[41]

Such a flexing of leadership muscle is not the normal procedure, but it illustrates the extent to which party leaders may control events on the floor. Johnson was reduced to this level of floor control only because his normal scheduling control had failed. The importance of scheduling in determining the outcome of a bill is indicated in Richard Fenno's comment that "the success of many a bill depends more upon when it was called up than on anything else."[42]

In addition to controlling when a measure reaches the floor, party leaders may exercise influence by determining the type of voting procedure. As mentioned earlier, party voting is most likely to be achieved when the procedure is not visible. Party leaders will often seek to have a voice, division, or teller vote, rather than a roll call, in order to maximize the number of party voters. Division and voice votes are often party votes because they happen so fast. Members often come to the floor unfamiliar with the measure to be voted on. In such cases, they often follow cues supplied by their party's floor manager or committee delegation.

The type of voting procedure used brings out the earlier discussed conflict between those emphasizing representational values and those stressing the importance of decision-making. Party leaders know that they are more likely to get a party vote if the visibility of voting is low, so they seek to have voice, division, or teller votes. This reduces the conflict which rank-and-file members might have between their party role and their role of constituency representative. But such a gain in decision-making ability is offset by the fact that low visibility voting makes it harder for a congressman's constitutents to determine whether he is really representing their interests. The 1970 rules change permitting twenty members to call for recorded teller votes was a clear victory for those stressing the representational function of Congress.

The importance of voting procedures is most clearly illustrated when the House or Senate reverses, by roll call vote, a decision earlier made by voice vote. This happened in 1971 when the House turned down, by a recorded teller vote, a proposal for funding the supersonic transport program which it had passed three times before on unrecorded votes.

Although the procedural changes in the 1970 Legislative Reorganization Act do reduce party leaders' influence over floor proceedings, the party leadership still retains a great deal of power over what happens on the floor of Congress. This power is generally manifested in three ways: party leaders can influence the presence or absence of particular members at the time of voting on the floor; they can determine when a measure will be brought to a floor vote; and they can attempt to control the visibility of the voting procedure so as to maximize party support.

12. *Structural changes.* If party leaders find themselves in a long-standing conflict with other power structures in Congress they may seek to have existing rules or structures changed in order to increase their own power. I have put this tactic last on the list because it represents an extreme case, one which rarely happens because party leaders generally work within the existing system. The example cited here is the case of party leaders changing the composition of the House Rules Committee in order to end a system wherein that committee was able to kill legislation sought by the Democratic leadership. That this tactic represents an extreme is suggested by the fact that the Rules Committee quite often is used as a leadership tool to influence scheduling of floor votes so that they take place when the party coalition vote is at its peak. In the Eighty-eighth Congress (1963–1964), for instance, the Rules Committee held up a Senate-passed mass transit bill for fifteen months until party leaders were able to produce enough votes to assure passage on the floor.

Because of an extended deadlock between party leadership and the House Rules Committee during the late 1950s, party leaders sought a change in committee membership so as to make it a more responsible arm of the Democratic leadership. In 1961, by increasing the size of the committee from 12 to 15, Democratic leaders were able to transform a 6-to-6 pro- and anti-leadership deadlock into an 8-to-7 pro-leadership margin. Other changes in the rules, such as the twenty-one day rule permitting the Speaker to pull a bill from the Rules Committee when its leaders have delayed acting on a bill for more than twenty-one days, have also been instituted in the past.

Generally speaking, party leaders are reluctant to use the tactic of structural change because it brings about a direct conflict between party leaders and those at the pinnacle of the committee power structure. The other tactics discussed in this section, ones which work within the existing system in which congressmen are willing to follow party cues only when there is no great conflict between their party role and their other roles, are more often used successfully by party leaders. Structural change tactics represent last ditch efforts to bring about party control when all else has failed.

This review of techniques available to party leaders suggests that leadership success depends on a great number of factors, some of which are beyond the control of leaders. The visibility of a particular issue may lead to voting patterns which the legislative party cannot control because of its commitment to the primary norm of reelection. In seeking to exercise control over voting patterns, the party leadership's most effective resource is its control over the flow of information. An effective party organization is one which becomes a reliable source of cues both as to the substance of a bill and as to the voting intentions of members. To provide reliable substantive cues the party leadership must work in conjunction with standing committee leadership. To be a source of reliable cues as to the disposition of members, the leadership must have an extensive intelligence network such as that developed by Lyndon Johnson in the 1950s.

Randall Ripley has observed that, in comparing the House and the Senate, "party leadership is likely to be more centralized, organized, effective in producing legislative results, and more meaningful to individual members in the House."[43] This difference between the House and Senate illustrates the importance of party organization as a source of cues. Because of the greater size and specialization in the House, representatives are in greater need of reliable information on which to make rational decisions. An effective party organization can supply these cues and greatly aid the individual member's decision-making.

By viewing the legislative party in Down's framework of information and decision-making, many of the seeming contradictions about American parties begin to make some sense. Serving as a reliable cue in elections, the political party makes it possible for the voter to cast a rational ballot on the basis of little information about candidates and issues. Similarly, the party within Congress can provide members with reliable cues for voting on bills about which they know little. In both cases, the party organization is able to exercise influence despite its lack of organizational sanctions.

Within Congress the party leadership, as we have seen, has a number of tactics which it can use to produce a party coalition even though it lacks the solid organization necessary for enforcing party discipline. The essence of these successful party tactics is their finding ways to avoid conflicts between the member's party role and the other roles which he must perform to be an effective legislator. Unlike party government advocates' proposals for fundamental changes in the existing system, these techniques of party leadership are ones which make use of sources of power extant within the present system. They do not produce a Congress capable of perfect decision-making to reflect electoral mandates, but neither do they deny the importance of a legislator's representational functions.

NOTES

1. Information regarding these races is drawn from many sources, including: *Congressional Quarterly Weekly Report,* July 24, 1970; R. W. Apple, Jr., "Nixon Guides G.O.P. on Senate Races," *New York Times,* April 6, 1970, pp. 1 and 12; Apple, "G.O.P. Picks 43 House Democrats as 1970 Targets," *New York Times,* January 4, 1970, p. 57; Warren Weaver, "Democrats Hope to Retain Senate," *New York Times,* April 20, 1970, p. 15; and Curtis J. Sitomer, "Western Shift to G.O.P. Tests Democrats," *Christian Science Monitor,* April 25, 1970, p. 3.

2. An account of both elections may be found in David Broder, "Nixon Puts Prestige on Line," *Boston Globe,* April 15, 1970, p. 23.

3. *New York Times,* January 4, 1970, p. 57.

4. *New York Times,* April 22, 1970, p. 1.

5. Quoted in *Congressional Quarterly Weekly Report,* Vol. 3, no. 46 (November 11, 1972), p. 2947.

6. Anthony Downs, *An Economic Theory of Democracy* (Harper & Row, 1957).

7. Fred Greenstein, *The American Party System and the American People* (Prentice-Hall, 1970), p. 36. Also see his *Children and Politics* (Yale University Press, 1965), Chapter 4.

8. The classic work on party identification in presidential elections is Angus Campbell et al., *The American Voter* (John Wiley, 1960) and the follow-up studies: Philip Converse et al., "Stability and Change in 1960: A Reinstating Election," *American Political Science Review,* Vol. 55 (June 1961), pp. 269–280; Aage Clauson et al., "Electoral Myth and Reality: The 1964 Election," *American Political Science Review,* Vol. 59, (June 1965), pp. 321–332; and Philip Converse et al., "Continuity and Change in American Politics: Parties and Issues in the 1968 Election," *American Political Science Review,* Vol. 63 (December 1969), pp. 1083–1105. For the role which issues play, see V. O. Key, Jr., *The Responsible Electorate* (Vintage, 1966). The increase in ticket splitting is discussed in Walter DeVries and Lance Tarrance, *The Ticket-Splitter* (William Eerdmans, 1972).

9. Donald Matthews and James Prothro, *Negroes and the New Southern Politics* (Harcourt, Brace & World, 1966), p. 383.

10. See Theodore Lowi, *The End of Liberalism* (W. W. Norton, 1969), p. 72.

11. *Congressional Quarterly Almanac,* 1968, p. 19.

12. *Congressional Record,* June 8, 1969, pp. H4937–H5004. Cited in Donald Matthews and James Stimson, "The Decision Making Approach to the Study of Legislative Behavior," paper delivered at the annual meeting of the American Political Science Association, New York, 1969, p. 9.

13. Both statements are from Matthews and Stimson, "The Decision Making Approach . . . ," pp. 8 and 10.

14. *Ibid.*

15. Randall B. Ripley, *Party Leaders in the House of Representatives* (The Brookings Institution, 1967), p. 141.

16. Quoted in *Christian Science Monitor,* March 21, 1970, p. 13.

17. Julius Turner, *Party and Constituency: Pressures on Congress* (The Johns Hopkins University Press, 1951), revised edition by Edward V. Schneier, Jr., 1970; Duncan MacRae, Jr., *Dimensions of Congressional Voting* (University of California Press, 1958); David B. Truman, *The Congressional Party* (John Wiley, 1959); Lewis Froman, Jr., *Congressmen and Their Constituencies* (Rand McNally, 1963); and Lewis Froman and Randall Ripley, "Conditions for Party Leadership; The Case of the House Democrats," *American Political Science Review,* Vol. 59, March 1965, pp. 52–63.

18. *Congressional Quarterly Almanac,* 1969, p. 1067.

19. Froman and Ripley, "Conditions for Party Leadership: The Case of the House Democrats."

20. *Congressional Quarterly Alamanac,* 1969, p. 1066.

21. Froman, *Congressmen and Their Constituencies,* p. 92.

22. Ripley, *Party Leaders in the House of Representatives,* p. 169.

23. Ralph K. Huitt, "Democratic Party Leadership in the Senate," in Huitt and Robert L. Peabody, *Congress: Two Decades of Analysis* (Harper & Row, 1969), p. 138.

24. "Leadership: An Interview with Senate Leader Lyndon Johnson," *U.S. News and World Report,* June 27, 1960, p. 89.

25. Ripley, *Party Leaders in the House of Representatives,* p. 149.

26. Quoted in George Goodwin, Jr., *The Little Legislatures: Committees of Congress* (University of Massachusetts Press, 1970), p. 176.

27. Ralph K. Huitt, "Democratic Party Leadership in the Senate," p. 148.

28. This discussion relies on Randall Ripley, *Majority Party Leadership in Congress* (Little, Brown, 1969), pp. 176ff.

29. Ripley, *Party Leaders in the House of Representatives,* p. 146.

30. Goodwin, *The Little Legislatures,* Chapter 4.

31. George W. Norris, quoted in Goodwin, *The Little Legislatures,* p. 70.

32. Richard Fenno, "The Internal Distribution of Influence: The House," in David Truman, ed., *The Congress and America's Future* (Prentice-Hall, 1965), pp. 64–65.

33. Rowland Evans and Robert Novak, *Lyndon B. Johnson: The Exercise of Power* (New American Library, 1966), p. 101.

34. Quoted by Arthur Krock, *New York Times,* April 8, 1958; also in Goodwin, *The Little Legislatures,* p. 73.

35. Quoted in Don Hadwiger and Ross Talbot, *Pressures and Protests* (Chandler, 1965), p. 118.

36. Quoted in Randall Ripley, "Techniques of Contemporary Leaders," in Raymond Wolfinger, ed., *Readings on Congress* (Prentice-Hall, 1971), p. 247.

37. Ralph K. Huitt, "Democratic Party Leadership in the Senate," pp. 149–150.

38. *New York Times,* April 9, 1970, p. 32.

39. *Washington Post,* April 12, 1970, p. A2.

40. Donald Matthews, *U.S. Senators and Their World* (Vintage, 1960), p. 129. For a full discussion of Johnson's co-optation

technique see Huitt's discussion in "Democratic Party Leadership in the Senate," pp. 150ff.

41. Rowland Evans and Robert Novak, *Lyndon B. Johnson: The Exercise of Power*, p. 96.

42. Fenno, "The Internal Distribution of Influence: The House," p. 63.

43. Ripley, *Majority Party Leadership in Congress*, p. 184.

CHAPTER 4

Committees

> Elsa and Ramona watched the Motorola television set in their
> pajamas.
> —What else is on? Elsa asked.
> Ramona looked in the newspaper.
> —On 7 there's "Johnny Allegro" with George Raft and Nina
> Foch. On 9 "Johnny Angel" with George Raft and Claire Trevor.
> On 11 there's "Johnny Apollo" with Tyrone Power and Dorothy La-
> mour. On 13 is "Johnny Concho" with Frank Sinatra and Phyllis
> Kirk. On 2 is "Johnny Dark" with Tony Curtis and Piper Laurie.
> On 4 is "Johnny Eager" with Robert Taylor and Lana Turner. On
> 5 is "Johnny O'Clock" with Dick Powell and Evelyn Keyes. On 31 is
> "Johnny Trouble" with Stuart Whitman and Ethel Barrymore.
> —What's this one we're watching?
> —What time is it?
> —Eleven-thirty-five.
> —"Johnny Guitar" with Joan Crawford and Sterling Hayden.
>
> Donald Barthelme
> *City Life*

As the Ninety-second Congress began organizing itself in January
1971, two representatives from Massachusetts indicated an interest in being on the House Armed Services Committee. Mrs.
Louise Day Hicks, who had defeated two liberal opponents on
the slogan, "You know where I stand," came from former Speaker
John McCormack's old district in Boston. The other contender
for the seat was Representative Michael Harrington, a liberal

113

maverick from the suburbs of Boston's north shore, who had won a special election in September 1969.

Hicks and Harrington were not only poles apart in the traditional liberal-conservative sense, they also represented quite different conceptions of the committee and the proper role of a member. Mrs. Hicks fit in with a majority on the Armed Services Committee in believing that a major function of the committee member is to make sure that his state and region receive their share of defense contracts and military bases. Then-chairman Mendel Rivers said that Mrs. Hicks was his kind of member and that he would welcome her to the committee. Harrington believed that the committee had not questioned military spending enough in the past. By being on Armed Services, he felt he could play an important critical role in reducing the $80 billion which was spent on defense every year. This, he felt, was more important than pork barrel questions of defense contracts and bases.

A key actor in the Hicks-Harrington contest was Representative James Burke from Milton, Massachusetts. Burke's power stemmed from his being the only New Englander on the Ways and Means Committee, the body which makes committee assignments for all House Democrats. In most cases Burke was able to decide where New England Democrats would go after consulting with House leaders. A close friend of the former number-two man on Armed Services, Philip Philbin, Burke was a defender of the House establishment and of the prevailing norms about Armed Services membership. At a White House reception before Christmas, Harrington mentioned his interest in the assignment to Burke and suggested that his seniority over Mrs. Hicks should give him the inside track. Since Harrington had been one of the most consistent critics of the seniority system in Congress, Burke was amused by Harrington's temporary conversion. He suggested that Massachusetts' problems, like declining defense contracts and the threatened closing of the Boston Naval Yard, might only be aggravated if Harrington were appointed to the committee.

It was clear that Burke felt a Hicks appointment would be better for the state and that he would support her candidacy. But the bargaining for this one seat soon became complicated by considerations relating to Massachusetts politics and tactics of the regional delegation. When the dust settled, Burke was arguing for a Harrington appointment before his Ways and Means colleagues.

One of the factors which perhaps made Representative Burke listen to Harrington's arguments for the assignment was the fact that the Massachusetts Senate, which would have a major role in redistricting Massachusetts to fit the 1970 census, was presided over by the congressman's cousin, Kevin Harrington. The president of the Massachusetts Senate possesses appointive powers which give him an unusual degree of influence for a state legislative leader. The legislature's ability to draw the boundaries of a congressional district so as to make it overwhelmingly Democratic or Republican, urban or rural, liberal or conservative, is an ever present threat to incumbent representatives.

The disagreement between Harrington and Burke about the Armed Services seat never reached a point where such a threat had to be brought into the open. Members of the New England delegation opposed to Harrington's getting the spot decided that they could both block his appointment and take Burke off the hook by having the delegation as a group vote to endorse a candidate for the committee. Harrington, after some hard campaigning, won the delegation's endorsement; Burke said he would abide by its decision and push Harrington's assignment in Ways and Means. But the campaign against Harrington continued and many influential congressmen suggested that he withdraw. This opposition often took the form of rumor: Ways and Means chairman Wilbur Mills was not happy with the prospect of a Harrington appointment to Armed Services; or the new Armed Services chairman, Edward Hebert of Louisiana, had indicated a preference for someone (anyone) else.

A junior representative is expected to realize that such opposition by influential members can only mean that a fight to gain the seat would be offset by alienating important members; that a temporary victory would be overshadowed by long lasting feelings of bitterness generated in the battle. Former Speaker Sam Rayburn's admonition to new members: "If you want to get along, go along," provides the rule of conduct in such cases. But Harrington refused to go along, and in the end he won the seat.

The struggle for a seat on Armed Services indicates the importance of committee assignments to congressmen. A member's entire career may be structured by the committee or committees to which he is initially assigned. The ability to serve constituency needs and be reelected, to begin developing the expertise needed for advancement in the congressional hierarchy, and to gain a forum providing the exposure necessary for a national or Senate campaign all depend on the committee on which the congressman is placed.

It is easy to understand, then, the frustration of Representative Herman Badillo of New York City after the Democratic members of Ways and Means assigned him to a committee which satisfied none of these needs, the House Agriculture Committee. "There's no point in dealing with these guys," he said. "They'll just put me on another silly committee."[1] Although Badillo later took his case to the full party caucus and won a seat on Education and Labor, other liberal Democrats did not fare so well. Outgoing Chairman of the liberal Democratic Study Group, Donald Fraser of Minnesota, lost his bid for election to the powerful Ways and Means Committee to Joe Waggonner of Louisiana. Representative Bella Abzug of New York failed to get her assignment changed from Government Operations to Armed Services.

Political scientists and other students of Congress have long shared members' appreciation of the importance of committees in the legislative process. Writing in 1884, Woodrow Wilson observed: "It is evident that there is one principle which runs through every stage of procedure, and which is never disallowed or abrogated—the principle that the Committee shall rule without let or hindrance. And this is a principle of extraordinary formative power. It is the mould of all legislation."[2]

Almost eighty years later Representative Clem Miller described Congress as "a collection of committees that come together in a chamber periodically to approve one another's actions."[3] However, discussions of congressional committees which talk about seniority, patterns of interaction, or the chairman's power as though all committees are pretty much the same tend to be misleading. For not only do House and Senate committees perform quite different functions in their respective chambers, but also, there is great variety in the roles played by different committees within each chamber.

House and Senate differences about the relative emphasis put on representation and lawmaking affect the roles which committees play in each chamber. Senate committees tend to maximize representational goals, while House committees are geared more to decision-making. House members can spend more time developing expertise relevant to the one or two committees on which they serve, while senators would find such a task impossible because of their serving on more committees. These differences are illustrated by looking at two Republicans from New York. The committee life of the state's senior senator goes something like this:

> New York's Jacob Javits sits on seven committees and nineteen subcommittees. He may be confronted with half a dozen hearings in a single morning; in which case he becomes a political wraith, floating from one to another, usually giving none of them more than thirty minutes. He makes the best of an impossible situation by assigning an aide to each of the hearings to keep tabs. When Javits arrives, the staff man greets him with a fast summary of what's been done. Javits tries to push in a question out of turn, to make the record reflect the presence of a body, then he is off to the next meeting.[4]

The opposite extreme is described by Representative Barber Conable of New York after he was appointed to the Ways and Means Committee in 1967:

> The assignment will change my work in the House of Representatives in many ways, not all of them good. I have had to give up my other committees and to curtail less important activities. The Ways and Means Committee is so demanding that I will not be able to get back to the district so often or do as much outside political work as previously. After one week on the Committee .ny staff already is looking startled every time I return to the office during the day.[5]

Committees are generally more important to individual House members than to senators, for they represent the only means of achieving power and policy goals within the lower chamber. House committees are also more important in determining the chamber's policy outcomes than are Senate committees because of House norms which tend to reinforce the acceptance of committee desisions on the floor. For these reasons, most of the following discussion will deal with House committees rather than their Senate counterparts.

There are many ways to classify committees. Some students of Congress focus on the "pecking order" and rank committees in terms of their prestige. Although there is disagreement as to exactly where a particular committee falls on these lists, most would agree with the general outline of Table 1.

Lists of this type reflect overall committee preferences for all members of Congress. They are based on studies of changing membership patterns and on reported preferences of congressmen and their staffs. What such a list fails to show, however, is the great degree of variation in personal preferences. While one former senator suggested that a member had to be "hog tied" in order to agree to go on Agriculture, many senators find this a most congenial committee for serving constituency interests and

---

TABLE 1 *The Hierarchy of Committee Preferences*

HOUSE	SENATE
1. Rules	1. Foreign Relations
2. Ways and Means	2. Finance
3. Appropriations	3. Commerce
4. Foreign Affairs	4. Judiciary
5. Armed Services	5. Appropriations
6. Interstate and Foreign Commerce	6. Armed Services
7. Judiciary	7. Agriculture and Forestry
8. Agriculture	8. Interior and Insular Affairs
9. Education and Labor	9. Banking and Currency
10. Banking and Currency	10. Labor and Public Welfare
11. Public Works	11. Public Works
12. Post Office and Civil Service	12. Government Operations
13. Science and Astronautics	13. Rules and Administration
14. Un-American Activities	14. Post Office and Civil Service
15. District of Columbia	15. District of Columbia
16. Interior and Insular Affairs	16. Aeronautical and Space Sciences
17. House Administration	
18. Government Operations	
19. Merchant Marine and Fisheries	
20. Veterans' Affairs	

SOURCE: William L. Morrow, *Congressional Committees* (Charles Scribner's Sons, 1969), pp. 42–43, reprinted by permission. For a somewhat different listing, see George Goodwin, Jr., *The Little Legislatures* (University of Massachusetts Press, 1970), pp. 114–115. All classifications of this type owe something to Donald Matthews's study of Senate committees. See his excellent discussion in *U.S. Senators and Their World* (Vintage, 1960), pp. 148–158. Also of interest is Louis Gawthrop's "Changing Membership Patterns in House Committees" *American Political Science Review,* June 1966, pp. 366–373.

influencing policy.[6] Westerners like Interior even though it is never at the top of any of these lists. Some representatives thrive on the din of ideological battles in Education and Labor; others consider it a sure cause of nervous exhaustion and electoral defeat.

Committees may also be classified in terms of the type of policy with which they deal. Donald Matthews's study of the Senate combined committee preferences and policy to come up with a four-fold typology of committees. These are: "top" committees (Foreign Relations, Appropriations, Armed Services, and Finance); "interest" committees (Agriculture, Banking and Currency, Interstate and Foreign Commerce, Judiciary, and Labor); "pork" committees (Interior, Post Office and Civil Service, and Public Works); and "duty" committees (Rules and Administration, Government Operations, and District of Columbia).[7] A more complete listing of committees in terms of the scope of issues handled is that of George Goodwin, shown in Table 2.

Classifying committees in terms of the type of policy which they handle is useful because it makes possible comparisons of committees and their counterpart institutions in other branches of government. A look at Table 2 also confirms the expected pattern of the most prestigious committees being those concerned with broad policy issues. But again, such a classifying scheme may often hide important differences among committees. Even though Education and Labor and Interior are both placed in the same category of clientele-oriented committees, for instance, they represent opposite extremes in terms of the degree of conflict found in committee activity. Whereas Education and Labor is consistently the scene of intense partisan and ideological conflict; Interior is best characterized by one of its members as "a neutral processing machine."[8]

Richard Fenno, in a paper seeking to provide a framework for comparative studies of congressional committees, suggests that a key factor in explaining differences among committees are the goals which a member seeks to accomplish by being on that committee. A member seeking internal influence in the House or Senate is drawn to different committees than those who seek to maximize constituency service or to draft good public policy. The difference between Interior and Education and Labor can be explained by the fact that members on the first want a low conflict

TABLE 2   *Committees Classified by Scope of Issues*

HOUSE	SENATE
National Issue Committees	
Science & Astronautics (Dis.)*	Aeronautical & Space Sciences
Appropriations (Dis.)	(Dis.)
Armed Services (Dis.)	Appropriations (Dis.)
Ways and Means (Redis.)	Armed Services (Dis.)
Foreign Affairs	Finance (Redis.)
Judiciary (Redis.)	Foreign Relations
Rules	Judiciary (Redis.)
Un-American Activities	
Clientele-oriented Committees	
Agriculture (Dis.)	Agriculture & Forestry (Dis.)
Banking & Currency (Reg. Redis.)	Banking & Currency (Reg. Redis.)
Interstate & Foreign Commerce	Commerce (Reg.)
(Reg.)	Interior & Insular Affairs (Dis.)
Interior & Insular Affairs (Dis.)	
Education & Labor (Reg. Redis.)	
Merchant Marine & Fisheries (Dis.)	
Public Works (Dis.)	
Veterans' Affairs (Dis.)	
Housekeeping Committees	
District of Columbia	District of Columbia
Government Operations	Government Operations
Post Office & Civil Service (Dis.)	Post Office & Civil Service (Dis.)
House Administration	Rules & Administration
Standards of Official Conduct	

SOURCE: George Goodwin, Jr., *The Little Legislatures* (University of Massachusetts Press, 1970), pp. 102–103, reprinted by permission.

*The abbreviations in parentheses refer to a classification of policies in terms of their impact on society. Professor Goodwin's source here is Theodore Lowi's review article, "American Business, Public Policy, Case Studies and Political Theory," *World Politics* (July 1964), pp. 677–715. Lowi discusses three types of policies: distributive, regulatory, and redistributive. Distributive policies are ones which give away some good, resource, or service which is in near-inexhaustible supply. Decisions are reached easily, through a patronage or pork barrel type of process, since no groups stand to lose by the decision. Rivers and harbors legislation is an example of this type of policy. Regulatory policies are those which apply general rules to individual cases. They tend to limit one group for the benefit of others or to expand the opportunities of one group at the expense of competing interests. The impact of such policies is broad and decisions are reached through a type of balance-of-power politics. Redistributive policies have the broadest impact on society. They are policies which take something of value from one large group (a social class, race, property owners, etc.) for the benefit of another. These are the hardest fought decisions and include such policies as civil rights, welfare programs, and basic fiscal matters such as the progressive income tax and revenue sharing.

committee which can provide lots of projects for home districts, while Education and Labor members are more concerned with drafting good legislation and are willing to engage in intense battles to do so.

Fenno studies six House committees by focusing on the following variables: committee member goals, environmental constraints, strategic premises, internal structure, and output. Committee members, it is suggested, will organize the committee so as to achieve their individual goals; they are limited in doing so, however, by other groups inside and outside of Congress who have particular expectations of that committee. In order to meet both individual goals and environmental expectations, members work out particular strategies which satisfy both. These strategies then become the bases on which committees are organized and these structures greatly determine the type of policy output coming from committees.[9]

As the Harrington-Hicks battle for the Armed Services seat demonstrated, members may have different reasons for being on the same committee. For most committees, however, there is some consensus as to why a congressman should seek appointment to that committee and what he can expect to get from it. On the basis of these shared member goals we can classify committees as power committees, policy committees, and constituency committees.

POWER COMMITTEES

Members seeking to maximize their influence within the House or Senate are naturally drawn to prestigious committees such as Appropriations, Ways and Means, and Rules. An overwhelming

---

The relationship between the Lowi and Goodwin classification schemes is described by Goodwin: "Distributive policies tend to be handled by clientele committees (Agriculture, Interior, Merchant Marine, Public Works, Veterans') though three national issue committees (Appropriations, Armed Services, Sciences) and one housekeeping committee (Post Office) are also involved. Regulatory policies tend to be handled by clientele committees (Banking, Commerce, Labor). Redistributive policies also tend to be handled by clientele committees (Banking, Labor), though two national issue committees are also involved (Finance for social insurance, Judiciary for civil rights)."

majority of the Appropriations and Ways and Means members in the Fenno study said that they sought "power," "prestige," or "importance" in joining that committee.[10] One Ways and Meanser sums up this attitude in discussing why he wanted on:

> Ways and Means is powerful around here because it's interpreted as being powerful. Power is interpretation around here; it's all interpretation. . . . The only way I can describe what I want to be is power. I don't know what I'd do with it when I got it, but I want to have it where I can reach out and use it when I want to.[11]

The fact that both committees deal with important money matters is obviously related to members' preferences; but the essential drive for membership is influence, not policy. If committees with totally different subject matter were to assume this position of importance in the chamber, then these members would easily shift their attention and aspirations to these other committees. Because most members of these committees hold relatively safe seats they do not need to worry a great deal about serving constituency interests; they are free to devote most of their time to the committee work which maintains their power.

There are four prominent groups of noncommittee members who often seek to influence committee behavior: members of the parent chamber, the executive branch, clientele groups, and party leaders. The relative importance of each of these groups will vary from committee to committee and issue to issue.

Since members of Ways and Means and Appropriations are most concerned with their influence in the House, the environmental group with which they are most concerned is other House members. The importance of the money committees within the House is directly related to the fact that these functions are the fundamental legislative powers which determine the importance of Congress in the larger political system. All congressmen want these committees to be powerful because the relative importance of Congress depends on it. In order to permit these two committees the independence deemed necessary for maintaining their influence, the House provides both with procedural rights denied other committees. Major bills from Ways and Means are brought to the floor under a closed rule which precludes amendments;

Appropriations is allowed to hold hearings in secret executive session; both committees are provided with large staffs.

In return for the great autonomy granted these committees, they are expected to be responsive to House desires. The primary means for assuring this responsiveness is control over assignment to the committee. Party leaders are very active in determining who will sit on these committees and will seek out legislators who have demonstrated a "responsible legislative style" emphasizing moderation and respect for the House as an institution.[12]

In seeking responsiveness, House members are more concerned with matters of style than they are with substantive policy questions. This means that other groups in the environment play a role in providing cues on substantive policy matters. Coalitions seeking to influence Appropriations decisions tend to be dominated by executive groups while those trying to influence Ways and Means are more likely to involve party leaders. The nature of the budgetary process dictates that clientele group demands be channeled through executive agencies; by the time these demands reach the Appropriations Committee they are chiefly executive requests. Although revenue matters also heavily involve executive groups, a key difference between these issues and questions of funding is the fact that revenue matters are regarded as having greater electoral impact. Basic disagreements on the issues of taxation, social security, medicare, and trade have long characterized American political parties. Because of the electoral importance of these issues, party leaders seek to have some influence over the substantive content of Ways and Means decisions.

Strategic premises for Appropriations members must meet the twin demands of influence and responsiveness. In order to maintain the influence which all House members desire, the committee must establish policy independence from the major actor in its environment, the executive branch. To do this the committee has adopted as a major strategic premise the idea that any and all budgets submitted by executive agencies should be cut. Fenno's earlier study of the Appropriations Committee led him to this description:

> The workaday lingo of the Committee member is replete with negative verbs, undesirable objects of attention, and effective instruments of action. Agency budgets are said to be filled with

"fat," "padding," "grease," "pork," "oleaginous substance," "water," "oil," "cushions," "avoirdupois," "waste tissue," and "soft spots." The action verbs most commonly used are "cut," "carve," "slice," "prune," "whittle," "squeeze," "wring," "trim," "lop off," "chop," "slash," "pare," "shave," "fry," and "whack." The tools of the trade are appropriately referred to as "knife," "blade," "meat axe," "scalpel," "meat cleaver," "hatchet," "shears," "wringer," and "fine-tooth comb." Members are hailed by their fellows as being "pretty sharp with the knife." Agencies may "have the meat axe thrown at them." Executives are urged to put their agencies "on a fat boy's diet." Budgets are praised when they are "cut to the bone." And members agree that "You can always get a little more fat out of a piece of pork if you fry it a little longer and a little harder."[13]

But if appropriations were to carry this norm of budget cutting too far it would fail to meet the other requirement which the parent chamber places on it: responsiveness. Support for Appropriations' budget cutting depends on the committee's providing adequate funding for programs which the House has authorized. This second strategic premise of adequate funding suggests that the committee must constantly search for a balance: cutting the budget enough to maintain its independence and influence, yet providing adequate funding to maintain the support of members interested in particular programs.

Ways and Means members are faced with a similar need for keeping their influence. To do this, members emphasize the technical complexity and political importance of their legislation and the need for independence so as to be able to deal adequately with such measures. Since the influence of Ways and Means would be greatly diminished by floor defeats, a major strategic premise is to write a bill that is not only technically sound, but also will pass the House. "It's a waste of time to bring out a bill if you can't pass it" is the attitude of Chairman Wilbur Mills. "As I see it our job is to work over a bill until our technical staff tells us it is ready and until I have reason to believe that it is going to have enough support to pass. Many of our bills must be brought out under a closed rule and to get and keep a closed rule, you must have a widely acceptable bill. It's as simple as that."[14]

John Manley's study of Ways and Means suggested to him that "a good bill that cannot pass the House is a contradiction in terms for most members of Ways and Means."[15] Since the other environmental group of concern to Ways and Means members consists of party leaders, the second strategic premise of committee members is to follow partisan policy choices when they are relevant. This is done, not with an eye toward committee influence, but rather to satisfy party leaders who were instrumental in each member's being on the committee and who seek to have clearly drawn partisan positions for electoral purposes.

The internal structure of committees may be analyzed in terms of partisanship, degree and types of participation/specialization as reflected in subcommittee structure, and patterns of leadership demonstrated by committee and subcommittee chairmen. Fenno measured internal partisanship by looking at committee reports on major legislation, measuring the number of reports on which there was recorded disagreement, and then measuring the number of recorded disagreements on which a majority of one party was in opposition to a majority of the other.

Ways and Means and Education and Labor are clearly the most partisan committees in this study. But there is a key difference. While Education and Labor decisions are reached in a constantly charged partisan atmosphere, Ways and Means members generally bring in partisan issues only after the major technical decisions have been made in a more neutral way. A Ways and Means staffer says of his group:

> I think you will find that Ways and Means is a partisan committee. There are usually minority reports. But partisanship is not that high when they discuss the bill and legislate. About 95 percent of the time, the members deliberate the bill in a nonpartisan way, discussing the facts calmly. Then toward the end (John) Byrnes (ranking Republican) and the Republicans may go partisan. But an awfully large part of it is nonpartisan.[16]

By following this pattern of "restrained partisanship," Ways and Means members are able to satisfy both party leaders' demands for making decisions along partisan lines and their own desires to reduce intracommittee conflict in the interest of maintaining committee influence. Education and Labor members, because they are more interested in policy than in committee influence, see no need to control partisanship in decision-making. Appropriations is the least partisan committee, and with good reason. Faced with the same demands as Ways and Meansers to maintain committee influence, but without having to satisfy party leaders' requests to structure conflicts in partisan terms, Appropriations members can best maintain their committees' mystique of expertise by minimizing partisanship. "This is one committee where you will find no partisan politics. We carry on the hearings and we mark up the bill and we compromise our differences. We bring a bill to the floor of the House each year with the unanimous approval of the committee members."[17] By having every member's approval of the bill and by minimizing partisanship, the Appropriations Committee is able to get its bills accepted by House members impressed by its "expert" nonpartisan decision-making and by its unanimity.

In the Ninety-second Congress (1971–1973), Appropriations had 55 members and Ways and Means 25. This size difference greatly affects the way the two committees work: Appropriations does all of its work through subcommittees; Ways and Means works through a full committee on all bills. The expertise which characterizes Appropriations members is upheld by a subcommittee system emphasizing independent subcommittee decisions that are recognized as authoritative by other subcommittees, the full committee, and the House. Such a system permits a high level of participation by members, but it is limited to subcommittees and issues on which the member has developed some expertise. This specialization greatly facilitates the committee's strategy of cutting budgets. By zeroing in on a narrow area, members are better able to locate unnecessary expenditures. It is easier to make appropriations policy through a series of independent decisions than to make tax, trade, or social security decisions the same way. "I'm so damn glad we don't have subcommittees," said a Ways and Means committeeman, "because if you broke things down into three or four parts you wouldn't know what's going on."[18] Because of its smaller size and because of the nature of its subject matter, Ways and Means is able to operate through full committee decisions. Committee influence is still dependent on members' knowledge of the subject, as in Appropriations, but this expertise is developed through participation in all decisions rather than through specialized subcommittees.

The preeminence of Ways and Means chairman Wilbur Mills has been widely recorded. A 1968 feature story in the *New York Times* called him "the most important man on Capitol Hill today;" a colleague said of his dealings with the chairman: "It's like being allowed to touch the hem of the Lord's gown."[19] Mills is able to exercise this leadership because he is in basic agreement with members' goals; he, too, wants to maintain committee prestige by writing bills that will pass the House and by following a pattern of restrained partisanship. His style of leadership is one favoring compromise and consensus. An HEW official who often deals with Ways and Means tells how the chairman seeks this consensus:

> Mills wants more than anything not to have a minority report. He wants at least twenty votes and one way he does it is to drop out anything controversial. I don't mean just major policy questions that may be controversial but anything. If they come across a provision and some member raises an objection, he'll drop it.[20]

Mills's influence on the committee stems not only from his seeking compromise and consensus, but also from his having superior information. Chairman since 1958, Mills's long service has given him a technical expertise which is unchallenged: "He knows the tax code inside and out and he knows what Ways and Means has done for the last twenty years. He can cite and does cite section after section of the code."[21] Another type of information possessed by the chairman is the distribution of opinion within the committee and in the House. A colleague says of Mills: "He counts the heads in the Committee and he counts the heads in the House, he's always counting."[22] Both sorts of information are key to the great influence which Chairman Mills has in Ways and Means and the parent chamber.

Recent Appropriations chairmen, Cannon and Mahon, have also sought compromise and consensus in their committees. But unlike Mills, neither has dominated the committee decision-making. This is so primarily because of the previously mentioned committee structure, with its emphasis on subcommittee autonomy, reciprocity, and specialization. The Appropriations chairman does have influence stemming from his power of appointment to subcommittees and his information about the activities of all subcommittees. But informal norms of the committee dictate minimal interference in subcommittee activity by the full committee chairman. This greatly circumscribes his range of activities and precludes the type of coalition formation exercised by the chairman of Ways and Means. The Appropriations chairman can best meet members' goals of House influence by supporting the specialized subcommittee structure and expertise on which that influence rests.

POLICY COMMITTEES

Committees such as Education and Labor, Foreign Affairs, Banking and Currency, and Government Operations are populated by members more interested in policy goals than in congressional influence or constituency projects. Fenno's study showed that not one member of Education and Labor or Foreign Affairs used the word "influential" or "powerful" to describe his committee.[23] Being on either committee generally has little or no effect on the members' standing in his district. "Politically, it's not a good committee for me. My constituents are interested in bread and butter, and there's no bread and butter on Foreign Affairs."[24] An Education and Labor Democrat expresses a similar attitude:

> I'm the most issue-oriented guy you'd ever want to meet. I know there won't be a Wagner Act with my name on it during my first term. But if I can get a few of my ideas in I'll be satisfied. Legislating in Washington, for the district and in the public interest. That's what interests me the most. Serving your constituency—that's a noble effort, too. But, frankly, I consider any time spent with a constituent as time wasted that I could have spent doing more important things.[25]

Freshman legislators seeking policy goals will generally request an assignment to Education and Labor, Foreign Affairs, or Banking and Currency. They do so because such an assignment offers them an opportunity to deal with exciting and controversial issues. When Abraham Ribicoff came to the Senate in 1962 he brought with him experience as governor of Connecticut and HEW secretary, and a great interest in urban poverty and unemployment. By being assigned to the Government Operations Committee Ribicoff, as a freshman senator, was able to hold extensive hearings on administrative organization in relation to urban problems. After thoroughly investigating problems such as those leading to the Watts riots of 1965, Ribicoff offered several bills designed to make government organization more responsive to urban problems.[26] The payoff of such activity is good policy, not Senate influence or constituency rewards.

The most important external groups for members of these committees are whichever ones dominate the policy coalitions for particular issues. Because they seek good policy rather than congressional influence, members of Foreign Affairs and Education and Labor are more sensitive to groups playing a major role in formulating policies than to fellow legislators. Congressmen who are not on these committees permit this attention to outside policy coalitions because neither welfare policies nor foreign affairs matters are regarded as key issues determining the relative influence of the House in the larger political system.[27]

The Foreign Affairs Committee deals with an environment dominated by the executive branch. The president's influence over foreign policy and the executive's near monopoly on information in this area make it the chief policy coalition with which Foreign Affairs must contend.[28] Education and Labor is confronted with an environment quite different from that of Foreign Affairs. Instead of facing a homogeneous policy coalition dominated by one actor, Education and Labor must deal with coalitions made up of executive officials, party leaders, clientele groups, and other House members. High priority presidential programs, such as Lyndon Johnson's poverty program, bring a flood of executive proposals and proponents to the committee. The importance of partisan disagreements on Education and Labor is shown in Table 3. The degree of clientele interest in the committee is suggested by the remark of an AFL-CIO official:

> We watch the Education and Labor Committee very carefully; but it's the only one we're interested in. Otherwise, you would spread yourself too thin. We have to control the labor committee. It's our life blood.[29]

Other House members are brought into the policy debate on issues facing Education and Labor because of the electoral and partisan importance of the issues considered by the committee. In contrast to the stable, executive-dominated environment of Foreign Affairs, then, members of Education and Labor face a constantly changing array of highly partisan policy coalitions.

Foreign Affairs members generally feel that they can best satisfy both their goal of good policy and the demands of their only important policy coalition by approving and building support for the administration's foreign aid program. Although the committee does provide a focus for opponents of foreign aid, most members see their role as one of making minor changes in the

TABLE 3 *Partisanship on Committees (1955–1965)*

	Total Major Legistlation	Percent Recorded Disagreements	Percent Party Disagreements	Party Disagreements as Percent of All Disagreements
Ways & Means	114	52%(59)	26%(30)	50%
Education & Labor	96	56 (54)	25 (27)	50
Interior	82	33 (27)	7 (6)	20
Post Office	42	38 (16)	7 (3)	19
Foreign Affairs	66	24 (16)	5 (3)	19
Appropriations	154*	7 (11)	0 (0)	0

*Original appropriations bills only.
SOURCE: Richard Fenno, "Congressional Committees: A Comparative View," paper delivered at the annual meeting of the American Political Science Association, Los Angeles, 1970, p. 54, reprinted by permission.

president's program and getting that bill passed. The nature of the subject matter, described by one committeeman as "all undefined and amorphous; all up in the air," makes it difficult for members to get the information and expertise needed to play a more active role.[30] Some Foreign Affairs members, because of their great interest in policy goals, do not like this executive dominance:

> I have the feeling that we sit over here like a lot of little birds getting fed, and if you are for the Administration then you are supposed to like the food. But I don't like that. Sure I'm for foreign aid, but is that all I'm supposed to do?[31]

There is no easy solution to this problem of presidential initiative and control over information. The subject matter and the policy goals of the members do not permit Foreign Affairs to adopt a blanket "cut the budget" norm like Appropriations. Expanding the committee staff would perhaps provide more technical information for members who wish to challenge the expertise of the administration. But even this staff must rely on information which comes primarily from executive sources.

Education and Labor reflects the depolarized, volatile nature of its environment. Highly charged issues are continually being brought to the committee by the numerous coalitions making demands upon it. The committee responds by emphasizing partisan and individualistic norms of behavior. "You can't get a resolution praising God through this Committee without having a 3-day battle over it."[32] Another committee member observes:

> Usually the Committee splits up the factions. They change from issue to issue, but on any one you know who they are. . . . Sometimes our side is so fragmented we have to pick up some votes on the other side. We go off in six directions at once.[33]

As Table 3 indicates, the issues splitting the committee generally do so along party lines. Because ideological positions and party labels do not always coincide, however, members sometimes find themselves on a different side of the fence from their own party leaders. Fenno suggests that Education and Labor norms support members pursuing their individual policy preferences in such situations. This can be justified because committee members have the experience and information to support their policy stands. Unlike Foreign Affairs where the committee faces a monolithic executive coalition with superior information and expertise, Education and Labor members can best pursue policy goals by becoming embroiled in the fragmented battles among many coalitions with relatively equal information resources.

The measures of internal structure—partisanship, participation/specialization, and leadership—show the different ways these two policy committees react to different environments. Foreign Affairs, like Appropriations, is a nonpartisan committee. "There's a feeling on the Committee that you don't want to exacerbate partisan feelings if you don't have to. Doc (the chairman) will say many times, 'It makes no difference; under Eisenhower, Kennedy, or Johnson we did this.' "[34]

Members of both parties are more liberal than their party colleagues in the House; they generally support the foreign aid program; and they believe that good policy in this area can best be reached by minimizing partisan differences. On Education and Labor, as we have observed, party cues are relevant to the individual member's policy position. The issues considered by the committee, because they touch on the basic differences between

Republicans and Democrats, preclude members adopting a non-partisan stance. "This is probably the most partisan committee in the House, because this is where the fundamental philosophical battles are fought."[35]

The subcommittee structures of the two policy committees are quite different: Education and Labor emphasizes subcommittee activity much like the Appropriations Committee, while Foreign Affairs completely ignores them. Listen to the comment of a Foreign Affairs committeeman:

> I've been on the European subcommittee for five months and I haven't even heard NATO mentioned, haven't even heard the word. I read my hometown newspaper to find out what's happening to NATO. The subcommittees have displayed absolute irrelevancy in foreign affairs, amazing irrelevancy."[36]

One of the reasons for Foreign Affairs' not working through a subcommittee system is the fact that it deals with only one big bill a year, the foreign aid bill. "If you had subcommittees," suggests a member, "the full committee would take it apart all over again. It's the one bill of the year. It's not like Education and Labor where you have all those big bills."[37]

Subcommittees are used on the Foreign Affairs Committee, but they are primarily a research tool: they hold hearings to gather information which might be of some use to the full committee; they do not legislate. The only important legislation with which the committee deals is the annual foreign aid bill, and this is handled by the full committee. All members participate in committee activity on this one bill. Because of the lack of subcommittee activity, there is no deference to "experts" who have spent a lot of time on one narrow aspect of the bill. All members are expected to participate in the full committee activity, but it is a closely limited participation designed to facilitate passage of the administration program. All members, for instance, are given only five minutes each for questioning witnesses in hearings on the foreign aid bill. Education and Labor represents a different extreme: subcommittees are the important arenas for policy debate, and all members enjoy a completely unrestricted participation in their activities. A somewhat surprised newcomer observes:

> I never dreamed the older members would have allowed us freshmen to contribute so much and participate and get into the legislative process as much as we have. I thought we would have to break the seniority system. But on my subcommittees I participate, get amendments passed and open doors I never thought I could. I was amazed at how little restraint and restriction is placed on us. I think Education and Labor is unique in the use that is made of freshmen.[38]

The committee uses subcommittees because the issues which come to Education and Labor can best be handled by allocating them to smaller units which isolate the conflicts surrounding a particular education or manpower program. The high participation level of all members is a direct result of committee members' emphasis on policy goals. There is no impetus to maintain committee prestige within the chamber by parading expertise, and there is no acceptance of the idea that one member's opinion is worth more than another's:

> Expertise? Hell, everyone thinks he's an expert on the questions before our Committee. On education, the problem is that everyone went to school. They all think that makes them experts on that. And labor matters are so polarized that everyone is committed. You take sides first and then you acquire expertise. So no one accepts anyone as impartial.[39]

Unlike Appropriations, where subcommittees are also important, Education and Labor subcommittees do not make decisions for the whole committee. There is no expertise mystique preventing other subcommittees and the full committee from questioning decisions made in Education and Labor subcommittees. "On some two bit, piddling little bill, the full committee will say, 'that's what the subcommittee recommends, we'll vote it through.' But on major bills, the subcommittee has no standing with the full committee."[40] Committee members' interest in good policy and the committee norm of maximizing pursuit of individual policy goals lead to high levels of individual participation not only within one's subcommittee, but also in considering the work of other subcommittees.

Leadership on the Foreign Affairs Committee fits in with members' goals of passing the president's foreign aid bill. The chairman, Thomas Morgan, is able to help members to achieve this goal. But beyond that, his influence over the broader issues of foreign policy is limited. The Senate Foreign Relations Committee dominates congressional debate in this area, and there is little the House committee can do to challenge the upper chamber's constitutional prerogatives. Fenno's interviews with committee members seeking a more active committee role showed some dissatisfaction with Chairman Morgan. "He's a perfectly delightful man," observed one, "so I have nothing against him personally; but he's the State Department's man. As a result, this precludes any aggressive or imaginative activity on the part of the Committee."[41]

Education and Labor presents quite a different picture. From 1953 to 1967, the committee was run by two men who, although poles apart ideologically, exercised great influence over the committee. Graham Barden of North Carolina chaired the committee for eight years. A conservative, Barden was able to control his committee by operating only through ad hoc subcommittees over which he kept a wary eye. Subcommittees were used as burial chambers for legislation opposed by the chairman.

In 1961, Adam Clayton Powell became chairman of Education and Labor. He expanded the number of subcommittees, but maintained his control by keeping their jurisdictions vague. There were three subcommittees for education and three for labor; two were called "general," two "special," and two "select." By expanding the number of subcommittees, Powell was able to elevate liberal Democrats to the position of subcommittee chairman. By keeping subcommittee jurisdictions unclear, he was able to determine where a bill would be sent. Powell's success as chairman relied on his giving the important coalitions affecting Education and Labor what they wanted: subcommittee members were able to have a hand in policy-making; the liberal Democratic coalition making demands on the committee was rewarded with volumes of legislation; and the chairman and his party received great publicity for their programs.

The importance of policy goals to members of Education and Labor is demonstrated by the fact that both chairmen were, in effect, deposed. Barden was upset because his conservative views clashed with the policy-oriented Democratic majority; Powell's influence was diminished after he alienated members of the liberal Democratic coalition by delaying action on bills dealing with the repeal of state right-to-work laws in 1965, a pro-labor picketing bill in 1966, and the poverty program of 1966. As long as the Education and Labor chairman's views coincide with the policy conscious majority on the committee, he has great influence over the fate of legislation coming to the committee. When he becomes separated from that majority, however, the individualistic policy norms of the committee require that he be outvoted and stripped of his power.

CONSTITUENCY COMMITTEES

Fenno's research showed that members of the Interior and Post Office committees are more concerned with serving constituency interests through committee work than with influence within the House or broad questions of public policy. Other studies of the Agriculture and Armed Services committees suggest that most members also think of them primarily as constituency committees.[42] People on these committees obviously have an interest in making "good" public policy. But unlike Foreign Affairs or Education and Labor committeemen, their policy interests are narrower and more tailored to interests of constituents. A representative sums up this attitude in telling Fenno why he wanted to be on Interior:

> I was attracted to it, very frankly, because it's a bread and butter committee for my state. I guess about the only thing about it that is not of great interest to my state is insular affairs. I was able to get two or three bills of great importance to my state through last year. I had vested interests I wanted to protect, to be frank.[43]

This concern with constituency interests is also reflected in comments by members of the Agriculture and Post Office committees:[44]

> I vote for what I think will be the best economic interests of my people. Throughout the years I have gained an idea of what those interests are. This is the way representative government should work.

We have over 10,000 civil service and postal employees in my state. While we are here first and foremost to represent the national interest, and while I'm a firm believer in that, nevertheless you have to look out for the interests of your people. Politics is a great way to promote your ideals, but first you have to be elected and then reelected and to do this you have to help your constituents.

Lewis Anthony Dexter's study of the House Armed Services Committee found members and staff men characterizing their committee as a "real estate committee." By that, notes Dexter, they meant that "the location of installations and related transfer, purchase, and sale of properties is the main concern of the House Armed Services Committee."[45]

The geographic distribution of seats on Interior, Armed Services, and Agriculture illustrates House acceptance of the idea that committees are primarily constituency committees. Fenno's analysis showed Interior to be the most unrepresentative of the six committees studied. Congressmen from western states accounted for 50 percent of the membership on Interior, while their percentage of seats in the whole House was only 14.[46] Over half of the Democrats on Armed Services and Agriculture in the Ninety-second Congress came from southern or border states. Charles Jones's study of Agriculture demonstrates how party affiliations and subcommittee assignments reinforce representation of constituency interests. Democrats dominate the tobacco, cotton, peanuts, and rice subcommittees which deal with commodities of interest to their constituents; Republicans have a similar edge on the corn, dairy, livestock and feed grains, and wheat subcommittees.[47]

The important environment groups for clientele committees are their respective policy constituencies, i.e., those groups which have electoral pull and certain demands on the committee. For the Post Office Committee these groups are postal employee unions (the National Association of Letter Carriers being the most important) who want higher wages, and mail user organizations (such as the Associated Third Class Users) who want lower postal rates. Both groups are continually locked in combat, not with other interest groups, but rather with the executive branch which opposes increased postal salaries and favors higher rates. The environment of Post Office, then, is a monolithic one similar to Foreign Affairs; but instead of dominance by the executive, it is faced with constant pressure from organized postal interests. Listen to one member's description of committee life:

> Nobody in the Congress or in the public gives a damn about what we do. Oh, once every few years, we have an orgy on junk mail, but other than that, nobody cares. We are wooed by the whole panoply of outside groups. There's always a dinner somewhere. They come in and fawn over your staff. There isn't a day that goes by that someone doesn't come in here wooing me. This is the dominant fact of life, the distinguishing characteristic of the Committee.[48]

Interior committeemen face a much more pluralistic environment: each issue brings many groups arrayed against one another. A debate over using public lands, for instance, will involve such groups as the National Lumber Manufacturers Association, the American Mining Congress, and the American Cattlemen's Association on one side, and the Wilderness Society, the Sierra Club, and the National Wildlife Federation on the other. The visibility of this pressure is muted, however, by the fact that members of Interior often act as spokesmen for these groups. The pluralist nature of the environment, the use of congressmen as spokesmen, and the predisposition of western legislators to favor most federal projects all contribute to members' feeling that they are subject to little pressure. "Maybe I don't know pressure when I see it," said one member in describing his contacts with clientele groups, "but all I ever get from them is information."[49] The Agriculture Committee shows a similar pattern of representation, one in which there is no need for overt pressure because the congressman himself recognizes and responds to the interests of his policy constituency:

> You are in the position to know, of course, on a lot of things. I live there—there are many things I just know. I don't have to ask anybody. There are very few bills where I have to guess. If I did, I wouldn't be here as the representative. I am a native of ———. I get letters—though I don't get very much mail. I have sent out questionnaires, but I don't now. It is just the fact that I know and I can judge their needs.[50]

The Interior Committee is faced both with a pluralistic environment and an overwhelming flood of legislation. One out of every five bills introduced in the House goes to Interior. In order to satisfy member goals of constituency service and the demands of clientele groups, the committee has adopted the basic strategic premise of passing all legislation sponsored by relevant constituents and supported by committee members. Such reciprocity does not preclude close scrutiny of legislation by the committee and it maximizes committee norms favoring the reelection of individual members. One result of adopting this strategy is that committee decisions generally favor western commercial interests over the competing claims of eastern conservation groups.

The Post Office Committee, with three-quarters of its members serving on other committees, is run by what Fenno calls an "efficient minority." Although some members object to the close ties between their colleagues and postal groups ("He's a bought man;" "He's in the pocket of the unions;" "He's in bed with all the groups; they raise money for him and he does their bidding"), this active minority is able to set the major strategic premise of the committee: support pay and benefit increases for postal employees and oppose all mail rate increases.[51]

One of the effects of the monolithic environment on the Post Office Committee is to make it a relatively nonpartisan committee. Like Foreign Affairs, party disagreements on the committee represented only 19 percent of all disagreements. This lack of partisanship is probably more a result of the environment of the committee than it is of the constituency orientation of committee members. By minimizing partisan conflict, the clientele groups which dominate committee activity are better able to present a united front. Introducing partisan debate would only serve to weaken the present lobbying monopoly enjoyed by postal employee and mail user groups.

Interior is also free of most partisan conflict, but for different reasons. It is the nature of the issues which the committee faces, rather than the character of the environment, which accounts for Interior's low partisanship. Its environment, like Education and Labor's, consists of many groups. But other than debate over public versus private power, the issues handled by Interior are not structured in ideological terms. Says one member:

There's a kind of cohesiveness in the Committee that overrides partisan considerations. The key here is that there aren't any ideological issues. You don't hear the Republicans saying we can't afford this or that. And the reason is that everyone has a project in his district that he wants or will want.[52]

Reciprocity norms and Interior members' desire to maintain House support for the committee in order to meet their goal of passing lots of bills also account for the relative lack of partisan conflict.

Until 1965, the Post Office Committee used only ad hoc subcommittees on legislative matters. The comments of one member suggest the ineffectiveness of this system: "Murray would appoint some fluffy subcommittee, a temporary sort of thing, with mostly newcomers. They'd issue some half-assed report which no one would read."[53]

A rules change in 1965 led to every member sitting on three subcommittees; freshmen were also given assignments designed to encourage participation in committee decision-making. But even with these changes, subcommittee activity on Post Office is not of great importance in affecting policy outcomes. This is the case, it would seem, because of the working alliance between outside groups and the efficient minority which runs the committee, and because most members of the committee take little interest in its work.

Subcommittees play an active part in Interior decision-making. The committee itself was formed in 1946 by combining six standing committees; these became the basis for subcommittees in the new Interior and Insular Affairs Committee. This emphasis on subcommittees is similar to that of Appropriations, but differs from the latter because it does not rely on the money committees' structure of subcommittee expertise and autonomy. There is specialization on Interior subcommittees, but it is more tailored to meeting members' constituency needs than to developing substantive expertise. As a result of this active subcommittee system and the lack of expertise norms, newcomers to Interior are able actively to participate in committee decisions. Every member respects the right of others, including freshmen, to work vigorously for projects at home. Because of this pattern of heavy participation by all members, incoming legislators feel that

Interior is "the best training ground for active participation and debate in the House."[54]

The Agriculture Committee's internal structure illustrates the importance of constituency matters to its members. There are two types of subcommittees: one deals with specific commodities and the other with general agricultural problems like farm production. Congressmen on the committee are much more interested in the commodity subcommittees, the subcommittee assignments almost always match representatives with products of importance to their district. Party ratios, however, require that some members be assigned to subcommittees of no importance to their constituents (midwestern Republicans on the cotton subcommittee; southern Democrats on the wheat subcommittee). Participation norms reinforce the importance of constituency matters in such cases, for as Professor Jones observes, "members who have little interest in the proceedings are expected either to remain silent during hearings or not to attend."[55]

Leadership on Post Office and Interior could not be more different. A member of both committees during the period studied by Fenno compared Interior Chairman Wayne Aspinall and former Post Office Chairman Tom Murray:

> Aspinall's a marvelous chairman. He knows more about that jurisdiction than any other person in the country, bar none. He's in at 8:00 a.m., works all day, no social life. He dominates those subcommittee chairmen; they have no autonomy at all. He's with them every step of the way. And everything's by the numbers, according to good parliamentary procedure. When we wanted rules for Post Office, we followed Aspinall's rules. He lets everybody talk, he's fair. He'll say if a freshman has anything to say, let's hear it. Aspinall's the best chairman anyone could have. It's time consuming, time consuming as hell; but it's run perfectly.
>
> On the other hand I'd go over to Post Office and it was a miserable mess. Everyone yelling and shouting, "Who's got the floor?" "I don't know." "Is there a quorum?" "Who cares." It was utter chaos—screaming, fighting, a miserable mess—and all old Murray would do is stare off into space. When we did want to do something, we'd meet in Morrison's office then leave by twos so no one would get suspicious. Then we'd come in, vote cloture and get a bill out. But even after we ran a steamroller over Murray in committee, we'd have to prod him to go before the Rules Committee for a God damn rule.[56]

Post Office members stripped Murray of almost all powers in 1965, not only because of the inertia caused by his age, but also because he tended to favor executive proposals and thus worked against the strategic premises of the majority.

Wayne Aspinall is often compared to Ways and Means' Wilbur Mills in the extent to which he controls Interior. He sits on all six subcommittees and actively participates; he makes the basic scheduling decisions which determine when a bill moves from subcommittee to committee to the floor; and he has an enormous reputation for success on the floor ("I don't think Aspinall has ever gone down on the floor, at least I can't remeber a time." "When you come to the floor with the Interior Committee, you feel like a member of the varsity team.")[57]

In the case of both Mills and Aspinall, they are successful chairmen because they share, and are able to help members meet, expectations about committee behavior. The floor success of both chairmen illustrates this: for Ways and Means such success is crucial for maintaining its influence within the House; for Interior, it is the only way that members can satisfy their goal of constituency projects.

CONCLUDING NOTE

We are left with an incomplete picture. Fenno's framework of comparative analysis in terms of members' goals helps in understanding similarities among committees which are quite different in many ways. But there have not been enough studies of particular committees to provide a thorough discussion of all committees in this manner. Manley's study of Ways and Means, Jones's of Agriculture, and Fenno's of these six House committees are important because they expose the complexity of the subject. This variety in types of committees and their functions makes the problems of evaluation and reform more difficult. A supporter of the Jeffersonian party government model, for instance, who uses the highly partisan Education and Labor committee to evaluate all committees neglects the importance of nonpartisan norms for the Appropriations Committee and the budgetary process. Similarly, adherents of the Hamiltonian model who seek centralized, responsive committees will find that while this might make sense for policy committees like Foreign Affairs and Education and Labor, it would be a silly expectation for representational, constituency committees like Agriculture or Interior.

To properly evaluate committees it is first necessary to understand this variety and then to judge each committee, not by a single yardstick applied to all committees, but rather in terms of how well it performs its particular functions. One of the reasons that congressional reform has been slow in coming, when it comes at all, is that reformers often have overlooked these differences among committees in prescribing changes in committee structure or procedure. When some broad reform is passed which conflicts with the functions of a particular committee, the effect of reform is abrogated by finding new ways to perform the old functions, or simply by ignoring the new rules.

The Legislative Reorganization Act of 1946, for instance, eliminated more than half of the standing committees; from a total of 81 to 34. Instead of really centralizing the committee structure and increasing its capacity for decision-making, though, the act lead to a great proliferation of subcommittees to perform most of the representational functions of the old committees. In 1945 there were 180 subcommittees, in 1970, 367. Ignoring reform procedures is an easy matter, as long as enough members agree. A 1969 survey by *Congressional Quarterly* found that most committees ignored the 1946 act's provision requiring that each committee schedule a regular meeting day.[58]

Floor action in the Senate on the 1967 reorganization bill illustrates how such reforms often overlook the special characteristics of particular committees. Finance Committee Chairman Russell Long offered 16 amendments dealing with matters important to that committee; William Fulbright of Foreign Relations put forward 10 amendments to make sure that the operations of his committee would not be hampered by reform; and Labor and Public Welfare committeeman Wayne Morse, in proposing 13 other amendments, criticized the "false assumption that a uniform procedure applicable to all committees under all conditions will improve the efficiency of the committee work."[59] When the Legislative Reorganization Bill finally passed the House, in October 1970, it did contain provisions affecting committee behavior. Included were rules that:[60]

1. Require that committees make public all roll call votes taken in committee.
2. Require that committee meetings and hearings be open to the public —unless the committee votes to close them.
3. Allow any open hearing to be broadcast or televised—if a majority of the committee approves.
4. Require that a committee report on a bill be filed within seven days after a majority of the committee asks that it be filed.
5. Outlaw proxy voting—unless the committee adopts a rule permitting such voting.
6. Require committees to announce hearings at least one week in advance—unless there is a good reason for beginning earlier.

What Congress did in passing the Legislative Reorganization Act of 1970 was to recognize the committee variety discussed in this chapter. The bill seeks to limit the arbitrary power of chairmen and to make committee proceedings more public. But it does this in such a way that each committee can bend the rules to suit its own purposes. Committee chairmen, with the support of a majority on their committees, can still close all meetings and hearings; they can refuse to have hearings televised or broadcast; and they can adopt their own rules regarding the use of proxies. The message here seems fairly clear: unless reforms of the congressional committee system, and the evaluations on which they are based, recognize the distinctive characteristics of particular committees, there is little hope that they can bring about meaningful changes in Congress.

NOTES

1. Quoted in *Boston Globe*, January 30, 1971, p. 2. A similar event occured two years earlier when Representative Shirley Chisholm from New York City was sent to the Agriculture Committee. "Apparently all they know in Washington about Brooklyn is that a tree grew there," was her reaction. "I can think of no other reason for assigning me to the House Agriculture Committee." *Washington Post*, January 30, 1969. Quoted in George Goodwin, Jr., *The Little Legislatures: Committees of Congress* (University of Massachusetts Press, 1970), p. 78n.

2. Woodrow Wilson, *Congressional Government* (Meridian, 1967), p. 66.

3. Clem Miller, *Member of the House*, edited by John Baker (Charles Scribner's Sons, 1962), p. 110.

4. Robert Sherrill, "Who Runs Congress?" *New York Times Magazine*, November 22, 1970, p. 65. George Goodwin's analysis of the Eightieth through Ninetieth Congresses showed "that a representative is likely to have two subcommittee assignments at the most, while a senator is likely to have at least six." See Goodwin, *The Little Legislatures*, p. 48.

5. Quoted in John Manley, *The Politics of Finance: The House Committee on Ways and Means* (Little, Brown, 1970), p. 84.

6. The regrettable pun is that of former Senator Joseph Clark of Pennsylvania. *Congressional Record*, 88th Congress, 1st Session, 1963, pp. 2559–2562. Quoted in Goodwin, *The Little Legislatures*, p. 111.

7. Donald R. Matthews, *U.S. Senators and Their World* (Vintage, 1960), pp. 154–155.

8. Quoted in Richard Fenno, "Congressional Committees: A Comparative View," paper delivered at the annual meeting of the American Political Science Association, Los Angeles, 1970.

9. *Ibid.;* see the discussion on pp. 22, 29, and 90–91 which puts the Fenno framework into the context of other studies of congressional committees. Although Fenno never gets around to discussing policy output in this paper, his general framework of analysis and application to the Appropriations, Education and Labor, Foreign Affairs, Interior and Insular Affairs, Post Office and Civil Service, and Ways and Means committees marks this paper as a pathbreaking analysis similar to his classic article on the Appropriation Committee. Most of this discussion of committee types defined in terms of member goals follows Fenno's perceptive analysis.

10. *Ibid.*, p. 3.

11. Manley, *The Politics of Finance*, p. 53.

12. For a more thorough discussion of this criterion, see Nicholas Masters, "Committee Assignments," in Robert Peabody and Nelson Polsby, eds., *New Perspectives on the House of Representatives* (Rand McNally, 1969), pp. 240ff.

13. Richard Fenno, "The Appropriations Committee as a Political System," in Peabody and Polsby, eds., *New Perspectives on the House of Representatives*, p. 129.

14. Manley, *The Politics of Finance,* pp. 111–112.

15. *Ibid.,* p. 218.

16. *Ibid.,* p. 67.

17. Quoted in Richard Fenno, *The Power of the Purse* (Little, Brown, 1966), p. 200.

18. Fenno, "Congressional Committees: A Comparative View," p. 69.

19. Julius Duscha, "The Most Important Man on Capitol Hill Today," *New York Times Magazine,* February 25, 1968; and Manley, *The Politics of Finance,* p. 137.

20. Quoted in Manley, *The Politics of Finance,* p. 113.

21. *Ibid.,* p. 125.

22. *Ibid.,* p. 107.

23. Fenno, "Congressional Committees: A Comparative View," p. 11.

24. *Ibid.,* p. 10.

25. *Ibid.,* p. 9.

26. William Morrow, *Congressional Committees* (Charles Scribner's Sons, 1969), p. 82. See also John Bibby and Roger Davidson, *On Capitol Hill* (Holt, Rinehart & Winston, 1967), pp. 30–52.

27. This is in contrast to the Senate Foreign Relations Committee which is charged with maintaining the Senate's constitutional powers in this area similar to the House money committees' function of preserving the House's fiscal powers outlined in the Constitution. See Fenno, "Congressional Committees: A Comparative View," p. 18.

28. For documentation and analysis of this presidential dominance see Holbert N. Carroll, *The House of Representatives and Foreign Affairs* (Little, Brown, 1966) and Michael K. O'Leary, *The Politics of American Foreign Aid* (Atherton, 1967).

29. Fenno, "Congressional Committees: A Comparative View," p. 20.

30. *Ibid.,* p. 48.

31. *Ibid.,* p. 47.

32. *Ibid.,* p. 56.

33. *Ibid.,* p. 50.

34. *Ibid.,* p. 59.

35. *Ibid.,* pp. 48–49.

36. *Ibid.,* p. 71.

37. *Ibid.,* p. 70.

38. *Ibid.,* p. 66.

39. *Ibid.,* p. 68.

40. *Ibid.,* p. 67.

41. *Ibid.,* p. 88.

42. Charles O. Jones, "The Agriculture Committee and the Problem of Representation," pp. 155–174, and Lewis Anthony Dexter, "Congressmen and the Making of Military Policy," pp. 175–96 in Peabody and Polsby, eds., *New Perspectives on the House of Representatives.* For a thorough analysis of the relationship between defense spending and Senate voting patterns, see Bruce M. Russett, *What Price Vigilance* (Yale University Press, 1970). Also James Phillips, "The Military Industrial Complex," *Congressional Quarterly Special Report,* May 24, 1968, pp. 1155–1178.

43. Fenno, "Congressional Committees: A Comparative View," p. 6.

44. Jones, "The Agriculture Committee and the Problem of Representation," p. 169 and Fenno, "Congressional Committees: A Comparative View," p. 6.

45. Dexter, "Congressmen and the Making of Military Policy," p. 182.

46. Fenno, "Congressional Committees: A Comparative View," p. 40. This is for the period covered by the Eighty-fourth-Eighty-ninth Congresses (1955–1966). In the Ninety-second Congress, 22 of the 38 members of Interior were from western states. All 15 of the members of the Senate Interior Committee represented western states.

47. Jones, "The Agriculture Committee and the Problem of Representation," pp. 158ff.

48. Fenno, "Congressional Committees, A Comparative View," p. 42.

49. *Ibid.,* p. 41.

50. Jones, "The Agriculture Committee and the Problem of Representation," pp. 170–171.

51. Fenno, "Congressional Committees: A Comparative View," pp. 41–42.

52. *Ibid.,* p. 60.

53. *Ibid.,* p. 73.

54. *Ibid.,* p. 65.

55. Jones, "The Agriculture Committee and the Problem of Representation," p. 160.

56. Fenno, "Congressional Committees: A Comparative View," p. 89.

57. *Ibid.*, p. 81.

58. *Congressional Quarterly Weekly Report*, December 25, 1970, p. 3062.

59. *Congressional Record*, February 3, 1967, p. S1495.

60. *Congressional Quarterly Weekly Report*, December 25, 1970, pp. 3062–3063.

CHAPTER 5

Rules and Norms

There was only one catch and that was Catch-22, which specified that a concern for one's own safety in the face of dangers that were real and immediate was the process of a rational mind. Orr was crazy and could be grounded. All he had to do was ask; and as soon as he did, he would no longer be crazy and would have to fly more missions. Orr would be crazy to fly more missions and sane if he didn't, but if he was sane he had to fly them. If he flew them he was crazy and didn't have to; but if he didn't want to he was sane and had to. Yossarian was moved very deeply by the absolute simplicity of this clause of Catch-22 and let out a respectful whistle.

Catch-22 did not exist, he was positive of that, but it made no difference. What did matter was that everyone thought it existed, and that was much worse, for there was no object or text to ridicule or refute, to accuse, criticize, attack, amend, hate, revile, spit at, rip to shreds, trample upon or burn up.

Joseph Heller
Catch 22

On June 30, 1970, the Senate passed the Cooper-Church amendment to the Military Sales Bill by a 58–37 roll call vote. The amendment stipulated that, as of July 1, 1970, no funds could be used for: (1) retaining U.S. forces in Cambodia, (2) paying any U.S. personnel engaged in military instruction to Cambodian forces or in combat activity supporting Cambodian forces, (3) entering into a contract providing military instruction or combat support for Cambodian forces, or (4) providing combat air support for Cambodian forces. The vote culminated seven weeks of

Senate debate. During those seven weeks supporters and opponents of the bill engaged in a wide-ranging discussion of the American presence in Indochina and of the proper roles of the president and Congress in setting foreign policy and making military decisions.

The House had passed the Military Sales Bill two months earlier. Because the House version did not contain the Cooper-Church amendment, however, the measure was returned to the House after Senate passage. The bill was brought to the House floor on July 9. Representative Thomas E. Morgan, chairman of the House Foreign Affairs Committee, offered a motion to send the bill to conference.

Although Morgan himself was opposed to Cooper-Church, he was resigned to the fact that House conferees would have to accept a modified version of the amendment in order to get the Military Sales Bill out of conference. A motion to send to conference is normally a debatable motion, and Morgan was allowed one hour of debating time. The chairman said that none of the House supporters of Cooper-Church had asked him for any time. Therefore, he moved the previous question which calls for an immediate vote. At least two representatives were on their feet to speak on the measure. They were not recognized, and Morgan's motion to send the bill to conference was passed, 247–143, without any debate on the matter. Immediately after the vote, Morgan asked for one hour of debating time. House rules give the minority party the right to make the first motion to instruct conferees. Republican Donald Riegle of Michigan, a supporter of Cooper-Church, then moved to instruct House conferees to retain the Cooper-Church amendment in the compromise bill worked out with the Senate. A motion to instruct conferees is also a debatable motion, and it seemed that the House was now ready to discuss the important issues involved in the Cooper-Church amendment. Debate on Riegle's motion was immediately cut off, however, when Representative Wayne Hays of Ohio, an opponent of Cooper-Church, moved to table the motion. A motion to table is not subject to debate. When some members objected to an immediate vote, Hays tried to withdraw his motion but he was overruled by the chair. The tabling motion carried, 237–153. Several members then asked for "unanimous consent" for an hour's debate on the matter. Only one member need object to kill this procedure, and in this instance unanimous consent was denied. The total amount of time spent by the House in considering Cooper-Church was less than one hour.

More recent attempts to have the House vote directly on the war were subject to the same sort of parliamentary jiggery-pokery. The House did not vote on the actual issue of cutting off funds until the Nedzi-Whalen amendment to the Military Procurement Act was defeated in June 1971. Ten years, 50,000 American lives, and $150 billion had already been spent on the Indochina War by the time the House voted directly on the matter.

In October 1971, the House considered the Senate-passed Mansfield amendment to set a date for ending United States participation in the war. Again House rules were used by the leadership to limit consideration of the measure. Representative Leslie Arends, the ranking Republican on Armed Services, offered a motion to instruct House conferees not to accept any "nongermane" amendments to the bill (this included the Mansfield amendment). Debate was limited to one hour and controlled by Arends. When a roll call vote was taken it was a "vote on the previous question" (sending House conferees to meet with Senate conferees) rather than a direct vote on the Mansfield amendment. The forces wanting to avoid a vote on the war issue won that roll call, 215–192.

The frustration of antiwar congressmen over the use of House rules to stifle debate on the war was expressed by two junior representatives: "Young men are in Vietnam this minute having their guts blown out," said Charles Whalen, "while we in the Congress argue about germaneness." Representative Pete McCloskey of California turned to Riegle of Michigan during one of these debates and muttered that "Old men babble while young men die."[1]

The contrast between the seven-week Senate debate and the one-hour "nondebate" in the House on the Cooper-Church amendment suggests that there are some fundamental differences between the two chambers. It is not simply that the Senate is more "responsive" to pressing social needs or that the House is always the more "conservative" body. Rather, the structure of each chamber and the rules of behavior related to that structure produce two quite different conceptions of the legislation function. In the first chapter, I discussed the sometimes conflicting functions of representation, or deliberation, and lawmaking. Although both chambers must perform both of these legislative functions, the structure and rules of the Senate emphasize that chamber's deliberative role, as seen in the long debate on the war, while House rules emphasize a lawmaking role which requires less talking and the speedier dispatch of legislative business. While the Senate is expected to be a great forum for debate and the representation of all interests and viewpoints in the nation as a whole, the House is regarded as a legislative mill which must process an overwhelming amount of technical legislation. These basic functional differences produce different rules and norms in the two bodies, and we will discuss some of the more important of these rules in this chapter. But first let us have a quick look at some of these basic differences between the two sides of Capitol Hill.

HOUSE-SENATE DIFFERENCES

"If the Senate has been the nation's great forum" a representative has written, "the House has been its workshop."[2] Although most of us tend to think of Congress as a whole and discuss it in terms of its shared characteristics (decentralization, seniority, the existence of two coequal chambers), there are important differences between the House and the Senate, and these differences are reinforced by the rules and norms governing legislative behavior in the two houses. Some of the more important ones are discussed below.[3]

Size

Most of the dissimilarity between the two chambers stems from the fact that the House is made up of 435 members elected for two-year terms while the Senate consists of 100 members elected for six-year terms. The impact of this fundamental difference is enormous. Senators, even newly elected ones, are much more "visible": they can more readily obtain media coverage when they want to discuss some issue; they rank higher in Washington's social protocol than do representatives; they have a larger allowance for staff and office expenditures; and the upper chamber is regarded as a prime source of candidates for the presidency.

Because the House is over four times the size of the Senate, it cannot operate in the informal relaxed manner characteristic of the upper chamber. The House is more formal, more impersonal, more hierarchically organized. There is a sharper division of labor in the House, and it is a decentralized system which maximizes the technical consideration of complex legislation by committee and subcommittee "experts."

Committees

As we saw in the last chapter, committee work is generally more important to a representative than to a senator. The House, with its 435 members, has 21 standing committees; the Senate, with 100 members, has 17. A senator therefore is likely to serve on three or four committees while a representative is on only one or two. The Senate's overlapping membership on many committees greatly reduces the mystique of committee expertise which is so important in the House. Committee membership in the Senate gives members a wider range of issues over which they can have some influence.

This greater dispersion of power in the Senate can be seen in Table 1 below. Senators of the majority party are more likely to be committee or subcommittee chairmen than are majority House members. While 93 percent of the Senate Democrats in the Ninety-second Congress had committee or subcommittee chairmanships, only 35 percent of House Democrats did. Also, in the Senate, 79 percent of the majority party membership had two or more chairmanships, while less than 8 percent of the House majority membership occupied two or more committee or subcommittee chairs.

Because there are fewer people competing for committee and subcommittee leadership positions in the Senate, the amount of time it takes to assume these positions is shorter for a senator than for a representative.[4] All of these factors, when put together, suggest the different impact of committees on legislative behavior in the two chambers and on the careers of senators and representatives. In the House, committees are primarily a place for legisla-

TABLE 1 *Distribution of Committee and Subcommittee Chairmanships among House and Senate Majority Members Ninety-Second Congress (1971–1972)*

Number of Committees and Subcommittees Chaired by Each Member	Senate	% of Democrats	House	% of Democrats
7	2	4	0	0
6	1	2	0	0
5	5	8	0	0
4	10	18	2	.5
3	13	23	5	1
2	13	23	20	6
1	8	14	98	27
0	4	7	235	65
	(N=56)		(N=360)	

SOURCE: Charles B. Bronson, *1972 Congressional Staff Record* (Washington, D.C., 1972), pp. 181–198 and 343–387. Lewis Froman did the same thing with data from the Eighty-eighth Congress (1964), and found the pattern which persists through 1972. Froman found that 78 percent of Senate Democrats had at least one committee or subcommittee chairmanship, while only 40 percent of House Democrats did. In the Senate, over 50 percent of the Democratic senators had two or more chairmanships, while only 12 percent of the representatives did. See Froman's, *The Legislative Process* (Little, Brown, 1967), pp. 11–12.

tive work, a place for senior members with great expertise to deal with complex matters of lawmaking. To have any real influence on policy an individual congressman must be on the committee which handles legislation in that area. While Senate committees must necessarily perform lawmaking functions, there is greater opportunity for senators to play a representational role in committee, and there is a better chance for a senator to have some influence over a wider range of policy areas.

Leadership Control

Because of its greater size the House must be organized in a more formal, hierarchical way than the Senate. This, in turn, requires that the leadership in the House be given more direct control over members than is given to Senate leaders. Both the formal rules and the unwritten norms of the two chambers support this difference, and we will be talking about some of them in this chapter.

A leading student of the Senate once described it as a place where "no one finally can make anyone else do anything."[5] Leadership in the Senate reflects this pattern of concern for the individual senator. In scheduling floor debate on a bill, for instance, majority party leaders will generally canvass the membership and arrange the timing of floor debate so as to suit all members' schedules. Such a practice would be impossible in the House; there, leaders schedule floor action after consultation only with the principal party and committee leaders. This, of course, leads to individual House members being subject to leadership control over their actions to a much greater extent than is true in the Senate.

Another indicator of the greater leadership control in the House is the amount of time both chambers spend on floor action. As we saw in the case of antiwar amendments, House leaders exercise great control over the time that the full chamber gives to floor consideration of a bill. In 1885 Woodrow Wilson observed that "the Senate commonly feels with the House, but it does not, so to say, feel as fast."[6]

House leaders' control over debate time is reflected in Table 2. The Senate spends many more hours in session than does the House, time that is controlled by the leadership in each chamber. This reflects not only the greater control over debate time by House leaders, but also the previously mentioned difference between the "representative," deliberative Senate and the "law-making," "rapid-dispatch-of-business" House.

Policy Roles

The House-Senate structural differences we have been discussing are closely tied to the roles each chamber plays in the policy process. In the next chapter we will be looking more closely at the fact that different types of policies are handled in different ways in the American system. Thus, it is difficult to generalize about some stable "policy-making process," and to discuss House and Senate roles in this process. In keeping with the structural differences already discussed, though, what we can do is suggest that the two chambers are best suited for two different sorts of policy-producing activities.

TABLE 2   *Days and Hours in Session Ninety-first Congress (1969–1970)*

	First Session		Second Session	
	Senate	*House*	*Senate*	*House*
Days in session	176	186	280	164
Time in session	926	747	1424	865

SOURCE: *Congressional Record Daily Digest*, Vol. 116, pt. 35, (January 19, 1970–January 2, 1971), p. 739. Again, I am following Lewis Froman's study of earlier Congresses here. In 1963 and 1964 the Senate spent a total of 375 days in session compared to the House's 334 days. But the Senate was in session 2,395 hours and the House only 1,250 hours. See *The Congressional Process*, p. 9.

The House, with its well-ordered division of labor based on the mastery of technical details by committee experts, is best able to play a policy role of drafting legislation in conjunction with subject matter experts in executive agencies and bureaus. Committees are the policy workshops of the House. And the career patterns based on seniority and subject matter expertise put highly placed House members on an equal footing with executive technicians in drafting legislation. When an executive spokesman goes before a House committee such as Ways and Means, a former Treasury official has observed, "he is confronted with an independent panel of specialized experts who usually possess vastly more experience than he."[7] The House role in policy-making, then, is primarily one of lawmaking. And it is carried on in committee by subject matter experts well versed in the technical details of complex legislation.

The Senate's policy role is different. As Nelson Polsby has written, " 'passing bills,' which is central to the life of the House, is peripheral to the Senate. In the Senate the three central activities are (1) cultivating national constituencies; (2) formulating questions for debate and discussion on a national scale (especially in opposition to the president); and (3) incubating new policy proposals that may at some future time find their way into legislation."[8] Policy incubation is the process of keeping a new proposal alive, of continuing to introduce a proposal until it gains enough supporters to assure passage or until the political climate has changed enough so that a proposal which at first seemed "radical" becomes accepted as a possibly rational solution to some problem. To accomplish these policy goals the Senate must emphasize representational values of extensive debate, of mutual deference to individual legislators rather than committees, and of an unstructured informal legislative chamber which gives as much time to discussing ideas as it does to passing legislation.

To become a law, policy proposals must pass both chambers and they must emerge from Congress in one form. If the Senate gives one nickel more than the House does in bills to finance a housing program, the housing policy does not come into being until the two chambers agree on an identical bill. After running the gamut of these two chambers with their different policy orientations, most important bills wind up in a joint House-Senate conference committee which must reconcile the differences between the chamber bills and produce a compromise bill that can win acceptance on both sides of Capitol Hill. Congressional rules and norms governing conference committees are thus a most important aspect of this chapter's discussion and will be discussed below.

A growing body of literature on conferences suggests that the Senate generally "wins" most conference battles with the House.[9] But these studies do not really mean that the upper chamber always has the upper hand in conflicts over policy. Rather, the Senate "victories" in conference are directly related to the different policy roles of the House and the Senate. I will discuss this more fully at the end of this chapter, but the immediate point is that Senate conferees follow a role of supporting broadly based proposals which have the backing of the whole chamber, while House conferees defend proposals advanced by committee experts which do not necessarily have widespread support among that chamber's membership. In other words, the policy role differences between the two chambers are carried on into the final interchamber bargaining sessions for producing bills.

So let us now turn to a quick review of some of the important rules governing legislative behavior in the House and in the Senate and some of the informal folkways practiced in one or both chambers, and then have a look at the "third house" which is charged with settling the differences between the other two.

HOUSE RULES

The conflicting demands of decision-making and representation which were discussed in Chapter 1 reappear when we consider

House and Senate rules. While Senate rules tend to support representational values, House rules are directed more toward decision-making. In both chambers there are many opportunities for delaying or defeating a measure. In the Senate, procedures favoring such dilatory tactics (the filibuster, for example) are defended in terms of their providing for personal and minority representation. However, House rules which have the same delaying effect more often stem from procedures intended to facilitate the decision-making function. The House Rules Committee, which on occasion has served to delay or defeat legislation, is designed to perform the important decision-making function of controlling the flow of legislation to the floor and the conditions under which it is considered. By performing this traffic cop function the Rules Committee plays a key role in moving bills along the legislative treadmill. But, because it is another point at which a decision must be made, the committee can be used to slow down or stop legislation. After receiving majorities in committees and on both floors, for example, the 1960 Federal Aid to Education Bill was stopped dead by a Rules Committee vote denying a rule sending the bill to conference.

In this brief section on House rules, we shall focus on rules and procedures affecting floor consideration of bills. Two aspects of House rules are most important here: calendars and the Rules Committee. When a bill has been cleared by committee and awaits floor action, it is placed on one of many lists of bills called calendars. The Union Calendar lists bills raising revenue, general appropriation bills, and other public bills which directly or indirectly appropriate money or property. The House Calendar lists public bills which do not raise revenue or directly or indirectly appropriate money or property. The Private Calendar lists bills which affect only those named in the bill. Bills which have appeared on the Union or House Calendars, but which are likely to be unopposed because of their minor character may be placed on the Consent Calendar.

Most bills which pass the House do so on the Private Calendar. Lewis Froman suggests that 300 to 500 private bills are reported by committee each session and placed on the Private Calendar. He found that over a third of the bills passed by the Eighty-eighth Congress were private bills.[10] There are two basic types of private bills: (1) those which pay an individual who has suffered personal injury, property damage, or nonpayment of benefits as a result of government action and (2) immigration bills which allow certain people to enter the country as exceptions to immigration quotas. Bills on the Private Calendar are called up on the first Tuesday of each month, and may also be called up on the third Tuesday of each month at the discretion of the Speaker. No other business may be considered on these days except by a two-thirds vote of the House. Each side is given five minutes to debate a bill. If two members object to consideration of a bill on the Private Calendar, it is returned to committee. Committees seldom report such a bill a second time. In essence, then, bills on the Private Calendar must be approved not just by a majority vote, but by unanimous consent. Because most members do not want to waste time on the floor during consideration of private bills, both parties designate official objectors to be present during the call of the Private Calendar. These objectors, acting for the party or for individual congressmen, are able to prevent passage of any unwanted private legislation.

A second calendar used to improve House efficiency in producing legislation is the Consent Calendar. Bills passed on the Consent Calendar are generally noncontroversial bills providing minor benefits to specific constituencies. Naming a VA hospital, making a minor administrative change in existing law, or disposing of public lands are all actions which might be handled in this way. The Consent Calendar is called on the first and third Mondays of each month. If one member objects to a bill called on the Consent Calendar, the bill is passed over to the next call of that calendar. Three members objecting at that time is enough to have the bill striken from the calendar. However, bills defeated on the Consent Calendar may be returned to the House or Union calendars and brought to the House floor in another way. Few members are on the House floor during consideration of Consent Calendar bills, and, as in the case of the Private Calendar, both parties have official objectors. In spite of these procedures allowing a small minority to reject a bill, the Consent Calendar accounts for the second largest number of bills passed by the House.

Both the Private Calendar and the Consent Calendar are devices for expediting the flow of legislation through the House. They permit minor and noncontroversial legislation to move through without taking up much of the members' time or clogging up channels needed for consideration of important legislation. Other procedures also exist for the purpose of bringing bills quickly to the floor. On the second and fourth Mondays of each month, bills reported by the District of Columbia Committee are privileged business. A procedure known as suspension of the rules is in order on the first and third Mondays of each month (the same days on which the Consent Calendar is called). Any member may move suspension of the rules on these days, but the Speaker's absolute discretion over recognition gives him tight control. Because a two-thirds vote is required to suspend the rules, this procedure is useful only for relatively noncontroversial bills. Bills which could not pass the unanimous consent requirements, but which are still relatively noncontroversial, may be passed under suspension of the rules.

Another way in which bills may be brought quickly to the floor is through a discharge petition. Any public bill that has been before a standing committee for 30 days or any committee-approved bill that has been before the Rules Committee for 7 days without receiving a rule may be brought to the floor through a discharge petition signed by a majority of the House (218 members). A petition gaining the necessary signatures is placed on the Discharge Calendar, which is privileged business on the second and fourth Mondays of each month. A majority vote on these days will bring the bill to the floor for immediate consideration. Since its adoption in 1910, however, the discharge petition has been successfully used only 24 times.[11]

In addition to District of Columbia day, suspension of the rules, and the discharge petition, House rules provide that certain committees are privileged to bring special types of legislation to the House floor at any time without having to gain a rule from the Rules Committee. The Appropriations Committee may report general appropriation bills; Ways and Means, revenue bills; Public Works, bills affecting rivers and harbors; Interior and Insular Affairs, bills affecting public lands and admission of new states; House Administration, bills on the seating of a member, enrolled bills, bills on printing and expenditures from the contingent fund of the House; and Veterans Affairs, general pension bills.[12] Even with this privileged status, however, committees may find it beneficial to go to the Rules Committee before going to the floor. Ways and Means, for example, will generally go the Rules Committee on revenue bills in order to get a closed rule barring floor amendments.

All of the procedures we have discussed so far provide for

ways to bring legislation to the floor without going to the Rules Committee. They are designed to help the House perform its legislative mill function by providing quick consideration of low conflict legislation. Most important legislation, however, does not follow this path. Instead, a rule from the Rules Committee is required to bring the bill from the House or Union calendar to the floor. The form of such a rule will vary, but the following example gives some indication of what a typical rule looks like:[13]

> *Resolved,* That upon the adoption of this resolution, it shall be in order to move that the House resolve itself into the Committee of the Whole House on the State of the Union for the consideration of the bill (H.R.——), entitled, etc. After general debate, which shall be confined to the bill, and continue not to exceed —— hours, to be equally divided and controlled by the chairman and the ranking minority member of the Committee on ———, the bill shall be read for amendment under the five-minute rule. At the conclusion of the consideration of the bill for amendment, the Committee shall rise and report the bill to the House with such amendments as may have been adopted and the previous question shall be considered as ordered on the bill, and amendments thereto to final passage without intervening motion except one motion to recommit with or without instructions.

There are four types of rules granted by the Rules Committee. Most legislation comes to the floor under an open rule which permits the House to amend the committee bill. An open rule helps organized minorities who are not satisfied with the committee bill, and wish to add or delete certain provisions.

A second type of rule granted by the committee is a closed rule which prohibits all, or certain types of, amendments. James Robinson's study of the Rules Committee showed that closed rules are seldom used; between 1939 and 1960, there were 1,128 open rules and 87 closed rules granted by the committee.[14] A closed rule is most often used in conjunction with bills coming from the Ways and Means Committee. Tax bills or social security legislation coming from this committee are both highly vulnerable to special interest demands and represent a delicate balance worked out by experts on Ways and Means. Floor amendments, it is argued, would upset that balance. As one member of the committee said: "It'd be suicide if you ever tried to write a tax or social security bill on the floor. We sit in there surrounded by experts to keep us from going off on a tangent so you can imagine what would happen on the floor.[15]

The third type of rule granted by the committee is one waiving points of order against a particular bill. This rule is used most often by the Appropriations Committee when it has a bill which contains legislative provisions as well as appropriations. House rules permit any member to raise a point of order against such legislative provisions in general appropriations bills. A single objection is enough to have the measure striken from the bill. In order to avoid this the Appropriations Committee asks for a rule waiving points of order against the bill. Because the inclusion of such provisions in an appropriations bill can produce serious conflict with the legislative committees, this procedure of waiving points of order for appropriations bills is used sparingly. During the period, 1939–1954, the Appropriations Committee received an average of two waiver rules per year.[16]

The fourth type of rule granted by the Rules Committee is one which sends a bill to conference when it has passed the House and Senate in different form. Prior to 1965, any member could object to sending a bill to conference, thus requiring that the Rules Committee grant a rule for sending the bill to conference. A rules change in that year provided that a majority of the House be able to send a House-passed bill with Senate amendments to a conference with the Senate, thus avoiding the Rules Committee.

Approximately 150 bills come to the Rules Committee each Congress. The committee denies a hearing on about twenty of these bills.[17] Such denials may represent a conflict between the committee or its chairman and party leaders. Chairman Smith's attempt to deny hearings in 1964 to both the civil rights bill and the poverty program stemmed from such a conflict. The committee's power to delay by denying a hearing can also be a useful tool for House leaders opposed to a particular bill or in favor of a bill which would not pass the House if brought to the floor at that time. Whip polls in 1964 showed that the administration's Area Redevelopment Bill would fail if brought to the floor. The Rules Committee was able to aid party leaders by denying a hearing on the bill.

In addition to the power to delay by denying hearings, the committee can exercise the threat of denying a rule after holding hearings on a bill. Although this occurs only about twelve times in each Congress, the threat of denial is useful to the Rules Committee when it seeks changes in the bill as reported by the substantive committee. In exchange for granting a rule, the committee may demand that certain amendments be accepted on the floor.

There are dramatic instances when the fifteen member Rules Committee has been able to defeat the intentions of a majority of the House. This type of conflict was quite visible during the 1950s. In 1961, the Democratic leadership won a close vote expanding the size of the committee and giving the leadership a one-vote margin. Overall, however, the most accurate description of the Rules Committee would be that it generally acts in accordance with both party and committee leadership. Because of its control over floor activity, the committee has a great deal of power in the House. This power is most often exercised in conjunction with the goals of the majority leadership and the substantive committees.

The House calendars and the Rules Committee are designed to increase the efficiency of House decision-making. By reducing the amount of floor time spent on minor legislation, these devices seek to increase the rationality of legislating. Any organization of this size must provide institutionalized procedures for decision-making. Most of the House rules seek to achieve this rationality by providing automatic procedures for handling legislation. Instead of each congressman being asked to make a political judgement on every bill, the structure of House rules provides a hierarchy of experts who make "rational" decisions after careful consideration of all factors. Specialization is reinforced by House rules which greatly limit the participation of "unqualified" members in legislative decisions. This type of organization makes sense, given the immense work load of Congress. But again we become aware of how an objective, rational solution to problems of decision-making can have implications which are not neutral in their effect.[18]

The Legislative Reorganization Act of 1970 contained a provision which has altered the strength of the House leadership over floor action. Upon request of one-fifth of a quorum (twenty members in the Committee of the Whole), the clerks can be directed to record the names and positions of members on a teller vote.

Previously, most bills were passed in the Committee of the Whole by a teller vote which did not show how individual members voted. As a result, generally less than one-fourth of the members would come to the floor for these votes, and floor activity could easily be dominated by the committee reporting the bill. This procedure tended to maximize the influence of committees and of the conservative coalition whose members were more likely to show up for such votes.[19] With recorded teller votes, however, more members take part in Committee of the Whole proceedings. Such participation reduces the influence of committees on these floor proceedings.

The 1972 report by Ralph Nader's Congress Project dramatically shows the impact of the teller vote change on House voting patterns. The authors observe:

> Before the advent of recorded "teller" voting in 1970 (previously votes on amendments which make up the bulk of our laws, had never been recorded), SST funding was easily approved, with only 118 members voting. But the very first year that members had to go on public record with the SST vote, it was defeated 217 to 203.
>
> *The Congressional Quarterly* found that attendance in 1971 on key issues doubled because of its rules change. "[Teller voting] means that the primary factor in your voting," said Congressman Charles Whalen, "is not whether you'll please Boggs or Albert or Gerry Ford; you've got to think about what your constituency wants."[20]

The teller vote rule change obviously moves in the direction of increasing House members' representational functions. But this one change alone does not alter the basic structure of the House. For House calendars and the Rules Committee still determine which matters will come to the floor for a vote, when they will come, and the conditions under which they will be considered by the whole chamber. As we saw in the antiwar amendment cases discussed at the start of this chapter, leadership control over the conditions of floor debate and floor voting is still formidable. And House leaders tend to accept the notion that the lower chamber is the place for making laws and that the luxury of extensively debating issues can only be afforded in the smaller Senate.

SENATE RULES

Bills are brought to the Senate floor in a simpler, more direct way than in the House. The Senate has no Private Calendar, Consent Calendar, District of Columbia Calendar, Discharge Calendar, or Rules Committee. Instead, there are only two Senate calendars: the Calendar of Business which lists all legislation and an Executive Calendar for nominations and treaties. When a bill has been reported by committee it goes on the appropriate calendar to await action by the majority party leadership. When the Democrats control the Senate, floor scheduling is handled by the Democrat Policy Committee, a nine member committee chaired by the majority leader. In practice, however, the scheduling is done by the majority leader after consultation with the minority leadership and other interested individual senators. When a bill is stalled between the committee report and floor action, it is not the result of a Rules Committee impeding action, but rather of the majority leadership's respect for minority wishes or the schedule of an individual senator. Another difference between the two chambers is that the Senate will have as many as five bills on the floor at the same time, while the House always limits itself to consideration of only one bill at a time.

Once a bill comes to the Senate floor, the differences between the two chambers become even more apparent. Two important rules governing Senate floor proceedings help to explain most of these differences. These are procedures relating to the germaneness of debate and to concluding debate.

Although the Senate adopted a germaneness rule in 1964, it is more often violated than followed. Because the Senate floor is viewed as an excellent forum for speeches, members want to be able to come to the floor and deliver a prepared speech at any time. If all such speeches had to be related to the topic under consideration, senators would have great difficulty meeting other commitments and still being on the floor when that particular topic came up. Because all senators know that they will be in this position sometime, they support any member's right to speak on any subject at any time by not objecting to unanimous consent to waive the germaneness rule. Although this practice often makes Senate floor proceedings seem chaotic compared to the

House, it does permit consideration of many measures at once and allows the Senate to function as the chamber of comprehensive debate.

In addition to normal violation of the germaneness of debate rule, Senate floor activity is kept open and unstructured by the fact that there is no rule prohibiting nongermane amendments to nonappropriation bills. A member can thus completely avoid the germaneness of debate rule by submitting a nongermane amendment to the bill under consideration and then speaking on that amendment. By offering nongermane amendments on the floor, senators are able to avoid hostile committees and immediately bring a matter to debate. Examples of this tactic include the 1960 Civil Rights Bill which was offered as an amendment to a minor bill to aid a Missouri school district and Senator Dirksen's two attempts to block Supreme Court rulings on state legislative reapportionment by offering amendments to the foreign aid authorization act in 1964 and to a resolution proclaiming National American Legion Baseball Week in 1965.

There are three ways to conclude debate in the Senate: unanimous consent, cloture, or everyone simply stops talking. Although unanimous consent is the most common means for bringing a matter to a vote, we are more interested here in the cloture rule because of the profound impact which it has on all Senate behavior. Rule 22 specifies that debate may be ended in the following manner: sixteen senators sign a cloture petition; on the second calendar day after the petition is filed the Senate votes on the motion to end debate; if two-thirds of those present and voting support the cloture motion then each senator may speak for one hour on the bill under consideration, no additional amendments may be offered, and only germane amendments may be voted on.

A cloture vote is regarded as a last resort measure by senators. It will occur only when there is intense conflict and after attempts to reach some agreement have failed. Even if supporters have a solid majority for their bill, they will often have great difficulty assembling the two-thirds needed to end debate. Many senators might favor the measure yet not support a cloture move because they consider unlimited debate to be an integral part of the Senate. In addition to these defections from the original majority, some members will be unwilling to go along with the compromises needed to build a two-thirds majority coalition. For these reasons, cloture votes are generally unsuccessful.

When the Senate twice defeated a cloture motion to end debate on electoral reform in September of 1970, it marked the thirty-ninth time that a cloture motion had been defeated on the floor since the rule was adopted in 1917. Only eight motions successfully passed the Senate during this period. The importance of rules, however, cannot be measured simply by looking at the times they are invoked. For by structuring Senate bargaining and by being available as a threat, the filibuster and cloture rule have a great impact even when they are not employed. Howard Shuman describes how the filibuster was important in passage of the 1957 Civil Rights Act by its not being used:

> Throughout the debate, and preceding the votes on Section III and the jury trial amendment, the threat of a filibuster was used to gain support for both these amendments. Senator Russell has since frankly admitted what many on the inside felt sure of at the time, namely, that the South would not filibuster and that the threat of doing so was more effective than the reality would have been.[21]

By guaranteeing the difficulty of limiting debate, Rule 22 affects every aspect of decision-making in the Senate. Lewis Froman has outlined five ways that the existence of this rule structures behavior:[22]

1. A relatively large minority (one-third plus one of those present and voting) opposed to a measure is able to prevent a majority from acting. In 1968, for instance, there were four cloture votes on the Open Housing Bill. On the first three votes a minority (37, 36, and 35 senators respectively) was able to prevent a majority (55, 56, and 59) from ending debate on the bill.

2. The threat of a filibuster can be used to gain concessions from the proponents of a bill. Although the filibuster was not used in passing the Civil Rights Act of 1957, opponents of the bill were able to exact major concessions by threatening a filibuster. The leader of the southern coalition termed it "the sweetest victory of my 25 years as a Senator from the State of Georgia."[23]

3. The problem of assembling a winning coalition is greatly increased by the possibility that a two-thirds majority will be

needed on the floor. As mentioned before, many members who support the original measure will oppose invoking cloture on procedural grounds. Proponents may also face defections by members unwilling to accept the compromises needed to expand the coalition.

4. The intensity of members' opinions on a measure becomes an important factor in determining the outcome. An intense minority may prevail over a relatively apathetic majority by threatening delay on all business until a particular matter is resolved.

5. Bargaining in the Senate is greatly facilitated by the fact that any group of senators may legitimately use the filibuster. Because all members would prefer to avoid the conflict and ordeal of a filibuster, senators are motivated to make the compromises needed to placate strong minority opposition. Bargaining in the Senate takes place among a shifting series of coalitions. This means that members of a majority coalition are likely to be part of a minority on another issue. Any attempt to limit minority action on this one measure could be used when members of the present majority are part of a minority on another bill. All parties to a conflict thus have reason to maintain the minority weapon of Rule 22 and to bargain within the framework it provides.

In concluding this section on Senate rules, it is perhaps worth mentioning again the basic difference between House and Senate rules. House rules are designed to allow a majority to work its will; they seek to facilitate decision-making. Rule 22 of the Senate, on the other hand, illustrates that chamber's emphasis on representation to the extent that a minority can prevent a decision being made.

It should also be clear that the net effect of the rules in both chambers is not neutral. The conservative implications of the House committee hierarchy has already been noted. The Senate filibuster similarly favors those who wish to maintain the status quo. This is so both in the obvious cases of southern opposition to civil rights bills, and in instances where northern liberals have filibustered to maintain the status quo established in Supreme Court reapportionment cases.

Those who seek to change the status quo must generally first seek to change the rules which work against them. This is hard to do for two reasons. First, a majority that could change the rules can generally exercise its will within the existing framework anyway. As the authors of a book on congressional reform put it:

> When majorities are able to work their will in Congress, they see little need for procedural change. When majorities are slender or unstable, the need for attaining high priority legislative goals diverts attention from reform efforts. Thus reform-minded Congressmen often find themselves in the dilemma of the old man with the leaky roof: when the sun was shining, there was no need for repair; when it was raining, it was too difficult to repair.[24]

A second reason for the difficulty of changing rules is found in the fact that one rule or procedure may have multiple purposes. A quorum call, for instance, can be both an effective tool for party leaders seeking to make sure the necessary supporters are present and a useful instrument of delay for those opposing the measure. When a rule has different purposes for different groups of members, it is difficult to reach consensus as to the implications of changing that rule.[25] As a result, it is hard to put together a majority coalition supporting the rule change.

HOUSE AND SENATE FOLKWAYS

On September 8, 1970, the Senate began debate on an amendment to replace the electoral college with direct popular election of the president. Consideration of the measure was done in the common "two-shift" schedule of the Senate; the electoral reform measure would be debated for a portion of the day, the Senate would move to other matters by unanimous consent, and the reform measure picked up again on the next day. A coalition of southern and small state senators opposed to the measure were successful in blocking a vote on the amendment by insisting that there had not been enough debate. A cloture vote to end this tacit filibuster failed by six votes on September 17, and the two-shift consideration continued. One week later, Senator Birch Bayh, floor manager for the bill, undertook a strategy designed to force a Senate decision. By objecting to unanimous consent requests that the Senate move to other business and by objecting to allowing committees to meet while the Senate was in session, Bayh was able to bring Senate business to a halt. From September

24 to 29, the senator from Indiana was able to force the Senate to debate his amendment exclusively. After a second cloture vote failed on September 29, Bayh admitted defeat by agreeing to unanimous consent that the amendment be put aside and the Senate move to other business.[26]

Individual actions of this kind are not confined to the Senate. After the House passed the Civil Rights Act of 1964, for instance, Representative John Bell Williams of Mississippi showed his disfavor by tieing up the House for an hour by similar objections to unanimous consent motions. The rules of both chambers make it possible for a single member to greatly hamstring his colleagues. Such measures are seldom used, however, and the reasons for this reflect the influence of unwritten norms, or "folkways," on the behavior of congressmen.

Any organization must develop norms of behavior which contribute to its achieving organizational goals. Such norms provide the stability and predictability necessary for the institution's maintenance and goal achievement. Donald Matthews's study of the postwar Senate is the primary source of any discussion about legislative folkways.[27] Other studies of the House of Representatives and state legislatures have uncovered similar patterns of expected behavior in these bodies.[28]

Although the relative importance of these folkways varies from chamber to chamber, the House and Senate will be discussed together here since these norms are found in both. Legislative norms may be classified in terms of the primary functions they perform; some contribute to that chamber's goal achievement in terms of decision-making or representation; others contribute to maintaining the existing system by regulating the level of conflict. Folkways which help Congress to perform its decision-making function are those of specialization, apprenticeship, and legislative work. The norm of reciprocity aids decision-making in the House, but seems to be more geared to achieving representational goals in the Senate. Folkways helping to maintain the existing system by controlling conflict are those of courtesy and institutional patriotism.

Specialization

Norms which contribute to the function of decision-making are more important in the House than in the Senate. Just as the larger chamber must have more thorough rules governing the handling of legislation, so it also must have informal norms supporting a more structured decision-making process. By encouraging congressmen to specialize in one or two subjects, House norms both prevent the chaos which would result from every member attempting to speak on each subject, and insure that there will be a number of experts on each subject coming before the House. The results of specialization were noted by one congressman in his observing: "There is always someone around here who's an expert on something you need to know. I dare say there is not one subject you could think of that doesn't have at least one member of the House particularly qualified to give you advice about it."[29] Matthews's study of the other chamber found general agreement that: "The really effective senators are those who speak only on the subjects they have been dealing with at close quarters, not those who are on their feet on almost every subject all the time."[30]

Even though we find a norm of specialization in both houses, specialization means different things in the House than it does in the Senate. In the House, specialization is tied to the importance of committee work, the development of subject matter expertise, and a division of labor necessary for accomplishing that chamber's lawmaking function. In the Senate, on the other hand, specialization is much less committee-oriented and is conceived mainly as expertise to enhance the senator's standing with a national constituency associated with that subject.[31] Senators' specialization helps that chamber to play a policy incubation role by insuring that there will be at least one senator to keep debate alive on an issue which does not yet command the majorities needed to become law. In short, the specialization norm in the House helps that chamber to fulfill its lawmaking responsibilities, while the specialization norm in the Senate helps that chamber to provide for the representation of many diverse interests throughout the country.

Apprenticeship-Seniority

The apprenticeship norm aids decision-making by weighting the impact on decisions in favor of those members who have been in Congress or on the committee the longest. It is another part of the process, described earlier by Charles Reich, of maximizing the influence of those "best qualified" to make each type of decision. Freshmen are limited in their participation by norms which suggest that the prudent first-termer is one who talks little, tends to his committee work, cooperates with his leaders, and spends his time learning how to be a good congressman. "Like children," one said, "we should be seen and not heard."[32]

At the other end of the hierarchy, apprenticeship norms are reflected in a seniority system which grants influence over policy chiefly on the basis of length of service. Defenders of the apprenticeship-seniority system suggest that Congress is no different from other organizations in this regard. As a former Speaker noted:

> No sane man would for one moment think of making a graduate from West Point a full general, or one from Annapolis an admiral, or one from any university or college chief of a great newspaper, magazine or business house. A priest or preacher who has just taken orders is not immediately made a bishop, archbishop or cardinal. In every walk of life, "men must tarry at Jericho till their beards are grown."[33]

Nelson Polsby, a leading scholar of Congress, has noted that "the great advantage of the seniority system is that it decentralizes power in the House of Representatives by creating multiple centers of policy influence and increasing the number of good Congressional jobs. This adds to the incentives of the Congressional career."[34] Defense of the seniority system generally follows this pattern; it focuses mainly on the House goal of lawmaking and on individual "House career" patterns to achieve that goal.

Among those who attack the seniority system are, not surprisingly, younger congressmen who seek to play a representative role and want to influence policy over a wide number of issues, rather than following a safe "House career" pattern. Or, they are journalists, citizen groups, or academicians who emphasize the unrepresentativeness of the seniority system because of its benefits to southern, rural, or one-party districts. Don Riegle of Michigan is an example of the first. In his book, *O Congress,* Riegle bemoans the fact that his five years as a congressman give him little influence over policy, and he places much of the blame on the situation produced by a congressional seniority system in which;

> A man can come to Congress when he's thirty-five, serve here twenty years and emerge, at age fifty-five, as the ablest man on his committee. But because he has to wait for all the members ahead of him to retire or die, he may have to wait another twenty years—until he's seventy-five—before he becomes a chairman. The practical and psychological implications of this are obvious.[35]

Ralph Nader's Congress Project represents the second group of critics of the seniority system. In *Who Runs Congress?*, they point out that the average committee chairmen a hundred years ago was in his forties, in 1910, he was fifty, and by 1972, he was sixty-seven; that 87 percent of the committee chairmen from 1950 to 1970 came from one-party districts; that in 1970, thirteen of twenty-one House committee chairmen came from rural districts; and that southerners held more than one-half of the committee chairmanships from 1921 to 1966.[36]

Although apprenticeship norms in the House continue to support a system of decision-making by experienced committee experts, the impact of a strict seniority system has been diminished. Studies of committee assignments, the distribution of power within committees, conference committees, and party leadership selection have suggested that the seniority system is a flexible one which permits consideration of factors other than just tenure.[37] Even in that one area where the seniority rule is most stringent, the selection of committee chairmen, the trend seems to be toward a more flexible system.

In 1971 both parties in the House adopted reforms in the seniority system for determining committee positions. The Democrats agreed that;

1. The Democratic Committee on Committees would recommend to the caucus nominees for the chairmanship and membership of each committee, and such recommendations need not necessarily follow seniority.
2. The Committee on Committees would make recommendations to the caucus, one committee at a time; upon the demand of 10 or more members, nominations could be debated and voted on.
3. If a nomination is rejected, the Committee on Committees would submit another nomination.

4. No member could be chairman of more than one legislative subcommittee.

Republicans in the Ninety-second Congress also adopted seniority reforms affecting the selection of ranking members. These reforms included the following guidelines:

1. The nomination for ranking Republican member of each committee would be put to an automatic vote of the entire Republican membership in the House.
2. The Republican membership would vote in secret on these nominations.
3. The member nominated need not be the member with the longest consecutive service on that committee.
4. If the nomination was rejected, the Republican Committee on Committees would submit another nomination.

These changes in the seniority system for selecting committee chairmen in the House serve to institutionalize the flexibility in the seniority norm which earlier studies had discovered. But they do not eliminate seniority as a norm which helps to determine who will have the most influence over certain policy areas. And again, the different structures of the two chambers lead to a different impact of the same norm in the House and the Senate.

Because it is a norm essential to lawmaking, to the maintenance of a hierarchical division of power, and to providing incentives for long-term careers, seniority has a more immediate effect on the individual representative than it does on the individual senator. The representational function of the Senate, its structure of overlapping committee membership, and its more diversified career patterns (based on higher visibility, the opportunity to cultivate national policy constituencies, and the possibility of using a Senate career as a launching pad for national office candidacies), all produce a higher tolerance for young "upstarts" in that chamber and a more flexible application of the seniority norm in term of controlling the behavior of members.

Legislative Work

A third norm crucial to decision-making is that of legislative work. Because most of the congressman's work is "highly detailed, dull, and politically unrewarding," it is important to the functioning of both chambers that the system reward those who put in the long hours needed to fashion sensible legislation.[39] Matthews's study of the Senate showed the importance of this norm to that body;

> The words used to describe those senators who seem to slight their legislative duties are harsh—"grandstanders," "demagogues," "headline hunters," "publicity seekers," "messiahs." They are said to do nothing but "play to the galleries," and not to be "team players." It is even occasionally hinted that they are mentally or emotionally deranged.[40]

In the House, the norm of legislative work is most clearly demonstrated in the case of such high prestige committees as Ways and Means or Appropriations. Richard Fenno's study of the latter led him to conclude; "By adopting the style of hard work, the Committee discourages highly individualized forms of legislative behavior, which could be disruptive within the Committee. It rewards its members with power, but it is power based rather on work inside the Committee than on the political glamour of activities carried on in the limelight of the mass media."[41]

This norm helps to account for the fact that some of the most influential members of the House are virtually unknown outside of it. Most of the important committee work is done backstage. And the member who increases his influence by diligence in committee work is unlikely to have much time left over to develop his media image. Indeed, as one legislator commented, "the very ingredients which make you a powerful House leader are the ones which keep you from being a public leader."[42]

Reciprocity

A reciprocity norm operates in both chambers, but with quite different effects. In the House, reciprocity is manifested in committees' respecting each others' specialities. As such, the norm functions to support decision-making in the House. An example of this type of reciprocity is that obtaining between a substantive committee and its counterpart appropriations subcommittee. According to Fenno, "there normally exists a mutual recognition that the Appropriations Committee should not define programs, i.e., legislate, in an appropriation bill and that the authorizing committee must accept the dollar figure set by the appropriating committee."[43]

Reciprocity in the Senate focuses more on the interaction between individuals than committees. Because senators serve on many committees, the membership of any one of them will represent a broad spectrum of other Senate committees. Unlike the House, where reciprocity operates through a specialized committee structure, Senate reciprocity works through a "relatively undifferentiated, interlocking decision-making structure."[44] The result is that senators will go out of their way to insure that every member's views are given a hearing, that there is "the maximum participation of a maximum number of its members" on every decision.[45] Senate reciprocity, rather than contributing to a smooth decision-making process, primarily serves the goal of representation.

Courtesy and Institutional Patriotism

Decision-making requires some conflict. The structure of Congress and such norms as specialization and legislative work provide a focus for conflict as part of the decision-making process. Because of the wide dispersion of power in both chambers, there is a great potential for conflict among individuals, committees, and between leaders and followers. In order to maintain itself as an institution capable of achieving decisional goals, Congress must keep this conflict within manageable bounds. Two folkways are most important here: courtesy and institutional patriotism.

The norm of courtesy prescribes that even the most intense conflict over issues should not lead to personal conflict. One way of accomplishing this is to maintain an impersonality in debate; to address an opponent as "the Senator from Maine," rather than "Mr. Muskie" or "Ed." At times this formality shades into the comic:

> Mr. JOHNSON of Texas. The Senator from Texas does not have any objection and the Senator from Texas wishes the Senator from California to know that the Senator from Texas knew the Senator from California did not criticize him. . . .[46]

"One's overwhelming first impression as a Member of Congress," observed the late Clem Miller of California, "is the aura of friendliness that surrounds the life of a congressman. No wonder that 'few die and none resign.' Almost everyone is unfailingly polite and courteous. Window washers, clerks, senators—it cuts all ways. We live in a cocoon of good feelings."[47] Another congressman captures this mood of good feeling which pervades the House in describing the scene when that chamber reconvened for its second session in January of 1972:

> The chamber buzzed with loud hellos, story-swapping and laughter and I was reminded once again how physical a place this is. Congressmen don't just speak to one another. They punch each other on the arm, slap each other on the knee, grab at each other's jackets and occasionally give each other a goose.[48]

This air is maintained by a courtesy norm which not only proscribes any sort of personal attack, but actively supports members' going out of their way to keep matters on a friendly plane:

> Mr. Chairman, at the appropriate time, I intend very humbly and very prayerfully to offer an amendment. I hope the gentleman from Texas, my distinguished intellectual leader and my athletic leader, will help me a little bit with it, and if he would I would bestow upon him the highest accolade of all and call him my spiritual leader, if he will help me to correct an injustice that I know he does not want to be meted out upon the gentlemen from Florida.[49]

Senator Edward Brooke of Massachusetts, after sitting through a long floor discussion shot through with such verbal manifestations of the courtesy norm, once suggested that if the word "distinguished" could be taken out of floor speeches legislators would save 10 percent of their time. Senate majority leader Mike Mansfield's response to the Brooke suggestion: "I appreciate the remarks of the distinguished senator from Massachusetts for his views."[50]

Although the results of this courtesy norm often strike the outside observer as a bit silly, the norm does greatly affect both the style and content of congressional debate. Just as the conversational style of the British House of Commons discourages demagogic speeches, so too does the courtesy folkway in Congress provide a limit to conflict. It is difficult to accuse a colleague of being either a Marxist or a Fascist after referring to him as "the distinguished senator from New York." Courtesy demands that congressmen avoid any sort of personal charges even if the matter is common knowledge. Thus, even though many senators considered the 1970 debate on providing $290 million for developing a supersonic transport airplane to be a question of helping out the influential Senators Jackson and Magnuson of Washington (home of Boeing Aircraft), they shuddered when Senator Proxmire of Wisconsin brought it into the open by remarking;

> There are just two very good reasons for the Federal financing of an SST. One is the senior senator from Washington and the other is the junior senator from Washington.[51]

Institutional patriotism is a second norm which helps to limit the level of conflict in Congress. It is most obvious in the Senate because of the higher status of that body and because House members are more likely to aspire to the Senate or to a governorship back home. Few things can so quickly unite the Senate as an attack on its integrity. A House chairman tried to force a settlement on the 1964 Appropriations Bill, then in conference, by noting; "Nobody on earth can find out names of everyone who is on a Senator's payroll. I personally know of a Senator who keeps two call girls on his office payroll. I know because I've been at parties where they've been."[52] The Senate reacted to this attack by defeating the conference report, two to eighty-eight. Similarly, when Senator Joseph McCarthy was censured in 1954 after browbeating witnesses and making unsubstantiated accusations of persons being Communists and traitors, the primary charge in the Senate's censure resolution was that McCarthy "acted contrary to Senatorial ethics and tended to bring the Senate into dishonor and disrepute."[53] The norm of institutional patriotism helps to reduce conflict within Congress by providing a shared sense of values which even the most hostile opponents can agree on. When it comes into play in House-Senate conflicts, it also provides a basis for unity in each chamber. Proponents of a measure can sometimes increase the size of their coalition by making it a matter of the House versus the Senate, or Congress versus the president.

All of the legislative folkways we have discussed serve more than just one function. The seniority system which is part of the apprenticeship norm, for instance, is defended not only in the decision-making terms already discussed, but also for contributing to conflict reduction. By making the selection of committee chairmen a relatively automatic process, this system allows Congress to avoid the potentially high conflict area of chairmen selection. The norm of reciprocity plays a similarly important role in maintaining a low conflict situation. The folkways of Congress are generally evaluated as being functional for the legislative system; that is to say, they help Congress to achieve its decision-making and representational goals and they help to maintain the existing legislative system. In an institution where the individual has power to block actions by the group, as in the case of Senator Bayh which opened this section, informal norms which keep individuals from exercising that power are crucial. Without such norms to constrain individualistic behavior, it is unlikely that Congress could achieve its decision-making tasks.

But what is functional for the legislative system is not necessarily functional for the larger society. Some critics argue that the high premium which congressmen place on cooperation and bargaining leads to their avoiding conflict by postponing or passing difficult or sensitive decisions on to others.[54] It is also suggested that these folkways help to maintain a conservative establishment or inner club which is out of touch with the needs of society in the 1970s.[55]

While there are all sorts of difficulties determining who is "in" or "out" of such an inner club, studies by both Donald Matthews and Wayne Swanson suggest that supporters of the status quo are able to minimize the influence of senators who do not conform to the established rules of the game.[56] Such nonconformists are usually the more liberal members of the House or Senate. It is not necessary to adopt a conspiratorial view to see that one effect of both the formal rules and the informal norms of Congress is to strengthen the hand of those who wish to maintain the status quo. By the time a congressman is in a position to exert major influence over important issues, he will have acquired a heavy stake in the existing system. Both in terms of legislation in his areas of expertise and in the existing distribution of influence within the chamber, the status quo is a means of evaluating him as a congressman.

CONFERENCE COMMITTEES

Most books about Congress discuss conference committees in the "committees" section of the book. That makes some sense because the members of these ad hoc committees responsible for settling House-Senate differences are drawn from the standing committees of the two chambers. But such treatment often overlooks some of the points raised earlier in this book: that the House and Senate play different roles in the policy process, that committees in the House have a more direct impact on representatives' policy influence and general legislative action, and that conference committee members are called upon to play different roles in settling interchamber disputes than they are in dealing with legislation in their respective standing committee bailiwicks. These differences are not completely a product of chamber rules governing conference committees, for the formal procedures of conference are generally similar in both the House and the Senate.

Conference Rules

When one chamber produces a bill which differs from a similar measure already passed by the other chamber, two things can happen: either the chamber which first passed the legislation concurs in the changes made in the second house and the bill goes to the White House for signing into law; or, both houses agree to set up a joint conference committee to compromise the differences and to produce one bill which both chambers can approve. About 15 percent of the laws passed by Congress go through the conference committee route, but this 15 percent often includes the major legislation handled in that session.[57] Because of the importance of this "third house" of Congress, about thirty pages of the House and Senate *Rules and Manuals* deal with the questions of who selects the conference delegates, who sits on conference, how they go about their business of drafting a compromise bill, and procedures for voting on the finished product of conference negotiations.

Conference rules in both chambers say that the presiding officer (i.e., the Speaker of the House and the president pro tem of the Senate) is given the power to appoint conferees. The actual appointment power, though, belongs to the chairmen of the

House and Senate committees which handled the legislation in their chamber. The committee leaders make up a list of conferees and give it to the presiding officers; the latter officers then "appoint" those people listed.

The Legislative Reorganization Act of 1946 provides that members of conference committees must have supported the legislation under consideration when it passed their respective chambers. This is not always the case, and has been the object of some concern. "If one wanted to stretch the point a little," remarks a student of Congress, "one might whimsically claim that any similarity between the views of the House or the Senate and those of the conferees is purely coincidental."[58] The villain in such cases is that old foil of reformers, the seniority system. When committee chairmen appoint conferees they normally select the most senior members from the committee or subcommittee responsible for that chamber's legislation. Because senior members are sometimes out of step with the party majorities in their chamber, following seniority in appointing conferees could mean that a majority of the conference delegation sent to uphold their chamber's version of the bill actually opposed that version in their own house.

The important question is how often this happens. Former Senator Joseph Clark thought it happened often enough to justify a strict interpretation of the 1946 provision, and cited a 1959 conference on an unemployment compensation bill where four of the five Senate conferees had opposed the Senate's adoption of the liberalizing McCarthy amendment to the bill. The stated position of the Senate was overturned in twenty minutes of conference deliberation.[59] A 1967 conference on the congressional redistricting bill also produced a weird situation where the leader of the Senate delegation, Sam Ervin, was arguing for the House version of the bill, while the leader of the House delegation, Emanuel Celler, supported the Senate version. To no one's surprise, the bill died in conference.

In spite of these isolated instances, recent research suggests that following seniority in appointing conferees does not often lead to conference delegations made up of members who opposed the bill in their chamber. A survey by the *Congressional Quarterly* in 1959 found only four instances where conference delegations included members who had opposed major provisions of the bill passed by their chamber.[60] In an earlier book on conference committees, I had a look at all conference delegations in five Congresses covering a twenty-year period, and found that committee chairmen, by following subcommittee rather than committee seniority or by skipping over some senior committee members in appointing conferees, were able to increase the number of bill supporters on the conference delegation. The mean percent of bill supporters on these delegations if strict committe seniority had been followed was 70 percent, while the actual mean percent brought about by the chairmen's screening of conferees was 82 percent.[61]

We have skipped lightly over many of the nuances involved in the procedures which determine who will sit on conference committees and the impact of the seniority norm on the makeup of these delegations. But it does seem clear, from the evidence we have today, that the membership of conference delegations is best characterized as being a collection of senior committee and subcommittee people who generally support their chamber's position in the interchamber dispute.

One of the most important rules governing conference behavior is that the deliberations are secret: no minutes or written records of conference proceedings are kept; the conference "reports," which are, in effect, the compromise bill, are simply the legislation drafted by the conference committee. House conferees also submit a statement about the effects of the compromise on the House-passed bill. But the actual conference deliberations: the votes of members, the arguments advanced for striking or retaining certain measures, the evidence supporting certain changes, all these are not made part of the public record. The secrecy of conference deliberations is often attacked by those seeking to open up legislative proceedings in order to maximize representational values. When Albert Gore of Tennessee left the Senate in 1970, he berated conference committees for being "secret meetings often not even announced until the last minute [where] a few men can sit down and undo in one hour the most painstaking work of months of effort by several standing committees and the full membership of both houses."[62]

The 1970 Reorganization Act included measures designed to open up the deliberations of standing committees: it required that committees make public all roll call votes taken in committee and that committee sessions be open to the public. These provisions are subject to approval by the committee chairmen and majority members, but even so, 64 percent of standing committee proceedings in 1971 were subject to public scrutiny.[63] None of the conference committee proceedings were.

So, what happens to conference reports when they come to the floor of their respective chambers? Most pass. In the Ninetieth Congress (1967–1968), for instance, 640 laws were enacted by Congress, 129 of these were the product of successful conferences, and only 6 unsuccessful conferences were held.[64] Part of the explanation for the success of conference bills in Congress lies in the timing of when these reports are brought to the floor, and part is related to the formal rules governing floor voting on conference bills.

About half of all conference reports are voted on during the last two months of each session. Debate, while formally unlimited, is often subject to a unanimous consent measure which sets a time limitation on floor debate. But the rule which has the most dramatic effect on floor consideration of conference bills is that which specifies that each chamber must accept or reject the compromise bill *in toto*. Members cannot support certain parts of a conference bill while objecting to other parts. The choice presented to congressmen is simple: they must vote yea or nay on the whole compromise bill. No amendments from the floor are accepted, and while some members might feel that their representatives could have done a better job of defending that chamber's version of the bill, they are faced basically with a choice of accepting the conference bill or having no bill at all that session. The only alternative open to congressmen who are not happy with the compromise worked out in conference is to pass a resolution instructing their chamber's delegation to retain or drop certain provisions or to raise a point of order against new material inserted in the conference bill.

Studies of conferences by Richard Fenno, David Paletz, and myself indicate that both chambers are reluctant to instruct their conference delegations.[65] This is so both because such instructions run counter to the basic norm of compromise which dominates conference activity and because motions to instruct a chamber delegation are regarded as a sign of little confidence in the bargaining ability of one's conference representatives. Section

135 of the Legislative Reorganization Act of 1946 provides that conference committees may not insert in the compromise bill new material which was not included in the bills passed by the two chambers. But this rule is often violated by conference committees' writing substitute bills which are quite different from either chamber bill. When this happens members may raise a point of order when the conference report is brought to the chamber floor. Like motions to instruct, though, points of order seldom are made. "The subjects are complex, debate time is limited, and most legislators are willing to believe their representatives on the conference committee have done as well as could be expected."[66]

We may summarize the rules governing conference committees by noting that they are made up of senior committee or subcommittee members chosen by the respective chairmen in each house; that conferees generally are supporters of the legislation as passed by their chamber; that conference meetings are secret bargaining sessions with each chamber's delegation voting as a unit; and that the rules governing floor consideration of conference bills lead to their high acceptance rate in both chambers. What we have yet to consider is how these rules affect the content of conference legislation, and how the House-Senate differences discussed earlier in this chapter are reflected in the nature of conference settlements.

Conference Settlements and House-Senate Policy Differences

One way of looking at conference committee outcomes is to ask which chamber most often "wins." That is, are conference bills generally closer to the original bill of the House or the Senate? Gilbert Steiner's study of conference committee outcomes in the period 1928–1948 found that the House won 57 percent of the conference battles, the Senate position prevailed in 27 percent, and that 16 percent of the conference settlements represented an even split between the two chamber positions.[67] Richard Fenno's study of appropriations conferences occurring between 1947 and 1962 came up with opposite findings: the Senate won 65 percent of the conferences in which one chamber's position prevailed, while the House won 35 percent.[68] I discovered a similar pattern to that uncovered by Fenno in my research of all conferences held

during five Congresses from 1945 to 1966. For the 297 conferences in which it was possible to compare conference outcomes
with each chamber's bill, 59 percent were Senate victories, 32 percent were House victories, and 9 percent evenly split the difference between the chamber positions.[69] John Manley's *The Politics
of Finance* also considered conference outcomes in the fields of
tax, social security, and trade legislation. He found that conference bills dealing with taxes were generally closer to the Senate
than to the House bill, that House conferees tended to prevail
over their Senate counterparts on social security legislation, and
that there was a mixed pattern of chamber dominance in conferences dealing with trade bills.[70] Finally, a study of congressional
action on defense budgets from 1960–1970 discovered overall
Senate dominance of the conference process. The House accepted
the Senate's position on budget levels 57 percent of the time,
while the Senate accepted House figures 23 percent of the time.[71]

A word of warning about interpreting these findings is in
order here. Fenno, Manley, and Kanter were quite explicit about
the problems of measuring conference outcomes in terms of relative chamber influence in conference, and about the danger of
assuming that a chamber's "winning" conferences in particular
policy areas meant that one chamber was more influential in overall policy-making in that area. While Senate conferees might more
often "win" defense appropriation conferences, as measured by
the number of Senate changes accepted in the final bill, it is often
the case that these Senate changes dealt with the least important,
most noncontroversial parts of the bill. In such cases, the House
has a greater impact on the overall defense budget policy process
in spite of the Senate's winning more points in the conference
struggle.

These studies which show Senate conference delegations mastery in retaining Senate bill provisions in the final conference bill
can be at least partially explained in terms of the differences
between the two chambers discussed earlier. Senate rules and
norms support members' fulfilling their representational role by
adding a wide variety of amendments to bills on the floor. Tax
bills, for instance, are brought to the House floor under a closed
rule which precludes amendments to the committee-approved
bill. In the Senate, though, as many as a hundred amendments
favoring interests in senators' home states are tacked on to the

Finance Committee bill. A conference compromise which accepts only half of these Senate amendments, then, will appear to be a Senate victory in conference.

When the House delegation prevails in conference, most observers attribute this to the superior expertise of House managers; "House conferees have usually spent more time studying the legislation and probably know the details better than the Senators, who after all, have more demands on their time than House members."[72] "By general agreement, the House conferees are better prepared, better organized, better informed, more single-minded in their interest, and employ a more belligerent bargaining style."[73] This expertise of House conferees is directly related to the greater specialization in the House illustrated in Table 1 of this chapter. Conference representation reflects the same pattern. Conference assignments are distributed more widely among the membership in the Senate than in the House. David Paletz found that in the Eighty-sixth through the Ninetieth Congresses, half of the members in the Senate had participated in six or more conferences, whereas the comparable figure for the House ranged from a low of 4.6 percent to a high of 14.25 percent.[74] House managers in conference, then, are generally subject matter experts who are there to protect policy decisions made in House committees.

The behavior of Senate conferees is quite different. Instead of representing a committee's decision made in the parent chamber, most Senate conferees emphasize that body's reciprocity norm and push for retaining all amendments accepted on the Senate floor. The comments of a House Appropriations Committee member and a Ways and Means Committee member are remarkably similar in describing how senators behave in conference;[75]

> We go over there and I say, "This item is not authorized. The Corps of Engineers hasn't agreed. It's ridiculous and I'm not going to vote for it." And they say, "Oh, that's Senator so and so's project; oh, that's Senator such and such's project. We can't touch that." They have a system over there where any Senator can get anything in a bill he wants—a gentleman's agreement.
>
> Someone on the other side will say, "Senator so and so wants this project or Senator so and so is interested in this item." That Senator isn't even on the Committee and hasn't attended the

hearings, but he wants something and the rest look out for him. He isn't physically in the conference room but he's in there just the same."

All the Senators are interested in getting their amendments into these tax bills, when we come to conference. They make no bones about it. They're very open. They'll sit down for God's sake and say, "Now let's see, whose amendment was this? Oh yes, it's ——— and I told him I would support it. We are going to stand firm on that."

Curiously, then, one explanation of Senate victories in this least visible arena of congressional activity can be found in the representational nature of Senate conferees' roles. Fenno suggests that "the Senate is stronger in conference because the Senate Committee and its conferees draw more directly and more completely upon the support of their parent chamber than do the House Committee and its conferees. . . . When the Senate conferees go to the conference room, they not only represent the Senate—they are the Senate. The position they defend will have been worked out with a maximum of participation by Senate members and will enjoy a maximum of support in that body."[76]

John Manley's study of tax legislation also points to the Senate's emphasis on the representational function in explaining Senate dominance in these conferences. "The reason the Senate does better in cases of conflict with the Ways and Means Committee is because politically Senate decisions are more in line with the demands of interest groups, lobbyists, and constituents than House decisions. Ways and Means decisions, made under the closed rule, tend to be less popular with relevant publics than Senate decisions."[77] While Fenno suggests that Senate conferees are more successful because they represent the entire chamber and not just the committee position in conference, Manley broadens the concept of representation as it applies to tax conferences: Senate conferees are more successful because they represent a wider range of interests in the general public while House conferees represent fiscal decisions arrived at in closed door Ways and Means Committee sessions.

This consideration of joint House-Senate interaction in conference committees brings us back to the observations made at the beginning of this chapter. The rules and norms governing the behavior of representatives and senators are different because the two chambers play different roles in the policy process. Congress must both pass laws and serve as a forum for the representation of a wide range of interests. The structure of the House of Representatives and rules and norms governing the behavior of its members serve to emphasize that body's concern with lawmaking. The Senate, on the other hand, is more suited to acting as a forum where the interests and ideas of a heterogeneous public are introduced into the political process. When these two chambers come together in conference to determine the final form of legislation, these differences are not eliminated, but maintained. House conferees come to the bargaining table to uphold bills fashioned in committee workshops; Senate conferees come to make sure that individual senators' provisions to help certain segments of the public are not dropped from the final bill.

But the important question about the final outcome is not just whether the Senate or House position is closest to the bill which emerges from conference. Rather, we are concerned with who gets helped and who gets hurt by the congressional policy decision. To attempt to answer that we must look at some of the policy outcomes of the congressional process, and we must consider the influence of noncongressional actors, such as lobbyists and the executive, in helping to shape policy. That is the task of Chapter 6.

NOTES

1. Quoted in Donald Riegle, *O Congress* (Doubleday, 1972), p. 172 and p. 69.

2. Charles L. Clapp, *The Congressman; His Work as He Sees It* (Anchor, 1964), p. 39.

3. Lewis Froman and Nelson Polsby discuss these differences in Froman's *The Congressional Process* (Little, Brown, 1967), pp. 5–151 and Polsby's *Congressional Behavior* (Random House, 1971), pp. 6–9.

4. Froman, *The Congressional Process*, p. 12.

5. Ralph K. Huitt, "The Internal Distribution of Influence: The Senate," in David Truman, ed., *The Congress and America's Future* (Prentice-Hall, 1965), p. 80.

6. Woodrow Wilson, *Congressional Government* (Meridan, 1967), p. 155.

7. Quoted in John Manley, *The Politics of Finance* (Little, Brown, 1970), p. 378.

8. Polsby, *Congressional Behavior*, p. 7.

9. Richard Fenno, *The Power of the Purse* (Little, Brown, 1966); John Manley, *The Politics of Finance* (Little, Brown, 1970); David Vogler, *The Third House* (Northwestern University Press, 1971); Arnold Kanter, "Congress and the Defense Budget," *American Political Science Review*, Vol. 66, no. 1 (March 1972), pp. 129–143.

10. Froman, *The Congressional Process*, pp. 44–45.

11. Representative Martha Griffiths successfully employed the discharge petition in July 1970 to bring the Women's Rights amendment out of the Judiciary Committee presided over by Chairman Emanuel Celler, a strong opponent of the measure. *Congressional Quarterly Weekly Report*, August 14, 1970, p. 2041.

12. Froman, *The Congressional Process*, p. 50.

13. *Ibid.*, p. 67.

14. James Robinson, *The House Rules Committee* (Bobbs-Merrill, 1963), p. 44.

15. Quoted in Manley, *The Politics of Finance*, p. 72.

16. Fenno, *The Power of the Purse*, p. 422.

17. Information in this section comes from Robinson, *The House Rules Committee* and discussions in Froman, *The Congressional Process*, pp. 52–61, and Robert Peabody, "The Enlarged Rules Committee" in Robert Peabody and Nelson Polsby, eds., *New Perspectives on the House of Representatives* (Rand McNally, 1963), pp. 129–164.

18. Charles Reich, "The Greening of America," *The New Yorker*, September 26, 1970, p. 50. Charles Reich, in an analysis of the "administrative state," points out the conservative bias in this "rational" system:

> Administration seeks to remove decision making from the area of politics to the area of "science." Democratic or popular choice is rejected in favor of a "rational" weighing of all the factors by experts. Procedures are set up by which decision making is channelled, and care is taken to define exactly which institution shall make which decisions. For each type of decision, there is someone "best" qualified to decide; administration avoids participation in decisions by the "less qualified." If followed, these procedures usually produce a decision that is a compromise or balance and that rejects any particular choice in its pure,

uncompromised form. Choice takes place within narrow limits. A weighing of all the factors produces a decision somewhere in between, rather than at one or another "extreme."

Administration has no value of its own, except the institutional ones just described. Theoretically, it could accept any values. In practice, however, it is strongly conservative. Things go more smoothly when the status quo is maintained, when change is slow, cautious, and evolutionary. The more elaborate the machinery of administration is, the less ready it is for new, disquieting values. And "rationality" finds some values easier to understand, to justfiy, to put into verbal terms than other values. It can understand quantity better than quality. Administration is neutral in favor of present policy.

19. Froman, *The Congressional Process*, pp. 77ff.

20. Mark Green, James Fallows, and David Swick, *Who Runs Congress?* (Bantam, 1972), p. 64.

21. Howard Shuman, "Senate Rules and the Civil Rights Bill: A Case Study," in Lawrence Pettit and Edward Keynes, eds., *The Legislative Process in the U.S. Senate* (Rand McNally, 1969), p. 104.

22. Froman, *The Congressional Process*, pp. 121–122.

23. Shuman, "Senate Rules and the Civil Rights Bill," pp. 121–122.

24. Roger Davidson, David Kovenock, and Michael O'Leary, *Congress in Crisis: Politics and Congressional Reform* (Wadsworth, 1966), p. 110.

25. Froman, *The Congressional Process*, p. 65.

26. *Congressional Quarterly Weekly Reports*, September 18, 1970, pp. 2239–2240; September 25, p. 2320; and October 2, p. 2396.

27. Donald Matthews, *U.S. Senators and Their World* (Vintage, 1960), pp. 92–117.

28. For House norms, see Richard Fenno, "The Appropriations Committee as a Political System," in Peabody and Polsby, eds. *New Perspectives on the House of Representatives*, pp. 124–154: *The Power of the Purse;* and "The Internal Distribution of Influence: The House," in Truman, ed., *The Congress and America's Future*, pp. 52–76.

A comparative study of four state legislatures found forty-two "rules of the game" mentioned by members. See John Wahlke, Heinz Eulau, William Buchanan, and Leroy Ferguson, *The Legislative System* (John Wiley, 1962), pp. 141–169. Although this list at times resembles the Scout Law, most of the rules of the game are similar to the broader categories delineated by Matthews.

29. Quoted in Clapp, *The Congressman: His Work as He Sees It,* p. 18.

30. Matthews, *U.S. Senators and Their Worlds,* p. 96.

31. See Nelson Polsby's discussion in *Congressional Behavior,* p. 7.

32. Matthews, *U.S. Senators and Their Worlds,* p. 93.

33. Champ Clark, *My Quarter Century of American Politics* (Harpers, 1920), Vol. I., p. 209. Quoted in George Goodwin, Jr., *The Little Legislatures* (University of Massachusetts Press, 1970), p. 118.

34. Polsby, *Congressional Behavior,* p. 13.

35. Riegle, *O Congress,* p. 141.

36. Green et al., *Who Runs Congress?* pp. 58–62.

37. For the relevant areas, see Nicholas Masters, "Committee Assignments in the House of Representatives," *American Political Science Review,* June 1961, pp. 345–357; Richard Fenno, "The House of Representatives and Federal Aid to Education," in Peabody and Polsby, eds., *New Perspectives on the House of Representatives,* pp. 195–235; David Vogler, "Flexibility in the Congressional Seniority System: Conference Representation," *Polity,* summer 1970, pp. 494–507. More general discussions of seniority are George Goodwin, Jr., "The Seniority System in Congress," *American Political Science Review,* 1959, pp. 412–436; Michael Abram and Joseph Cooper, "The Rise of Seniority in the House of Representatives," *Polity,* fall 1968, pp. 52–85; and Nelson Polsby, Miriam Gallaher, and Barry Rundquist, "The Growth of the Seniority System in the U.S. House of Representatives, *American Political Science Review,* September 1969, pp. 787–807.

38. *Congressional Quarterly Weekly Reports,* Vol. 29, nos. 3 and 4 (January 15, January 22, 1971) pp. 134–137 and 177–179.

39. Matthews, *U.S. Senators and Their Worlds,* p. 94.

40. *Ibid.,* p. 95.

41. Fenno, "The Appropriations Committee as a Political System," p. 133.

42. Clapp, *The Congressman: His Work as He Sees It,* p. 23.

43. Fenno, "The Internal Distribution of Influence," p. 73.

44. The description is Fenno's in *The Power of the Purse,* p. 511.

45. *Ibid.,* p. 509.

46. *Congressional Record,* April 24, 1956, p. 6148. Quoted in Matthews, *U.S. Senators and Their World,* pp. 97–98.

47. Clem Miller, *Member of the House,* (Charles Scribner's Sons, 1962), p. 93.

48. Riegle, *O Congress,* p. 252.

49. Miller, *Member of the House,* p. 40.

50. Quoted in Green et al., *Who Runs Congress?* p. 167.

51. Quoted in *Boston Globe,* December 6, 1970, p. 23.

52. Quoted in *Congressional Quarterly Almanac,* 1963, p. 177.

53. Richard Rovere, *Senator Joe McCarthy* (Vintage, 1960), p. 230.

54. Theodore Lowi, *The End of Liberalism* (W. W. Norton, 1969).

55. Representative are Joseph Clark, *The Senate Establishment* (Hill and Wang, 1963) and Douglass Cater, "Spotlight on the House," *The Reporter,* September 28, 1961.

56. Matthews, *U.S. Senators and Their World,* pp. 112–117; Wayne Swanson, "Committee Assignments and the Nonconformist Legislator: Democrats in the U.S. Senate," *Midwest Journal of Political Science,* February 1969, pp. 84–94.

57. Goodwin, *The Little Legislatures,* p. 242. My earlier study reported a lower percentage, but agreed with Goodwin's evaluation of the importance of legislation passing through conference. See Vogler, *The Third House,* p. 4.

58. Bertram Gross, *The Legislative Struggle* (McGraw-Hill, 1953), p. 321.

59. Joseph Clark, *Congress: The Sapless Branch* (Harper & Row, 1964), p. 11.

60. *Congressional Quarterly Weekly Report,* Vol. 17, no. 18, May 1, 1959, pp. 597–598.

61. Vogler, *The Third House,* pp. 45–48.

62. Quoted in Green et al., *Who Runs Congress?* p. 63.

63. *Ibid.,* p. 62–63.

64. Goodwin, *The Little Legislatures,* p. 243.

65. Fenno, *The Power of the Purse,* pp. 657ff; David Paletz, "Influence in Congress: An Analysis of the Nature and Effects of Conference Committees," Paper delivered at the 66th Annual Meeting of the American Political Science Association, Los Angeles, September 1970, pp. 9 and 11; Vogler, *The Third House,* pp. 94ff.

66. Clapp, *The Congressman: His Work as He Sees It,* p. 279. See also Malcolm Jewell and Samuel Patterson, *The Legislative Process in the United States* (Random House, 1966), p. 481.

67. Gilbert Steiner, *The Congressional Conference Committee: Seventieth to Eightieth Congresses* (University of Illinois Press, 1950), pp. 170–172.

68. Fenno, *The Power of the Purse,* p. 662.

69. Vogler, *The Third House,* p. 55.

70. Manley, *The Politics of Finance,* pp. 269–294.

71. Arnold Kanter, "Congress and the Defense Budget: 1960–1970," *American Political Science Review,* Vol. 66, no. 1 (March 1972), pp. 129–143.

72. Manley, *The Politics of Finance,* p. 293.

73. Fenno, *The Power of the Purse,* p. 668.

74. Paletz, "Influence in Congress," p. 3. See also Goodwin, *The Little Legislatures,* p. 245.

75. Fenno, *The Power of the Purse,* pp. 627–628 and Manley, *The Politics of Finance,* p. 269.

76. Fenno, *The Power of the Purse,* pp. 668–669.

77. Manley, *The Politics of Finance,* p. 279.

CHAPTER 6

Policies, Pressure Groups, and Presidents

> *I speak Spanish to God, Italian to women, French to men,
> and German to my horse.*
>
> Charles V of France

The last four chapters have focused on structural and behavioral patterns which make up congressional politics. We have looked at the legislative process, but little has been said about the policies which emerge from that process. In a way this is unfortunate. For the ultimate criteria needed to evaluate Congress are the policies that come out of the legislative mill, regardless of how these policies were shaped and formed by structural factors which are more or less "representative" or "efficient" than they should or could be. Judgements about the representativeness of elections, the need for effective party leadership, the decentralized system of fiefdoms created by the committee and seniority systems, and the effects of institutionalized House procedures and personalized Senate procedures all rest on some evaluation of the laws made by Congress. It is acknowledged that the structure greatly determines the content of policies, but a direct link between certain behavioral patterns and legislative outputs is difficult to establish.

Both political scientists and the general public give more attention to the way Congress makes decisions than they do to the content of these policies. Public opinion polls conducted since the 1940s consistently show that negative feelings about Congress are generally expressed in terms of the delay associated with the legislative process rather than being tied to specific policies. A 1944 survey, for instance, showed that 41 percent of those who thought Congress was doing a fair or poor job expressed criticism of the way Congress goes about its business ("too much argument, politics, lack of leadership"), while only 7 percent raised objections to specific acts or policies.[1] Twenty years later a poll by Louis Harris showed a similar pattern. "In general, the public expects Congress to pass rather than hold up legislation. And to a much lesser degree, Congress is evaluated for the specific programs which it does or does not enact. . . . For those expressing negative reactions to Congress (51 percent of the sample), the chief irritant was obviously the dilatory handling of the lawmaking function: 'not done much,' 'avoided major bills,' 'too slow,' and 'everything stalled' were most frequently mentioned."[2]

When political scientists look at Congress there is the same tendency to focus more on structure and procedures than to evaluate the institution in terms of its policies. In 1964, the American Political Science Association received a $230,000 grant from the Carnegie Corporation to study Congress. The director of the APSA Study of Congress, Ralph K. Huitt from the University of Wisconsin, brought together eighteen young political scientists who had established themselves as leading students of Congress. A glance at the topics chosen by these scholars reveals the discipline's emphasis on process: (1) the seniority system; (2) comparative study of committees; (3) legislative oversight; (4) congressional rules and procedures; (5) minority party leadership; (6) Ways and Means Committee; (7) taxation and appropriation policy; (8) congressmen and local party organization; (9) defense policy; (10) committee staffing; (11) House-Senate relationships; (12) institutionalization of the House; (13) foreign policy; (14) majority party leadership; (15) congressional policy-making and urban-rural conflict; (16) the evaluation of congressional effectiveness; (17) centralization of power, presidential and congressional leadership.[3] Although the published results of the APSA studies have gone a long way toward meeting Huitt's stated goal of finding out "how Congress works," many people agree with Donald Matthews's observation that "knowledge about the internal workings of Congress takes on significance only as it helps explain the policies which emerge from the institution."[4]

While there is an obvious difference in the information levels of the general public and political scientists when they look at congressional processes, the fact remains that most of the scholarly attention given to Congress has focused on process rather than policy. Introductory textbooks on American politics almost always include a chart on "how a bill becomes a law" and an intricate description of the legislative maze through which a bill must pass. These books reflect the emphasis which research on Congress places on describing the legislative process rather than the content of the laws which come out of that process.

There are, though, a number of studies which zero in on a particular policy and follow it through the legislative process. The Employment Act of 1946, civil rights legislation in 1960 and 1964, the poverty program of 1964, and the Elementary and Secondary Education Act of 1965 have all been subjects for this type of study.[5] A theme which runs throughout these case studies is that by looking at a single piece of legislation, the authors can provide insights into the congressional policy-making process. "Certain inferences can be made about Congressional policy-making from the study of one bill," says one. "An attempt was made to explain the functioning of Congress by describing the way in which a particular bill became a law" reports another. The two political scientists looking at education bills point out that their "major purpose is to offer a working description of the American policy process by focusing on the issue of federal aid to education."[6]

When people do look at congressional policies, then, it is generally part of an attempt to explain the congressional policy-making process. The same may be said about most discussions of the role of lobbyists and the executive in helping to form legislative policies. Some observers decry the great influence of lobbyists over the content of bills; yet, a number of studies find the power of lobbyists to be much more limited than is generally supposed. While many scholars contend that the president has achieved such a dominant position in the legislative process as to render the Congress an ineffective, second-rate partner in policy-making, others find the reports of Congress's death greatly exaggerated.

One reason for the confusing and contradictory evaluations

195

TABLE 1   *Policies and their Politics*

DISTRIBUTIVE

Examples: Rivers and harbors legislation, tax loopholes, government services such as post office, agricultural subsidies, area redevelopment, defense procurement

Nature of Policy:

1. Short-run decisions made without regard to limited resources.
2. Easy to separate overall policy into component parts and to distribute unit by unit.
3. There is no "general rule" to determine distribution.
4. Decisions are highly individualized.
5. There is no direct confrontation between those who gain something from the policy and those who lose something.
6. It is difficult to locate the "deprived" groups because they can be accommodated by a further separation of policy into component parts and further distribution of benefits.

Nature of political activity:

1. There are a large number of small, intensely organized interests; a politics of "every man for himself"; the single person or single firm or group are the major political actors.
2. The politics is one of "mutual noninterference," *i.e.,* each actor seeks his own rewards but does not oppose other's seeking theirs. It is a low-conflict political process.
3. Coalitions are made up of unlike interests; "logrolling" is the most common form of political interaction.
4. The congressional committee or subcommittee is the most important official decision-maker.
5. The individualized nature of the political conflict provides a basis for very stable coalitions that are not affected by the larger policy outcomes.

REGULATORY

Examples: Trade policies since 1960s, federal aid to education, campaign finance regulations, medicare

Nature of policy

1. Like distributive policies in that they are specific and individual in their impact, but they are not capable of being separated into component parts to the same degree as are distributive policies.
2. Laws are stated in general terms, but their impact is to directly raise costs and/or reduce or expand alternatives of private individuals.
3. Differs from distributive because in the short run it involves a direct choice as to who will receive benefits and who will pay costs.
4. Decision-making involves the application of a "general rule" to specific cases.
5. Policy is cumulative and is made up of a series of individual decisions involving similar groups.

Nature of Political Activity:

1. There are a number of groups organized on the basis of shared attitudes rather than just narrow economic interests.
2. Coalitions are formed on the basis of conflict and compromise among groups which share some common attitudes; "bargaining" is the most common form of political interaction.
3. Policy tends to be the residue of the interplay of group conflict.
4. The power structure is not as stable as that dealing with distributive policies; there are shifting coalitions which must compromise to build majorities on each particular issue.
5. Congress, as a whole, is the chief decision-maker.

REDISTRIBUTIVE

Examples: Employment Act of 1946, civil rights legislation, strategic defense policies, 1964 poverty program

Nature of Policy:

1. Similar to regulatory in the sense that individual decisions are interrelated.
2. The policy affects broad groups of society ("haves" and "have nots," big business and small business, whites and nonwhites, bourgeoisie and proletariat).
3. The policy involves not just the use of property, but the possession or transfer of property itself.
4. The nature of a redistributive issue is not determined by how redistributive it actually is, but rather how redistributive it could become in the future.

Nature of Political Activity

1. The group conflict involves "peak associations" (those who speak for very broad sectors of society such as the National Association of Manufacturers, the Chamber of Commerce, the AFL-CIO); there is a high degree of cohesion within these groups on *redistributive* issues and their demands are generally expressed in ideological terms.
2. There are never more than two sides of the conflict over redistributive issues.
3. Negotiation is possible only in terms of softening or strengthening the impact on society; neither logrolling nor bargaining characterize political interaction.
4. The power structure is very stable and is made up of basically institutionalized factors.
5. Differences among related but competing groups are likely to be settled outside the realm of government.
6. Because of the centralization of conflict and the need for overall balancing and decision-making, Congress plays only a minor role. Decisions are more likely to be made in the executive branch or in the private sector. Congressional policies may provide some exceptions to the general principles established by redistributive policies, but does not decide on the basic principles themselves.

of the influence of Congress, lobbyists, and the president on policy is the tendency to treat policy as a dependent variable. Policy is the thing to be "explained" by reference to the legislative process. If we reverse this formulation and consider policies as independent variables, however, we uncover new ground for understanding the politics of Congress. Certain types of policies produce certain types of congressional politics. Rivers and harbors bills, for instance, create a legislative process in which the roles and relative influence of lobbyists and the president are quite different from the configurations arising from a civil rights bill or strategic defense policies.

There are a number of ways to classify policies. One of the most useful classification schemes, is that suggested by Theodore Lowi in a 1964 review essay of a book on trade policy.[7] Lowi classified policies as distributive, regulatory, or redistributive depending on their relative impact on society. Distributive policies directly affect the fewest people in society, while at the other end of the continuum, redistributive policies are those having the broadest impact on the whole society. An essential point of the Lowi formulation is that "these areas of policy or government activity constitute real arenas of power. Each arena tends to develop its own characteristic political structure, political process, elites, and group relations."[8] In Table 1, I have provided a summary of the major characteristics of each policy type and of the nature of political activity associated with each type.

Table 1 is a very rough outline of Lowi's classification of policies. The reader should keep in mind that these different policy types are not distinct and mutually exclusive, but rather points on a continuum reflecting the impact of policies on society. It is not easy to fit all laws passed by Congress into one or another of these categories. Some exhibit characteristics of both distributive and regulatory policies, or both regulatory and redistributive policies. Tax legislation, for instance, is distributive in its granting loopholes and exemptions to some groups, regulatory in its providing "general rules" to be applied to individual decisions, and redistributive in its underlying principle of a graduated federal income tax. In addition, policies change over time. Lowi suggests, for instance, that trade policies, which were distributive in an earlier part of this century began to be handled as regulatory policies after World War II and had bcome completely regulatory by the time of the Trade Expansion Act of 1962.

Lowi's scheme is certainly not the last word on policy classifications. It raises a number of questions about how policies move from one arena to another, about the distribution of power throughout society which determines how policies are defined, and about the exact dimensions of policies which are being measured in this schema. A number of political scientists have considered these matters in evaluating and refining Lowi's basic framework.[9]

I have introduced Lowi's classification of policies in this last chapter because I think it provides a useful organizational focus for looking at the role of lobbyists and the president in the congressional policy-making process. Confronted with some studies which assert that lobbyists have a great deal of influence over legislative policies and others which suggest that lobbyists play only a minimal role, we can try to answer the question of who is right. The answer might indeed be that they all are; that some types of policies are dealt with in a process which gives special interest groups a lot of influence in determining the eventual outcome, while others are decided in a manner which minimizes the lobbyists' impact. Similarly, we might find that the executive has a great deal of influence in some areas of congressional policy-making, while in others he plays a minor role. So let us turn now to a consideration of lobbyists and the executive, first in a general sense, and then in terms of these three different policy classifications and their politics.

PRESSURE GROUPS AND CONGRESS

In 1906, David Graham Phillips wrote a book about senators and special interests. Twenty-one senators were accused of serving big economic concerns in return for favors or money. A senator from Texas, for example, was said to have received over $225,000 from oil interests in just a matter of months. The title of Phillips polemic suggests its tone: *Treason of the Senate.* Seven years later, the *New York World* ran a series of articles claiming that the

National Association of Manufacturers had given "financial reward for services rendered for political purposes" to nine congressmen and former congressmen and to their chief pages in the House.[10] Some more recent studies of Congress have also painted a picture emphasizing the power of pressure groups on Capitol Hill. Ralph Nader's Congress Project issued a report in 1972 called *Who Runs Congress? The President, Big Business or You?* "With the lobbies' pressure bearing in from all sides," the authors note, "Congress ends up, for the most part, responding to the heaviest push."[11] Drew Pearson and Jack Anderson have also characterized the modern lobbyist and his techniques:

> Today's successful lobbyists are more likely to be smooth professionals, skilled in the "soft sell." They seldom engage in blatant currying of favor. Well-tailored and turned out, they will make thier pitches subtly over martinis at the posh Metropolitan Club or over golf balls at the exclusive Burning Tree course. But they can also retain a Senator's law firm or deliver cash in a paper sack to those who prefer that sort of gross transaction.[12]

Congressional reaction to these various charges of influence by special interests and their lobbyists has remained fairly consistent over time. Senator William Borah's reaction to the 1913 *World* articles is typical:

> I suppose in popular parlance we mean by "lobbyist" a man who is employed, paid professionally, to influence legislation concerning a matter not because he is interested in the matter, not necessarily because he thinks it is right, but because he desires to earn his salary, and is paid like a lawyer sometimes to argue a bad case, to do the best he can in the situation. That is my idea of a lobbyist, and I have not seen any around here this year, although they may be here.[13]

Half a century later, political scientists still find most congressmen denying the importance of lobbyists. "You know, that's an amazing thing," marveled one senator in an interview with Donald Matthews, "I hardly ever see a lobbyist. I don't know—maybe they think I'm a poor target but I seldom see them. During this entire natural-gas battle (in which he was a prominent figure) I was not approached by either side."[14]

In 1967, 439 individuals were registered as lobbyists in Washington. They reported spending over $4 million.[15] The extent and flavor of lobbying on the hill is suggested by looking at the top 26 spenders among the 274 organizations filing reports in 1967:

Organization	*1967 spending*
United Federation of Postal Clerks	$227,524
AFL-CIO (national headquarters)	165,505
Record Industry Assn. of America	139,919
National Assn. of Letter Carriers	133,877
American Farm Bureau Federation	133,777
United States Saving and Loan League	108,485
American Legion	106,088
National Automobile Dealers Assn.	101,707
National Federation of Independent Businesses	96,701
National Housing Conference	91,995
National Farmers Union	86,994
Central Arizona Project Assn.	78,867
Retired Officers Assn.	78,213
Council for a Livable World	77,470
National Committee for the Recording Arts	77,040
National Education Assn. (State & Federal Rel.)	73,612
American Trucking Assns., Inc.	61,718
National Assn. of Electric Companies	61,382
Liberty Lobby	61,341
American Hospital Assn.	61,283
American Medical Assn.	58,378
American Textile Manufacturers Inst.	57,394
Brotherhood of Locomotive Firemen & Enginemen	56,109
International Brotherhood of Teamsters	54,091
American Library Assn.	53,483
Brotherhood of Railway, Airline & Steamship Clerks, Freight Handlers, Express & Station Employees	53,352

SOURCE: Congressional Quarterly Service, *Legislators and Lobbyists* (May 1968), p. 37.

When congressmen downplay the importance of interest groups in the face of documented expenditures by lobbyists, it is not because they are lying, but rather that they do not think of most of this activity as lobbying. A union lobbyist tells this tale:

> One time during the minimum wage battle, Senator ——— began to weaken on the $1.00 minimum. Someone had touched his sympathy with a picture of what the bill would do to the sawmills of the South. He told me that he was contemplating making an exception in their case. I said, "——— (first name), if you even hint that you might back down from your previous position, this place will be swarming with lobbyists!" "Lobbyists," he said, looking around him, "I don't see any lobbyists around here." Then he realized that I was one and laughed. Hell, we don't think of ourselves as lobbyists![16]

Recent political science research on the role of interest groups in Congress gives some support to legislators' own descriptions of the lobbying process. In contrast to the muckraking descriptions of payoffs and the popular notion of congressmen giving in to pressure, these studies suggest a network of accommodation and mutual assistance between lobbyists and legislators.[17] A general overall description of the normal interaction between groups and congressmen, and some of the reasons why earlier descriptions are inaccurate, will be presented in the next few pages.

Most lobbying activity is directed toward reinforcing the opinions of legislators who are in basic agreement with the group position anyway. Instead of attempting to convert congressmen, lobbyists seek to hold supporters in line or to activate congressmen who agree with the group position but who might not vote unless convinced of the importance of that vote. This focus on legislators in agreement with them is a result both of lobbyists' believing that most votes are already pretty well set long before an issue comes to a vote and of their desire to avoid uncertain or high conflict situations. A major study of trade policy found that:

> Lobbyists fear to enter where they may find a hostile reception. Since uncertainty is greatest precisely regarding those who are undecided, the lobbyist is apt to neglect contact with those very persons who he might be able to influence.

It is so much easier to carry on activities within the circle of those who agree and encourage you than it is to break out and find potential proselytes, that the day-to-day routine and pressure of business tend to shunt those more painful activities aside. The result is that the lobbyist becomes in effect a service bureau of those congressmen already agreeing with him, rather than an agent of direct persuasion.[18]

When Congressmen respond to questions about lobbying, they think in terms of cases where an organization had attempted to change their vote. This happens rarely enough that most solons consider themselves relatively free of such pressures. The main task of lobbyists, that of providing information and rationales to justify a congressman's already decided vote, is not considered lobbying by those on the receiving end. Although performing such functions might not change any votes, it does provide an important service for legislators.

A study of the Illinois legislature shows the importance of giving representatives "reasons" for having voted the way they did. In this case, a legislator brought in a law professor to testify against a tax bill; neither the legislator nor the professor felt that this testimony had really changed any votes on the bill.

However (the legislator pointed out), do not undersell the significance of the presentation. Our arrangements (for votes) were concluded before the hearing ever started, but it was absolutely essential that members who had agreed to vote against the bill be furnished with a "cover"—with an impressive witness whose competence was unquestioned so that they could offer an explanation of their votes. The professor furnished that "cover." When we return the favor on legislation in which others are interested, we shall expect to be furnished with a "cover."[19]

A second reason why most lobbying is not perceived as such by members of Congress relates to the system of cue networks discussed in Chapter 3. Since most voting by legislators is done in a low-information situation, congressmen come to depend on a network of cue sources for reliable information as to how they should vote. Constituents, lobbyists, staff members, and party leaders all serve as cue sources for particular legislators on certain issues. But the most consistent source of cues for legislative voting is other senators and representatives. The information a congressman relies on to support his position will have come primarily from within the Capitol Hill network rather than from external sources.[20] The most successful lobbies are thus quite often the least visible. "The key point of contact is usually between a highly specialized lobbyist and the specialized staff people of a standing committee. Intimate friendships spring up there—it's the rivet point."[21] Because of the importance of a congressmen's staff, lobbyists often prefer to talk to a senator or representative's aides rather than to him.[22] This indirect approach fits in better with the internal information system of Congress.

Sitting congressmen are the best lobbyists, the most influential being legislative leaders who can exert internal influence beneficial to particular interests. During the 1950s, for example, the triumvirate leadership of Senators Robert Kerr of Oklahoma and Lyndon Johnson of Texas and Speaker Sam Rayburn of Texas was able to protect the interests of the oil industry by controlling membership on key committees. This was far more effective than any outside lobbying could have possibly have been.

"Inside lobbying" by other congressmen is generally viewed as a form of legitimate representation by members of Congress. Whether a legislator's ties to a particular group stem from his own occupational background or from that group's being an important part of his constituency, it is expected that he will try to convince colleagues to support that group's legislative goals. "Lobbying by other congressmen is the most difficult for me to resist," is the way one legislator put it.[23] Another comment:

> Congressmen tend to have a high regard for one another, and if someone has a pet bill, you tend to make efforts to accommodate him if it is at all possible. When Congressman ——— had his cranberry bill, everybody said, "let's do something for good old Nick," and so they passed the bill. It wasn't a very good bill and probably shouldn't have passed; but the "good old Nick" slogan was enough to do it. No lobby could have pushed that bill through. It was just a personal hand for a member.[24]

Drew Pearson and Jack Anderson's delightfully muckraking book, *The Case Against Congress,* shows how occupational links and financial interests often relate to a legislator's position on many issues. The authors studied fifty typical law firms with partners in Congress. Forty of the firms represented banks, 31 represented insurance companies, 11 represented gas and oil companies, and 10 represented real estate firms.

> Some of the biggest corporate names in America are listed as clients of Congressman's law firms in such out-of-the-way places, say, as Nicholasville, Kentucky, and Pascagoula, Mississippi. To name just a few, there are General Motors, Ford, Standard Oil, Gulf Oil, Sinclair Refining, Aluminum Company of America, Baltimore & Ohio Railroad, Western Union, International Harvester, Seagram distillers, Coca-Cola, Equitable Life. The Travelers Corporation, for one, has retained legal counsel in such unlikely places as Piqua and Findlay, Ohio, where the company's political radar led them straight to the law firms of Representatives William McCulloch and Jackson Betts, respectively. The same insurance company was also guided unerringly to the law firm of Representatives James Harvey in Saginaw, Michigan, and Wendell Wyatt in Astoria, Oregon. Solid Republicans all, the four have always managed to find in their hearts an extraordinary sympathy for the corporate view on insurance problems. Betts has been particularly effective as a champion of the insurance industry on the law-writing Ways and Means Committee.[25]

In addition to interest representation provided through member's law firms, there are more direct links which produce inside lobbyists such as the large agricultural holdings already discussed, or the fact that a senator or representative's money was earned by careful investment in particular industries. There was no need for the oil and natural gas industries to lobby the late Senator Robert Kerr of Oklahoma, for example, because the bulk of his fortune of over $15 million had been accumulated in those areas.

The vivid description of "inside lobbying" and legislators' conflicts of interest drawn by Pearson and Anderson should be tempered somewhat by considering the findings of a committee of New York lawyers reported in *Congress and the Public Trust*. Their study of the Ninetieth Congress is based on interviews with twenty-three senators and ninety-seven representatives. Only 37 percent of the lawyer-legislators in their sample continued some form of law practice. The majority of congressmen have given up their law practice and the fact that such self-regulation is the congressional norm is supported by their finding that most of the practicing lawyer-legislators were junior members. Financial interests in certain types of business reveal a somewhat different picture, however, and lend support to the "inside lobbying" notion of congressional biases.

> Nineteen of the 23 senators and 59 of the 97 representatives mentioned investments in securities or in real estate other than personal residences. Twenty-nine representatives, including a number who also rely on other investments, indicated an outside income from business or farming. Five senators indicated income from operating a business or farm. Of those interviewed, no senator and only 10 representatives indicated a total lack of significant income other than their salaries.[26]

Even if there are no existing ties with a particular interest, a member's background may predispose him to support the goals of an industry or social group with which he identifies. "I was born over a retail store and raised in one," a senator told Matthews. "The retailers don't have to pressure me into seeing things their way. If anything, I'm lobbying them, telling them to get on the ball. And when their man comes around to see me, I don't think of him as a lobbyist with an ax to grind but as a man with sound judgement and good will."[27]

A third reason why lobbying activity is often hard to find stems from the nature of the political process both within Congress and in the larger system. Inside the legislature, members are socialized into a body emphasizing reciprocity and bargaining. These norms, coupled with a specialization which precludes a member's having a broad general overview of the cumulative effects of public policies, help to explain how special interests are able to achieve their legislative goals. Stanley Surrey points out how the nature of legislative politics brings about tax loopholes:

> The desire—sometimes the need—of a congressman to be useful often places a congressman who sits on one of the tax committees, the House Committee on Ways and Means or the Senate Committee on Finance, in a difficult position. A fellow congressman who sits on the Public Works Committee, for example, can respond to constituency pressure by approving the project involved; a member of the Appropriations Committee can

respond by a favorable vote on a specific appropriation. But a congressman on a tax committee can respond only by pushing through a special tax provision.

His legislative stock in trade, so to speak, is special tax treatment. This difficulty is especially acute in the case of those congressmen who come to sit on a tax committee only after they have been members of other committees and have become so accustomed to using their committee powers in helpful ways that the habit persists."[28]

Legislative bargaining among elites requires that congressmen deliver tangible rewards. Although the mass public may accept symbolic rewards given in response to demands for policy benefits, legislators and lobbyists who are active in political bargaining cannot be so easily pacified. Instead of being satisfied with programs promising to maintain a "progressive" income tax, or agricultural price supports figured on "parity," political elites active in legislative bargaining seek specific tax provisions and price supports for particular crops. As Surrey's description of the tax committees suggests, bargaining is the exchange of tangible benefits among political elites. Most of this process is regarded not as lobbying by interest groups, but as normal legislative politics. The results in terms of policy payoffs for particular groups, however, are much the same.

In an insightful analysis of American politics, E. E. Schattschneider has suggested that any political system develops a set of predominant values, beliefs, rituals, and rules of the game which benefit certain groups at the expense of others.[29] This "mobilization of bias" is staunchly defended by those groups who benefit from the status quo. Professors Peter Bachrach and Morton Baratz suggest that this mobilization of bias is maintained through a process of "nondecison-making" by which challenges to the values or interests of the decision-maker or other political elites are suppressed or thwarted. "To be more nearly explicit," they continue, "nondecision-making is a means by which demands for change in the existing allocation of benefits and privileges in the community can be suffocated before they are even voiced; or kept covert; or killed before they gain access to the relevant decision-making arena; or, failing all these things, maimed or destroyed in the decision-implementing stage of the policy process."[30]

One effect of this conception of power is to greatly broaden the definition of politics; instead of focusing only on concrete decision-making by a political body, analysts must look at popular values which preclude certain issues from being seriously raised or permit their being dismissed after only superficial consideration. The power of the American Medical Association in blocking medicare for over twenty years, for instance, partially reflects the importance of such values as individualism (or "volunteerism") and belief in the free enterprise system. Because of widespread acceptance of these values, the AMA for a long time was able successfully to oppose all medicare programs by attacking them, at the symbolic level, as being "socialized medicine."[31]

Similar values affect the distribution of power within the political system: "volunteerism" made it difficult for organized labor to gain power in the United States and still affects the way in which labor legislation is administered;[32] "anticommunism" benefits those groups seeking a larger defense budget and government contracts; "economic growth" helps larger corporations in their pursuit of tax breaks for expansion and research;[33] the capitalist tenet that great risks should be greatly rewarded helps the oil industry to keep its depletion allowance despite the fact that those large companies which take the fewest risks benefit the most. The widespread acceptance of these values gives certain groups advantages in the political process which other groups lack. Those who profit from the existing distribution of values do not need actively to seek congressional support for beneficial programs, because the existing programs already help them. Their power is a diffuse veto power embodied in the political culture. It is exercised whenever policies which would challenge the status quo are eliminated prior to public debate or defeated by linking them with vague negative symbols. It is a kind of power which political analysts who focus on overt lobbying and concrete decision-making situations are likely to overlook or to underestimate.

A last consideration which we should include in this general discussion of interest groups and Congress is the series of descriptions and evaluations of lobbying put forward by those people identified with the pluralist school of thought in American politics. In Chapter 1 we had a brief look at these ideas and some of the criticism leveled against them. But because so much of

Madison's argument in Federalist paper #10, and later discussions of the public interest which rely on a process of special interests checking one another, have to do with the role of interest representation in Congress, it seems appropriate to end this section with some thoughts about these pluralist notions of how things work.

The competition of disparate groups seems to be a key element of pluralist thought. As long as congressmen must pay heed to the demands of a wide range of groups present in heterogeneous constituencies, they will tend to support policies which satisfy the greatest number of individual demands. Pluralist explanations of lobbying emphasize the heterogeneity of constituencies and the fact that a congressman must balance the conflicting demands of many groups. This discontinuity among groups is also extended into the Congress itself, and used to explain why individual legislators are relatively free from influence by any one group. "If Congressman A listens when the Fruitgrowers Association speaks," conclude the authors of one study, "Congressmen B, C, D, E, and F are indifferent to the pleas of the Association. Congressman B, in turn, might be vulnerable to a second group to which his colleagues A, C, D, E, and F are indifferent. When the patterns of individual vulnerability are overlaid on one another, so to speak, it is clear that relatively few Congressmen are vulnerable to any given group. Individual vulnerabilities cancel each other out to a considerable extent and are lost in the indifference, inertia, and invulnerability of Congress as a whole."[34]

There seem to be two weaknesses in this type of pluralist description of lobbying in Congress. First, the collusion of seemingly disparate groups and trade-offs in different policy areas is downplayed or ignored. Second, there is an assumption that competing groups will prevent any one interest from dominating a particular policy subsystem, that most policy areas involve opposing groups which serve to check the demands of others. Some general studies about group interaction in American politics and specific instances of congressional lobbying illustrate how either collusion among groups or norms of mutual noninterference greatly dilute the idea of groups checking one another.

Murray Edelman's description of management-labor "disputes" shows how even these very different interests may evolve a pattern of settlement which gives each side expanded benefits, and indicates the scope of intergroup collusion:

> A major function of much union-management bargaining in the late fifties and sixties has been to provide a ritual which must be acted out as a prerequisite for the quiescent acceptance of higher prices and higher wages by those directly involved. Nor is it surprising that the rite is most formalized precisely in the industries in which the bargaining and the speculation about the likelihood of a strike are most widely publicized: steel, autos, meat packing, heavy machinery, electronics.[35]

In 1964, the tobacco industry and the American Medical Association joined forces to do battle against health warnings on cigarettes and medicare legislation. The primary source for those who argued for regulating the cigarette industry was the Surgeon General's report linking smoking with cancer. The AMA had earlier halted research on the effects of smoking because it only would have duplicated the government study. But in February 1964, the association accepted a $10 million grant from six cigarette companies to conduct tobacco research. Three weeks later the AMA sent a letter to the Federal Trade Commission opposing the health warning on cigarette packages. "More than 90 million persons in the United States use tobacco in some form," the doctors' group reported, "and, of these, 72 million use cigarettes. . . . The economic lives of tobacco growers, processors, and merchants are entwined in the industry; and local, state, and federal governments are the recipients of and dependent upon many millions of dollars of tax revenue."[36]

Explanations of interest group activity in the legislature which emphasize the countervailing effects of different lobbies underestimate the power of these coalitions. Although an individual congressman may not be vulnerable to any given group, if many groups get together to support each other's legislative goals they may represent a political force which no elected official can ignore.

Group theorists who talk of countervailing interests also generally assume that there is some sort of representational balance which produces the "public interest." But again, studies of interest representation in Congress do not support such a view. In congressional hearings on tax laws, for instance, "there is practically no one, except perhaps the Treasury, available to represent the public." As William Cary observes:

> Perhaps the reason is that all of the pressure group proposals are of such character that no one of them would have a large adverse effect on the tax bill of any individual. Hence counter-pressure groups seldom develop.
>
> A second reason why the public is not more frequently represented is the difficulty of forming pressure groups around general interests. The concentration of business organizations on appeals brought to Congress and the emphasis placed on specific and often very technical information makes it difficult even for the members of the tax committees to secure a balanced view of what is the general interest, what the public wants or, indeed, what the public would want if it were informed as to the facts.[37]

A Ways and Means staffer made a similar point after watching futile efforts to generate public support for tax reform in 1963: "The average American doesn't mind other people having their own loopholes—he only cares about getting his."[38]

The organized interests who do lobby in Congress are, generally speaking, economic groups concerned with aspects of production. Larger public groups such as consumers or those who would benefit from tax reforms are not organized as effective lobbies. This is so both because of the size of these groups and because members are not motivated to pay the costs necessary for obtaining a policy benefit which would go to all members of a particular group regardless of their activity in behalf of the group. It is not "rational," for instance, for a consumer to devote a lot of time lobbying for reduced food prices; they represent only a fraction of his total budget, and he will share in any reduced prices whether he has worked to bring them about or not. It is "rational" for the producers of a particular commodity to organize, however, because these prices represent total income and are worth the costs of organization.[39]

Organized economic interests are able to get tangible rewards from the legislature, not by bribing legislators, but rather by using the advantages which the political system gives them. By providing information which reinforces the position of their supporters, by relying on inside lobbyists, by invoking legislative norms and political values which strengthen their position, and by working in conjunction with other political elites for shared benefits, these groups are able to benefit from policies coming out of particular subsystems.

But, as this general review of lobbying in Congress has shown, there is not complete agreement as to the effects of lobbying on legislators' behavior and the content of legislative policies. Sometimes those who emphasize the great influence of pressure groups seem to be right. At other times those who downplay their importance seem more nearly correct. It is time, then, to recognize that different types of policies are handled in different ways by Congress, and that these differences greatly affect the relative influence of lobbyists on legislation.[40] In the next few pages I have organized the discussion in terms of Lowi's classification of policy types and drawn on some studies of interest group activities in different policy areas. The purpose here is not to present an authoritative statement on lobbying in Congress, but rather to show the great variety of interest group behavior and influence. By employing Lowi's framework, it is hoped that some of the seeming contradictions about the importance of lobbyists in Congress will be cleared up.

Distributive Policies and Pressure Groups

A glance back at Figure 1 will remind you that distributive policies are those which generally involve the awarding of material benefits to some narrow segment of the general population. Awarding federal funds for the development of a harbor or building a bridge, maintaining or reducing postal rates for bulk mailers, granting tax loopholes for certain industries or occupations, keeping price supports at a certain level for particular crops, or awarding defense contracts or military bases to a congressman's district are all examples of this type of policy. They are generally characterized by the government's giving something away. And the politics of distributive policies focuses more on "Who gets what?" than it does on "Who pays?"

When we look at those accounts of lobbying in Congress which stress the influence of groups on policy outcomes we find that the vast majority of them are dealing with issues which are distributive. Both the Nader group study and Drew Pearson and Jack Anderson's *The Case Against Congress* sprinkle their descriptions of lobbying with examples drawn from distributive policy areas. The authors of *Who Runs Congress?* talk about the oil lobby, the military armaments lobby, the tobacco lobby, the automobile lobby, and the National Rifle Association among others. Their picture of lobbying is perhaps best illustrated in their character-ization of the oil lobby as one which "has plenty to gun with."

> When fully mobilized, oil can send into action lawyers from the most respectable law firms, public relations consultants, numer-ous ex-government officials, newsmen who serve as "advisors," company executives, corporate legal departments, government officials in several of the executive departments, trade associa-tion representatives, and—though only a small fraction of the total—men who actually register as lobbyists. Whenever legisla-tion affecting oil is on the docket, the oilers can easily afford to have a corporate vice-president or similarly impressive offi-cial assigned to persuade every member of every relevant com-mittee. If reinforcements should be needed, the industry can call on a vast reserve of sales agents, filling station operators, and other small businessmen.[41]

Pearson and Anderson's description of lobbyists' success in getting tax loopholes written into law in 1966 provides an even more lurid picture of the impact lobbyists can have on policy:

> It started through the legislative mill innocently enough as a tax measure to help the elderly. By the time it reached the Sen-ate floor, it was loaded down with forty-nine riders, none of them germane, most of them intended as Christmas gifts for the lobbyists' clients. Only the elderly wound up with nothing.
>
> Perhaps the most glittering ornament, worth an estimated $2 million to Harvey Aluminum Company, was strung on the Christmas tree by Senator Vance Hartke, D-Ind. This provided a retroactive tax reduction for the company by extending the investment tax credit to the Virgin Islands, where Harvey was building an aluminum plant. The company has no holdings in Hartke's home state, but its man in Washington, Keith Linden, has helped Hartke raise campaign funds. It was a strange pres-ent to a strange company.
>
> The lobbyists for three other giant metal firms—Anaconda, Reynolds Metals and Alcoa—petulantly demand equal favors from Santa Claus. Anaconda's lobbyist, Henry Gardiner, spoke to Senator Herman Talmadge, D-Ga., about increasing the depletion allowance on the Georgia clay from which the com-pany extracted aluminum. Reynolds and Alcoa hurried over to

the office of Senator J. William Fullbright, D-Ark., and demanded similar deals on Arkansas ores which they happened to be mining. "There was agreement among the three companies, I'll be blunt about that," admitted a Talmadge aide. "We thought it would help us. Ways and Means Chairman Wilbur Mills is from Arkansas, and he was the key man on the House side." On Christmas morning, the three big metal manufacturers were not disappointed; each received a sugar plum in the form of higher depletion allowances on aluminum ores.

The clay pipe industry, feeling left out, appealed to Hartke, who did more Christmas tree trimming than anyone else. He attached an amendment tripling the industry's depletion allowance. "The suggested wording," admitted the National Clay Pipe Institute's G. A. Robinson, "came from our depletion committee." The approach to Hartke, however, was made by Edward Clements, head of Can-Tex Industries of Cannelton, Indiana, which manufactures clay sewer pipes.

While he was decorating the tree, Hartke also added an excise tax reduction for hearses. He explained to the Senate, deadpan, that the tax break was needed to revive "a dying industry." Lawyer lobbyist William Geoghegan acknowledged that he had asked Hartke to sponsor the amendment. As justification, he explained that most hearses are made in Indiana and Ohio.

A group of deprived clay, shale and slate producers from Kansas took *their* hard-luck story to Senator Frank Carlson, R-Kans., who, in the Christmas spirit, arranged a small increase in *their* depletion allowance. And Russell Long, as the Senate Santa in charge of decorating the Christmas tree, could hardly return to his native Louisiana without something for the home folks. As an appropriate bauble, Lieutenant General Walter K. Wilson, Jr., the retired chief of the Army Engineers, helpfully suggested raising the depletion allowance for clam and oyster shells. He had taken a sudden interest in the tax status of the mollusks after joining Southern Industries, which processes oyster shells for cement. To the rejoicing of Louisiana's clam and oyster shell producers, Long tripled their depletion allowance from 5 to 15 percent.[42]

More systematic studies of legislative action on tax bills lend some support to the vivid descriptions of lobbyists' influence in this policy process. Both John Pechman and John Manley discuss the important role groups play in making sure that special tax provisions are maintained or inserted in tax bills before Congress. These loopholes most often come in the form of amendments to the bill and are generally inserted on the Senate floor. Senators proposed 111 amendments, and accepted 70, to the 1969 Tax Reform Act in less than two weeks of debate.[43] The importance of these special tax provisions cannot be overstated. They create a system in which small businessmen and wage earners pay about 20 percent of their gross income in federal income taxes, the average corporation pays almost 50 percent and the large oil refiners pay less than 10 percent.[44] In 1963, these myriad loopholes accounted for $6.4 billion in revenue lost to the Treasury.[45] Patterns of committee selection and committee structure and the differing roles of the two chambers in the policy process, which were discussed in earlier chapters, also tend to reinforce the access which special interests have to legislators involved with tax legislation.

Other examples of lobbyists directly influencing legislators and policies tend to come from similarly distributive policy fields. In 1972, a former senator from Maryland was found guilty of accepting an unlawful gratuity from a Washington lobbyist to influence his vote on postal rate legislation. The lobbyist represented a Chicago mail business to whom every one-penny increase in third class postal rates would cost $1 million a year. During the trial the senator's former chief assistant described his legislative office as "one where lobbyists wrote speeches, where a Federal job was purchased for cash, where money flowed into his and the Senator's pockets and where the Senator's signature was so widely copied by staff members that they even signed it to (the Senator's) final divorce decree."[46] Postal rates, like tax loopholes, are distributive policies in the sense that they have an important impact on only a narrow segment of the society (bulk mailers) and that the most intensively concerned interests are producer interests.

Farm price supports provide another example of policies which are influenced by single-issue economic interests. In addition, this policy area illustrates how the concept of representation and committee structure may make the need for overt lobbying by concerned interests unnecessary. As we saw in Chapter 4, the House Agriculture Committee is very much a "constituency" committee: congressmen tend to sit on commodity subcommittees which permit them to have some say over price supports for crops which are important in their districts. The distribution of benefits which this system produces is similar to that of tax loopholes. Most of the benefits go to the biggest economic interests in the constituencies. A recent study showed, for instance, that the wealthiest 25 percent of the farmers received 75 percent of the subsidy payments. Thus, in 1968, the largest 264 farms received $52 million in government aid, as did the 540,000 smallest farms. "This meant an average government payment of $197,000 to the wealthiest farmers, an average of $96 for the half million small farmers,"[47]

We do not presently have enough studies of lobbyists and legislators covering a sufficiently wide array of different policy areas to make sound generalizations about the overall impact on legislative policies. But when we encounter statements like this: "It's like there's a bushel basket in the middle of the table. Everybody is trying to throw as many of their things into the barrel as they can," there is a good chance that the speaker is describing a distributive policy-making process.[48] Similarly, when we see descriptions which emphasize the influence of lobbyists on legislation or when we hear congressmen suggest that they are not subjected to much "pressure" to vote one way or another, it is likely that legislative politics dealing with a distributive issue is the subject of attention. For the nature of interest group activity in distributive policy-making is such that there are both close links between concerned economic interests and members of relevant committees or subcommittees and that the narrow scope of the issue provides that only a limited number of lawmakers need be directly involved.

The outline presented in Table 1 provides a summary of interest group activity in the distributive policy arena. There are a large number of small, intensely organized interests based on narrow economic grounds; these groups pursue their interests in a low-conflict political process which stresses the norm of mutual noninterference; when coalitions form, they consist of unlike interests brought together through a logrolling process; and the primary focus is on the subcommittee or committee which has jurisdiction over that policy area.

Regulatory Policies and Pressure Groups

Those who study Congress often bring with them the distributive model of lobbying in their research. As Lewis Anthony Dexter notes, " 'pressure' and 'pressure politics' are regarded by most 'sophisticated' people today as 'explaining' a great deal that happens."[49] There is the expectation that affected interests will marshal their forces to directly influence congressmen on the matter, and that the level of lobbying activity will be related to the economic stakes which those interests have in the issue. The authors (Raymond Bauer, Ithiel de Sola Pool, and Lewis Anthony Dexter) of a prize-winning book on trade policy, for example, have pointed out that they "started with the notion that public officials would see themselves as under almost constant pressure from those who have a stake in the decisions they make."[50]

But what sometimes happens is that these scholars find much less lobbying (in the distributive sense) than they expected. This happened with the 1963 study of trade policy, and with a more recent study of the 1970 Political Broadcast Act limiting campaign spending. In the latter, the authors observe: "Probably the most striking aspect of pressure group activity in this case was the lack of it. Considering the importance of the measure and the potential impact of the various versions of the bill upon the broadcasting industry, it is somewhat surprising that more intense lobbying did not occur."[51] Lowi suggests that the reason Bauer, Pool, and Dexter found little pressure group activity in their study of postwar trade policies is because trade policy, which had long been regarded as distributive policy, was becoming regulatory in the 1950s and 1960s. Instead of being conceived as domestic policy which was designed to serve the interests of a vast array of unrelated native industries, trade policy came to be regarded as an instrument of foreign policy which required cohesion and the application of a general rule to all trade decisions. A look at Table 1 again will indicate how interest group activity in the case of regulatory policies differs from that of distributive policies.

In regulatory policy-making, interest groups are based on shared attitudes rather than just narrow economic interests. Coalitions of groups are formed through a bargaining process of conflict and compromise over goals rather than a logrolling process which produces mutual noninterference in each group's seeking its own goals. These coalitions change with different issues, but all groups in a coalition seek to build a majority on the issue by compromising with other groups in the coalition. Lastly, these groups focus their activity on the whole chamber and not just the concerned committees.

Suggested in Table 1 as some examples of regulatory policies are trade policies since the 1960s, federal aid to education, campaign finance regulations, and medicare. By drawing on case studies dealing with these types of policies, we can provide some general observations about the nature of pressure group activity in regulatory policy-making.

First, a characteristic of interest group activity in the regulatory arena seems to be that groups are seeking broad social goals and not just their own economic advantage. Congress passed the Medicare Bill in 1965. All studies of this public health legislation point to the importance of the AFL-CIO's campaign. Says one: "It [medicare] was carried by the AFL-CIO all the way to the bill-drafting stage, and for the first few months, at least, it had only nominal sponsorship by a congressman who had doubts about it and did little to promote it."[52]

The battle over medicare produced coalitions of interest groups that were concerned with more than just the immediate delivery of benefits from the government. On one side was a coalition made up of the AFL-CIO, the National Council of Senior Citizens, and members of the Democratic political coalition and administration. The coalition of opposition included the American Medical Association (which reported spending several millions of dollars), the American Dental Association, the American Hospital Association, and the American Nursing Homes Association. The fact that medicare was passed and that the AFL-CIO won, gives credence to the Nader group's evaluation of the effectiveness of the labor lobby that "labor has been stymied on many strictly labor issues, where the unions find themselves without allies, but has had some striking successes as part of coalitions working on broader social issues."[53] The essence of these interest group coalitions which form around regulatory policies seems to be the fact that they are based on a shared attitude toward some broad policy issue and not just collections of people who agree to stay out of each other's affairs.

When we consider regulatory policies and lobbying, another characteristic comes to mind which might help to explain the fact that there is seldom a feeling among congressmen that they are being "pressured" to vote a particular way in an immediate sense. And that is that coalitions of interests on regulatory policies tend to form a long time before a bill on the issue is subject to a vote.

A case study of the Elementary and Secondary Education Act of 1965 reports that "the private groups that had represented the varieties of opinion on federal aid legislation began their realignment a full year before the Eighty-ninth Congress convened."[54] Similarly, labor group activity in behalf of medicare began nine years before the legislation was passed.

This early formation of coalitions on regulatory policies is related both to the need to develop compromise positions among members of the coalition and to the fact that these interest groups must deal with bills when they reach the chamber floor and not just in their committee or subcommittee stage. Reaching a compromise position among different elements in a coalition obviously takes longer than mobilizing interests with the same economic base. For there is bound to be some disagreement about political attitudes on broad policy, while all members of the same economic interest can readily agree on their shared interests. Effective lobbying on regulatory policies also involves the mobilization of public opinion and the building of a broader base of support than does lobbying for distributive issues.[55] Both processes take more time than do those associated with distributive policies where interested groups need only make sure that they have the standing commitment of subcommittee and committee decision-makers. In addition, effective lobbying for regulatory policies entails utilizing the internal cue network of Congress in which legislative colleagues lobby one another and public opinion campaigns reinforce the congressman's feeling that he is supporting constituency interests.

A classic statement of pressure groups and distributive policies was E. E. Schattshneider's 1935 study, *Politics, Pressure, and the Tariff.*[56] The author uncovered a lobbying process which sought to keep the boundaries of conflict limited to appropriate subcommittees, took the form of logrolling, and relied on a standing pattern of agreement between industries seeking tariff protection and subcommittee members. The differences between this type of pressure group activity and that which we find in regulatory areas are summed up in the case study of recent federal aid to education legislation. "Our observation of the education issue in 1965–67 does not accord with Schattshneider's major theme of the pressure groups coercing Congress into action along lines they desire." "Rather," the authors note, "we saw the network of forces surrounding the Congress and education pressure groups blending into a policy climate that required certain prior arrangements among the pressure groups in order for Congress to act out its role."[57]

Once again, we become aware of the gap between general statements about lobbying and Congress and case studies of specific policies. There still are not enough studies on lobbying to provide comprehensive understanding of this part of the legislative process and the impact on policies. But this comparison between distributive and regulatory policy-making and the role of interest groups in each does suggest that some of the disparities among the different pictures of pressure groups' influence on legislation that we do have stem from the fact that people are talking about different types of policies. Let us continue this train of thought by looking at the last type of policy discussed in the Lowi essay and seeing what the pattern of lobbying in Congress is there.

Redistributive Policies and Pressure Groups

The earlier types of policy we looked at represent the "normal" ones handled by the legislative system. Redistributive policies, on the other hand, come along less often and are seen as policies to meet some crisis. We would expect, therefore, the nature of politics surrounding redistributive policies to be quite different from the politics of distributive or regulatory policies. Stephen Bailey has characterized "normal" legislative politics this way: "In the absence of a widely recognized crisis, legislative policy making tends to be fought out at the level of largely irresponsible personal and group stratagems and compromises based upon temporary power coalitions of political, administrative, and non-governmental interests."[58] Redistributive policies are handled in a different way. They are designed to meet some crisis, whether it is widespread unemployment and economic stagnation, patterns of racial discrimination, or extensive poverty in a seemingly wealthy society.

There are in the political science literature on Congress some fine case studies to which we can turn in attempting to sketch out how pressure groups influence legislative policies of a redistributive type. Stephen Bailey's *Congress Makes a Law* looks at the Employment Act of 1946; Daniel Berman's *A Bill Becomes a Law* deals with civil rights legislation in the early 1960s; and there are a number of studies of the 1964 poverty program which provide useful descriptions of the legislative policy process.[59]

Briefly, we can say this about legislative politics surrounding redistributive policies: the group conflict involves large coalitions made up of "peak associations" (such as the National Association of Manufacturers, the Chamber of Commerce, the AFL-CIO) which share a broad consensus on goals to be achieved; both sides of the conflict advance ideological, rather than self-interest, arguments; much of the discussion revolves around the possible long-term effects of the proposed policies; and the president generally plays an active role in the legislative process.

In discussing pressure group activity surrounding the Employment Act of 1946, Bailey devotes a chapter to the "Lib-Lab Lobby," which he sees as being similar to the broad reform coalition of Liberal and Labour interests operating in late nineteenth century Britain. The 1946 "Lib-Lab Lobby" consisted primarily of the Union for Democratic Action, the CIO political action committee, the American Federation of Labor, and an ad hoc collection of interests known as the Continuations Group. A simple listing of the organizations represented in this Continuations Group shows the breadth of this coalition. Included were: the American Federation of Labor; Americans United for World Organization; the Brotherhood of Maintenance of Way Employees; the Brotherhood of Railway Trainmen; Business of America, Inc.; the Congress of Industrial Organizations; the Council for Social Action of the Congregational Christian Churches; the Independent Citizens Committee of the Arts, Sciences, and Professions; the National Association for the Advancement of Colored People; the Y.W.C.A.; the National Catholic Welfare Conference; the National Conference of Jewish Women; the National Farmers Union; the National Women's Trade Union League of America; the Railway Labor Executive Association; the Union for Democratic Action; and the National League of Women Shoppers.[60] In addition, support for the bill came from a variety of other groups such as university professors; religious, racial, and educational groups; veterans; welfare workers; the National Lawyers Guild; and independent businessmen. Opposition to the bill also drew on a broad coalition of interests including the National Association of Manufacturers, Chambers of Commerce, the Committee for Constitutional Government, and the American Farm Bureau Federation.

Pressure group activity for the Civil Rights Act of 1964 and the poverty program show a pattern similar to that of the Employment Act. The most active lobby for civil rights legislation was the Leadership Conference on Civil Rights which was a broad coalition of labor, liberal, race, and church groups. By 1963, a total of 79 organizations were represented in the Leadership Conference. The endless parade of witnesses for the bill provided by the Leadership Conference led one southern congressman to scold those "cardinals, bishops, elders, stated clerks, common preachers, priests, and rabbis" coming to Washington to support the bill.[61] When a House subcommittee began hearings on the Economic Opportunity Act of 1964, the lead-off witnesses supporting the measure included the Secretaries of Defense, Labor, Commerce, Agriculture, HEW, and the Attorney General. "Later, spokesmen for an impressive range of civic, welfare, and religious groups appeared to endorse the bill. AFL-CIO President George Meany and the National Urban League's executive director, Whitney Young, Jr., led off, followed by representatives of such groups as the National Council of Churches, the National Catholic Welfare Council, the National Education Association, the American Public Welfare Association, the National Farmers Union, the National Grange, the American Friends Service Committee, and the General Federation of Women's Clubs."[62]

We saw earlier that pressure group activity for regulatory policies differed from that of distributive policies. When a distributive issue is involved, the outside interests seeking to influence Congress generally represent a single economic interest or industry which is seeking only to maximize the benefits it receives from government. There is a little concern for what others are doing, and any group coalitions that do form are based on an agreement not to interfere with each other's interests. Regulatory policies, however, saw some broadening of group goals and a tendency for groups sharing some common social policy to compromise their differences and jointly seek legislative action. The nature of group activity in relation to redistributive policies is a continuation of this expansion of the scope of the conflict and the breadth of the coalitions involved. This is clearly seen in the above descriptions of the composition of pressure group alliances formed over the Employment Act, Civil Rights Acts, and the Economic Opportunity Act. Differences in the structure of the group conflict are also accompanied by differences in the form of the debate.

Arguments advanced by both sides in considering redistributive policies are much broader and ideological than those put forward in debates over distributive policies ("this is in the interest of cotton growers, the construction industry, etc.") or regulatory policies ("this is in the interest of certain broad segments of the population such as school children or the elderly"). The participants in redistributive policy-making invoke broad ideological symbols such as "free enterprise," "the right to work," or "political freedom versus totalitarianism." A sampling of the arguments put forward in the Employment Act and Civil Rights Act debates clearly shows the ideological nature of the debate and a concern for the possible long-term effects of these policies.

The hearings of the House committee on the Employment Act contained the following statement issued by the Ohio Chamber of Commerce:

> The Communist-sparked C.I.O.-P.A.C., aided by its political fellow-travelers, is now making the drive which has been in preparation for years. Everything that has happened up to now has been but a preliminary.
>
> This is the hour, almost the moment, of historic decision. The basic goal of C.I.O.-P.A.C. is to overturn our system of competitive, private enterprise and substitute for it complete government control over capital and labor alike. . . .
>
> Keystone of the new group of "crisis" legislative enactments, devised by the same cunning brains that have guided this boasted bloodless revolution, is the full employment bill, now being seriously considered in Washington.
>
> Labeled in fraud and deception as a bill designed to preserve private enterprise, if enacted, it would be the scaffold on which private enterprise could be dropped to its death. . . .[63]

The Committee for Constitutional Government, in opposing the bill, said that it "may turn America permanently from constitutional private enterprise toward a system of collective statism."

The National Association of Manufacturers talked about "state socialism" in their literature against the bill. And other opponents emphasized the potential long-term effects of the bill in suggesting that "there is an implicit threat that if 'free private enterprise' cannot supply jobs, then the task will be taken over by the government. The final step would be for the government to provide all the employment there is."[64]

The conflict over civil rights legislation reveals the same sort of emphasis on ideological concerns. Proponents of legislation talked in terms of constitutional guarantees, equality, and the moral responsibilites of the government. Those who opposed the various bills invoked the same values of freedom from federal government coercion seen in the Employment Act debate. A quick quote, again, seems the best way to capture the tone of the debate:

> We can keep our country free if we keep our elections free. We cannot keep our elections free if the electorate is to be determined by registration officials who owe their allegiance to a President who owes his allegiance to a political party which elected him. To those who think otherwise, I would point out the stark fact of history that Adolf Hitler's dictatorship became absolute when he was given power to appoint members of the German Reichstag.[68]

Assorted quotes are not, of course, sufficient evidence to prove or disprove any proposition. At best, they can only suggest a pattern. But it does seem clear that redistributive policy-making is not the same as distributive or regulatory policy-making. And part of the difference is reflected in pressure group activities and their influence on legislative policy.

In the first sections of this chapter we had a look at some of the different evaluations of pressure groups' impact on legislative policy. They ranged from "no impact" to "a great deal"; from pictures of benign lobbyists helping the congressman do a better job, to conspiratorial rumblings about boodlers, bagmen, and sell-outs to the highest bidder. By recognizing that different types of policies are handled in different ways, we have perhaps made a small step toward understanding the contradictory reports about lobbyists and legislators. Pressure groups do have some influence, but the nature and effectiveness of that influence will vary with the type of policy being considered. Senator Borah was not lying when he said that he "hadn't seen any lobbyists around here this year," nor was Senator Richard Russell when he talked about the "most intensive, extensive, and effective lobby assembled in Washington in many years."[66] They were talking about different types of legislative policy-making.

So the conclusion is mixed: on some types of issues pressure groups do seem to be able to influence the votes of legislators and the eventual policy outcome; on others, "special interests," pressure groups, and lobbyists are relatively ineffective. The same sort of discrepancies that we find in the literature on lobbies exist in studies of the influence of the president and the executive branch, other "outside actors" on legislative policy-making. And again, consideration of the different types of politics surrounding different types of policies is useful for some understanding of the role of the president in legislative policy-making. So let us conclude this chapter with a look at the executive role in the congressional policy process.

EXECUTIVE IMPACT ON LEGISLATIVE POLICIES

The Ralph Nader Congress Project's book, *Who Runs Congress?*, says that "no matter how hard the Congress may struggle on one issue, it is overwhelmed by the vastly greater forces of the presidency. Whether Congress wins or loses, the president ends up on top."[67] Yet a study published the same year concludes: "Congress in the 1960s did not docilely accept and ratify the defense policy positions of the executive. On the contrary, it played a relatively lively role in particular policies, an activism whose level seemed to be associated with a perceived inadequacy of presidential decisions and actions."[68]

A glance at other discussions of the president and Congress reveals that such contradictory evaluations of presidential influence on legislation are quite common. Some examples:

> It is a simple fact that for the past thirty-six years, Congress has become almost exclusively dependent on the Executive Branch for any forward motion.
>
> If Congress legislates, it subordinates itself to the President; if it refuses to legislate, it alienates itself from public opinion.
>
> Within American political institutions, the center of initiative and decision has shifted from the Congress to the executive.[69]

On the other hand, we have these assessments made by a political scientist, a former White House staffer, and a former president:[70]

> While the legislators do not obstruct, neither do they surrender. At times it has been they who led and the President who followed. The substantial contributions of members of Congress to legislation on air and water pollution, civil rights, education, medicare, and other measures come nearer to genuine partnership than to subordination.
>
> The President does not "control" Congress at any time, not even at periods of great popularity when it is politic for most legislators to go along with him. His true relationship to Congress is basically that of a highly important factor which the legislators must take into account.
>
> The fact is, I think, the Congress looks more powerful sitting here than it did when I was there in Congress. But that is because when you are in the Congress you are one of a hundred in the Senate or one of 435 in the House. So that the power is so divided. But from here I look at a Congress, and I look at the collective power of the Congress, particularly the bloc action, and it is a substantial power.

Assessments of executive influence on legislation, then, show a similarity to assessments of pressure groups' influence on legislation. Some observers, looking at particular instances, find that the president and the executive bureaucracy wield great power; others, focusing on different issues or different periods of time, find that the impact of these outside actors on legislation is not very great. We hear warnings about the president becoming an absolute monarch who can completely ignore Congress and make policies by executive fiat, about an emerging dictatorship of the bureaucrats which would relegate both the president and Congress to minor roles in the policy-making process, and about a powerful but unresponsive Congress which fails to tailor policies to meet pressing social needs and prevents the president from doing so.

Earlier in this chapter we saw that it sometimes helps to understand differing estimates of outside influence on legislative policies by recognizing that different types of policies are handled in different ways by the same political system. Discussions of presidential power relative to Congress are also more valuable when a distinction is made among different types of policies. We find, for instance, that people who stress the president's growing dominance of the policy process often point to foreign policy or strategic defense issues to support their assertions. The use of executive agreements rather than treaties, dispatching troops to the Dominican Republic, and the minor congressional role in making decisions about the war in Vietnam are all excellent cases to support the suggestion that Congress has little say in the policy process. "The United States has one President, but it has two presidencies," says Aaron Wildavsky. "One presidency is for domestic affairs, and the other is concerned with defense and foreign policy. Since World War II, Presidents have had much greater success in controlling the nation's defense and foreign policies than in dominating its domestic policies."[71] In discussing the relative influence of the executive and the legislature over policies, then, it is useful to distinguish between foreign and domestic policies. The president seems to have the upper hand in the first, while Congress is generally agreed to have some say-so over the second.

Another distinction among types of policies is that of Samuel Huntington in *The Common Defense*. He suggests that there are two quite different types of defense policies. One is "strategic" and deals with questions about the strength of military forces, their makeup and ability to be deployed, choices about the development of certain weapons and matters having to do with the development of military forces. The other is "structural" and concerns the amount of money to be spent to maintain overall levels of men and material and how these force levels should be organized. Congress plays a major role in deciding structural issues, but the focus of decision on strategic matters lies within the executive branch. As Huntington notes, "structural issues of military policy are usually handled through what might be termed the domestic legislative process," while strategic issues fit more correctly into the foreign policy category.[72]

Distinguishing between foreign and domestic policies and between strategic and structural defense policies certainly makes sense when talking about the relative influence of the executive and legislative branches on policies. But, I think we might go beyond this and consider different types of domestic policies as well. Lowi's distinction among distributive, regulatory, and redistributive policies again seems useful here. His essay consciously omits foreign policy in classifying different policy types. If we think of the continuum moving from distributive to redistributive policies as reflecting a broadening of the scope of issues and the number of people directly affected by them, however, we might tentatively throw foreign policy and strategic defense issues in with redistributive policies and use the Lowi framework as a way to organize the discussion of executive influence on congressional policies. Again, I should warn that these policy classifications are not mutually exclusive, that there is some overlap among the different categories. What the scheme helps us to do is to move away from overly general statements that Congress has lost all influence over policies to the executive or that the legislative branch maintains a decisive role in all policy-making.

Three major actors need to be considered in any discussion of relative executive-legislative influence on policy: the president and his administration officials, who represent the president's political source of power; the executive bureaucracy, whose source of power is its expertise based on long-term association with a government agency working in some specialized field; and the legislature, which consists of members who represent both expertise in some areas based on extended familiarity with a policy area and a political base which might be quite different from that of the president. We have, in short, a political world which is much more complicated than that represented by evening news shows' portrayals of an ideologically committed president versus a recalcitrant Congress or an arrogant president being held in line by the wisdom of a thoughtful Congress. The battles about who should determine policies are more likely to involve many people in both the executive and legislative branches rather than to be a battle between the president and Congress.

Using the Lowi classification as a starting point, we might venture the following generalizations. Distributive policies are determined chiefly by subgovernments made up of congressional subcommittees and representatives of executive bureaus, with little direct intervention by the president. Regulatory policies are more likely to involve political actors in the president's administration, with the president himself often playing a direct role in the legislative process, and to be decided by the whole Congress rather than by committees or subcommittees. Redistributive domestic policies and foreign policies are settled in a process which comes closest to being one of executive dominance. The executive's near monopoly on information in this last policy category often leaves Congress with a minor role of legitimizing decisions made elsewhere. Having said this, let us now turn to some examples of presidential, bureaucratic, and congressional interaction in these different areas. We shall find again that not all cases fit so neatly into the overall framework nor always support my generalizations about the different types of policy-making. Organizing the discussion in this way does help us to realize, though, that the influence of the executive on legislative policies varies with the types of policies under consideration.

Distributive Policies and Subgovernments

President Kennedy sometimes responded to policy suggestions put forward by friends or advisors with this comment: "Well, I agree with you, but I'm not sure the government will."[73] The "government" to which the president was referring has been variously called "subsystems," "subgovernments," and "whirlpools" by political anlaysts. To understand why some policies come out the way they do we have to look not just at the president and Congress, but at the collection of actors who make up these subgovernments. This includes: "(1) a federal administrative agency within the executive branch; (2) a heavily committed group of congressmen, usually members of a particular committee or subcommittee; (3) a private (or quasi-private) association representing the agency clientele; (4) a quite homogeneous constituency usually composed of local elites."[74]

The types of policies which are dealt with in such subsystems are generally distributive ones: use of public lands, rivers and harbors, agricultural subsidies, and specific tax benefits. Douglass Cater gives us a graphic description of the "tight little subgovernment which rules the nation's sugar economy."

> Political power within the sugar subgovernment is largely vested in the chairman of the House Agricultural Committee who works out the schedule of quotas. It is shared by a veteran civil servant, the Director of the Sugar Division in the U. S. Department of Agriculture, who provides the necessary "expert" advice for such a complex marketing arrangement. Further advice is provided by Washington representatives of the . . . producers.[75]

All farm subsidies reflect the same sort of policy-making by subgovernments. The president generally plays no direct role in the policy process, nor does Congress as a whole. Decisions about how to allocate the bulk of government expenditures through the Department of Agriculture are made by a subgovernment consisting of bureaucrats in the central agency, legislators on appropriate committees and subcommittees, and local farmer committees.

> These self-governing agriculture systems have such institutional legitimacy that they have become practically insulated from the three central sources of democratic political responsibility: (1) Within the Executive, they are autonomous. Secretaries of Agriculture have tried and failed to consolidate or even to coordinate related programs. (2) Within Congress, they are sufficiently powerful within their own domain to be able to exercise an effective veto or to create a stalemate. (3) Agriculture activities and agencies are almost totally removed from the view of the general public.[76]

All of the characteristics we associate with distributive policies are there in such discussions of policy-making by subgovernments. The nature of the overall policy is such that it can be separated into component parts and dealt with in piecemeal fashion. Only special segments of the general population are concerned with the policy outcome. The policy is a low-visibility one which carries with it no great political implications for the president or most congressmen. The normal legislative process for dealing with such policies is that of logrolling, of gaining support from unconcerned interests in return for support on other issues important to them. Because the outcome is of no great moment for either the president or for most congressmen, influence over distributive policies goes, by default, to bureaucrats, some legislators, and interest groups who do have a stake in the policy outcome.

Distributive policy-making, then, is not one which reflects a growing dominance of the president in legislative decision-making. For the most part, he stays out. If we want to find out who does determine the eventual policy outcome in these areas, we should look to both the executive and legislative bureaucracy. For the currency of power in distributive policy decisions seems to be one of technical information and expertise. The top assistant to a senator captures the essence of this reliance on bureaucrats and their expertise when he observes:

It's not bad enough that the Senators rely so totally on us. We rely on the executive branch's bureaucracy downtown. I can't tell you if we need a bill for V.A. benefits until I check with the Veterans Administration. We make hundreds of calls a day to the agencies. All these bills are so complex that we can't understand them without help from the bureaucrats.[77]

The executive impact on distributive policies is not manifested by a strong president's wielding power over congressmen. Rather, it is a process in which "experts" from executive agencies, congressional committees and subcommittees, and concerned interest groups come together to determine who gets what from the government larder. Descriptions emphasizing an overall diminution of legislative influence relative to that of the president's are not accurate portrayals of distributive policy-making. Those who talk about the increasing power of the executive bureaucracy are probably closest to home in describing the distributive policy process. This is not always the case, however, and we will see that the president's influence on legislative policy follows a somewhat different pattern in relation to regulatory and redistributive issues.

Regulatory Policies: Passing Laws and Implementing Them

When we look at the president's role in the policy process dealing with regulatory policies such as medicare or federal aid to education we find that he is more actively involved than was the case with distributive policies. Initiative on such programs generally rests with the president, and when a policy finally emerges it is the product of what James Sundquist calls the "dual legislative process." Policy consideration within the executive branch is similar to that within Congress. "In both branches, information is gathered and appraised, experts are consulted, formal or informal committees are created to draft bills, political prospects and consequences are weighed, and finally decisions are made."[78]

A major difference between distributive policies and regulatory policies, you will recall, is that the former consists of many small decisions affecting only special publics while the latter represents a coordinated, overall policy affecting most or all of the public. The president's role in regulatory policy-making seems to be that of coordinating the different demands made by various interests and shaping some compromise legislative program through a process of bargaining. Studies of the 1965 Elementary and Secondary Education Act illustrate the president's important coordinating role in the early stages of the legislative process. A central conflict in this case was over whether the bill should apply only to public schools or to parochial schools as well. One study sums up the president's mediating role in observing: "The most significant contribution the President made to the passage of the 1965 act was his initial effort to work out a bill which would appeal to federal aid advocates and avoid the church-state controversy."[79] The bill which came from the White House was said to have "just enough aid to parochial schools to push away the veto of the Roman Catholic Church but not enough to drive away the support of the National Education Association."[80]

Sometimes we find that the president's role in regulatory policy-making goes beyond that of serving to mediate and compromise conflicting demands. President Johnson's activities in behalf of medicare are a case in point. Richard Harris describes the highly visible efforts put forward by Johnson in this case:

> Leaving nothing to chance, President Johnson went on television at eleven o'clock on the morning of March 26th to describe the new bill. After giving a brief account of its provisions, he introduced nine other Democrats—from the House there were Mills, Speaker McCormack, Majority Whip Boggs, and Majority Leader Albert; and from the Senate there were Anderson, Smathers, Majority Leader Mike Mansfield, and Byrd. All but Byrd spoke glowingly of the new measure—even Smathers said, "I'm delighted with the bill." Then the President turned to Byrd, who had opposed all the earlier, and far more modest, versions of the bill, and who, it was feared, as chairman of the Senate Committee on Finance, might hold up the present version by postponing hearings on it.
>
> In a dialogue that Representative Albert described later as not only an outstanding example of the famous "Johnson treatment" but the first instance of it ever to be shown on a national television hookup, the President smiled at Byrd and said, "I know that you will take an interest in the orderly scheduling of this matter and give it a thorough hearing." Byrd looked at nim blankly, whereupon Mr. Johnson asked, "Would you care to make an observation?"

Byrd, who had engaged in many conversations with Presidents but never before with millions of people watching, shook his head. "There is no observation I can make now, because the bill hasn't come before the Senate," he replied gruffly. "Naturally, I'm not familiar with it."

President Johnson pressed on. "And you have nothing that you know of that would prevent (hearings) coming about in reasonable time, not anything ahead of it in the committee?" he asked.

"Nothing in the committee now," Byrd answered, shifting uneasily.

"So when the House acts and it is referred to the Senate Finance Committee, you will arrange for prompt hearings and thorough hearings?" the President asked, leaning forward intently.

Senator Byrd, in a voice that was barely audible, said, "Yes."[81]

Those who talk about the increasing power of the president to influence legislation, no doubt have such instances as this in mind. But even here the president does not "control" the eventual policy outcome. Rather, he is able to coordinate different elements in the policy initiation stage so as to present Congress with an overall legislative package and to overcome the fragmentation inherent in congressional structure. At times the president visibly invokes the symbol of his representing a truly national constituency and being the spokesman for the general public interest, as in the medicare example above. At other times the president's role is the less visible one of compromising the many group demands made during the policy initiation stage, as in the case of federal aid to education.

A major area of regulatory policy important to this consideration of executive influence is that of expenditures for programs approved by Congress. Because the president is the chief political officer held responsible for maintaining a healthy economy, he may sometimes decide not to spend funds allocated for certain programs. The justification for such impounding of funds is generally that they would exceed the limits of the federal budget and be inflationary. The Nixon administration asked for $2 billion for the food stamp program in 1972; Congress added $200 million more for the program; the president told the Office of Management and Budget to allow only $2 billion to be spent. Congress appropriated $800 million for water pollution control in 1970, yet the administration spent only $262 million. Of the $1 billion appropriated for the same purpose in 1971, the administration spent only $475 million. Urban renewal and mass transit programs showed the same pattern of the executive branch spending less than was appropriated by Congress. The total amount of funds impounded by the executive were found to be $12 billion in 1971.[82] When Congress passed the 1972 Water Pollution Control Act, it appropriated $18 billion to be spent for that purpose, $6 billion more than the president had requested. The president vetoed the bill, but Congress overrode the veto. The president's response was to direct that only $12 billion be spent for the program. Some senators talked about the "presidential arrogance" of such tactics and suggested that the constitutional issue raised by such a practice was grave enough to be a matter for Supreme Court decision.

Whatever the eventual outcome, this practice of the executive determining the real impact of policies by withholding funds and transferring money from one agency to another has been a common practice since World War II and represents another facet of presidential power to affect policies. Although executive impounding of funds is found in both distributive and redistributive areas, it seems to me that the general practice is one which reflects characteristics of regulatory policies more than these others. For while the effects of impounding funds might be felt in specific and narrow programs to give funds to specialized segments of the population, the guiding principle behind such withholdings is the regulatory one of maintaining fiscal integrity and controlling overall government spending.

A final consideration of this section is the implementation of laws passed by Congress. For the real impact of some policies is determined not by how the legislation is worded when it emerges from Congress, but rather how those who implement the policy interpret the legislation. Murray Edelman's *The Symbolic Uses of Politics* is a handy guide for analysis here.

Legislation is framed in what Edelman calls "legal language." This style is one combining definitional ambiguity with superficially precise directives to administrators who must execute the law. The symbolic directives reinforce the general public's belief that its representatives are controlling the activities of the government, while definitional ambiguity permits the "experts" from the executive branch to determine the real impact of policy by defining terms. Let me give you some examples.

The 1938 Food, Drug, and Cosmetic Act was designed to promote "honesty and fair dealing in the interest of consumers." Section 401 of the statute seems to provide quite precise directives about the labeling of ingredients: "In prescribing any definition and standard of identity for any food or class of food in which optional ingredients are permitted, the Secretary shall, for the purpose of promoting honesty and fair dealing in the interest of consumers, designate the optional ingredients which shall be named on the label."[83] The Food and Drug Administration has interpreted this section of the law to mean that the agency could require manufacturers to list "optional ingredients," but could not require them to list "mandatory ingredients" of a particular product. It is the FDA which determines mandatory ingredients, and the way in which an executive agency can make the law is shown by the directive issued by the FDA on January 21, 1966. That directive culminated a successful campaign of twenty-eight years by Coca-Cola and other cola manufacturers to prevent their having to label the fact that their drinks contained caffeine. It read: "Soda water designated by a name including any proprietary name . . . which includes the word 'cola' or a designation as a 'pepper' beverage that, for years, has become well known as being made with kola nut extract and/or other natural caffeine-containing extracts, and thus as a caffeine-containing drink, shall contain caffeine in a quantity not to exceed 0.02 percent by weight." By making caffeine mandatory, the FDA permitted the cola manufacturers to escape from the labeling provisions of the law. This same pattern is demonstrated by the FDA's list of "permissible ingredients," over 200 different ingredients which may be added to food without being listed on the label. Congress passed the law, but it is the executive agency which really determines what that law is by giving meaning to the ambiguous language of the statute.

Another example of executive "lawmaking" was uncovered by Representative Silvio Conte in the spring of 1970. The Massachusetts Republican was shocked to find that nearly $160 million worth of military supplies had been shipped to Nationalist China during the previous year. This did not seem to be in keeping with congressional intent, as the Military Assistance Program had been subject to continually diminishing authorizations by Congress. Authorized spending for the program had dropped from a high of almost $6 billion in 1952, to $350 million for 1971. Yet the normal procedures for congressional control seemed to have been followed: Congress had appropriated precise dollar amounts to particular countries, and annual reports had been submitted to Congress listing spending for particular programs. Administrators of the program felt that these authorizations were not "adequate to permit optimum use of military assistance." "Therefore," the Defense Department noted, "efforts along other lines to augment the amount of material which may be used to increase that support are proving productive. One such source is Department of Defense stocks in long supply and excess."[84] Equipment which is declared used military surplus has an assigned utility value one-third that of the new equipment. By working within the statutory ambiguity present even when precise dollar amounts are listed, executive branch administrators were able to triple the amount of military assistance provided.

This bending of the law and distortion of legislative intent does not occur because of secret cabals working in the night. Rather, it takes place in an atmosphere crowded with information and open exchanges between executive and legislative officials. The military assistance case, for instance, was one in which the Defense Department had submitted to Congress voluminous classified and unclassified reports on the military assistance program. "It's not our fault if people don't bother to read them," said one Defense Department expert after the Conte exposé. Reading is one thing and understanding another. Even if congressmen were to read the reports of agencies administering the laws, it is doubtful that they could understand many of the details of administration. "The agencies' work is pretty technical," confessed one legislator. "Most of us just don't know enough about it to even begin to ask intelligent questions." Listen to a senator on the problems of controlling administrative agencies:

> Even when we suspect something's not right (in the agencies) what can we do about it? It would take forever to really get into the thing. First we'd get a long run-around in and out of the statute. There's always some little provision that nobody

knew was there, except the bureaucrat who pulls it out of the hat—"but, Senator, the law does require that we do such and such." Before we finish they have us thinking it's all because of the terrible law we wrote and nothing at all to do with how they treated it.[85]

We will see many of the same patterns in our consideration of redistributive and foreign policy-making. But let us first summarize the general characteristics of executive influence over regulatory policies which we have looked at. First, the president plays a more direct and active role in regulatory policy-making than he did in distributive policies. Sometimes this is chiefly a coordinating role of bringing in various interests' demands in the bill drafting stage and working out a compromise through a bargaining process. At other times, the president plays a more public role and uses his office to build support for a measure pending in Congress. The executive also influences these policies through their implementation. The president's withholding of funds appropriated for specific programs can permit him to buck the will of Congress and to determine, by himself, what the level of government effort in these areas shall be. The executive bureaucracy can also influence congressional policies by determining what the language in a bill means as far as its implementation. As we move from distributive to redistributive policies, then, we find that the president's influence increases. The expanded power of the executive which we have seen in the regulatory area becomes even more pronounced when we look at redistributive and foreign policy-making.

Presidential Influence over Redistributive and Foreign Policies

Both domestic redistributive policies and foreign policies are somehow "different" from those that we have been considering. Many of the distributive and regulatory issues discussed so far are relatively unimportant, the sort of thing that presidents might ignore without serious repercussions. Most domestic policies in the United States, if they represent change at all, are incremental in nature. They are what one political scientist has called "experimental adjustments to an existing situation."[86] But both redistributive policies and foreign policies carry with them the sense of being irrevocable. They call for basic decisions which will in turn affect other policies for a long time in the future, and they are seen as commitments to follow through with basic value decisions involved in that one particular choice. Earlier in this chapter I mentioned the fact that the tone of policy debate over redistributive policies is determined more by what the policy "might lead to" than by what the immediate policy decision could involve in the more distant future. There is, then, a sense of importance about redistributive issues which greatly surpasses that of distributive or regulatory policies. The same sort of aura hangs about foreign policy decisions. As President Kennedy observed: "Domestic policy . . . can only defeat us; foreign policy can kill us."[87]

Because of the great importance attached to such decisions, we find that both redistributive and foreign policies are not generally determined in a political process demonstrating either the logrolling we saw in distributive policy-making or the bargaining we saw in regulatory policy-making. For these types of policies require that both Congress and the president make some *overall* commitment to the general direction of policy in that area. There is no room to say "Yes, but . . ." or to accept parts of a policy while delaying decision on others to a future time, in order to reach an immediate compromise. This overall coherence of redistributive and foreign policies is further reflected in the ideological slant to the debate surrounding them. In earlier parts of this chapter we saw the ideological nature of the arguments presented by interest groups for and against the Employment Act of 1946 and the Civil Rights Act of 1964. Such a characteristic means that political leaders may do one of two things. Either they disagree with the basic value premises embodied in a policy proposal and fight it on ideological grounds or they accept the basic ideological framework and concern themselves with the best means for achieving the accepted end. In either case, congressmen are in an inferior position relative to the president. If they choose to fight on ideological grounds they face an elected official who can claim to represent the general electorate's basic ideological sense of direction, no matter how crudely expressed. If they accept the executive's delineation of goals, they are subjected to the fact that the executive branch has overwhelmingly superior sources of information on which to base his specification of means for best achieving those agreed-upon ends.

Those who talk about growing presidential domination of Congress in the policy process, then, are probably closest to the mark in defining the existing redistributive and foreign policy process. For it is here that we find legislators playing a relatively passive role of ratifying decisions made in the executive branch. We said earlier that some examples of redistributive policies were the Economic Opportunity Act of 1964 and the Civil Rights Bill of the same year. Case studies of both of these programs suggest the extent of presidential influence on the eventual outcomes. In discussing the 1964 poverty program, James Donovan notes that "the Congressional role in developing the Economic Opportunity Act was essentially a minor one . . . it was written in the executive branch and subsequently endorsed by Congress."[88] "The most significant feature of the Economic Opportunity Act," report the authors of another study, "was that it was legislated almost entirely within the executive branch and, indeed, virtually without prodding from Congressional or other outside clienteles. . . . Thus, Congress was asked not to draft the war on poverty, but rather, to ratify a fully prepared Administration program, and invited, though hardly encouraged, to propose marginal changes."[89] James Sundquist observes in his review of policies during the sixties: "The war on poverty represents the most extreme case of legislative initiative by the President almost to the exclusion of Congress."[90]

President Johnson's role in securing passage of the Civil Rights Act of 1964 demonstrates both the great influence of the executive in redistributive policies and the aforementioned characteristic of such policies that they be decided *in toto*, with no side bargains to eliminate certain aspects of the issue. One of the best descriptions of the president's role here is provided by Washington journalists, Rowland Evans and Robert Novak:

> Johnson's contribution—and it was a highly significant one—was to pass the Civil Rights bill *without* much horse-trading. "Part III" (giving the federal government power to intervene in Civil Rights cases) had been added to the bill in the House Judiciary Committee and FEPC was adopted on the House floor, bringing the bill up to the highest hopes of the Civil Rights leaders. . . .
>
> Even before the bill passed the House on February 10 by a vote of 290 to 130, Johnson had laid down the no-compromise edict. In a private session in his office with Clarence Mitchell of the NAACP and Joseph Rauh of ADA, Johnson pledged

there would be no changes in the bill even if that required sus-
pending all other activity in the Senate for months.
. . . Johnson reiterated he wanted the Senate to pass the bill
intact.[91]

The relatively minor role which Congress plays in the foreign
policy process has been noted by both legislators and political scientists. Representative Donald Riegle of Michigan talks about his
experiences on the Foreign Operations Subcommittee. "The
House has long since abandoned its responsibility to dig into
policies of the executive branch. While he can be a scrooge on
specific items in the budget, Otto Passman (the subcommittee
chairman) makes it clear he has little interest in pursuing policy
questions, and today he used the reform rules to effectively
squelch any penetrating cross-examination of the Secretary."
Riegle goes on to describe his frustrated attempts to gain information from Secretary of State William Rogers during the latter's
testimony before the subcommittee:

> When my turn came to cross-examine, I thanked the Secretary
> for his initiatives in the Middle East, then asked immediately
> about his testimony before the subcommittee last year, which
> had been stricken verbatim from the public record. Rogers had
> appeared before us six days prior to the U.S. move into Cam-
> bodia. At that time he had indicated, rather forcefully, that the
> U.S. was not contemplating sending troops into Cambodia. He
> said emphatically that such a move would "destroy our Viet-
> namization program." If circumstances changed, he added, and
> the Administration decided to enter Cambodia, either he or
> someone else would surely inform Congress in advance—and
> seek Congressional authorization.
> Six days later the U.S. did precisely what Rogers had said the
> U.S wouldn't do. The Congress had been misled. So this morn-
> ing I read portions of last year's classified transcript aloud and
> asked Rogers why his testimony had been so unreliable. Then
> I asked, "Has sufficient time passed for this material to be de-
> classified and printed in the record?"
> Passman fidgeted and came to the Secretary's defense. That
> testimony should remain classified, he said. It was necessary to
> protect "national security."
> I continued to press Rogers, asking for explanations. He
> smiled and hemmed and hawed and offered only vague and
> indirect responses.
> "The gentleman from Michigan," Passman interrupted, "has
> now consumed *seven* minutes."

Rogers knew my time was up and that I'd have no further chance to cross-examine him this year. He smiled at Passman appreciatively."[92]

James Robinson's study, *Congress and Foreign Policy-Making*, comes to similar conclusions about the minor role played by Congress in this process. "The role of Congress in the U.S. system of government," he suggests, "has been shifting gradually away from the initiation of public policies toward the legitimization and emendation of policies originally devised in the executive branch. This alteration of the major role in the legislative process has been especially notable in foreign affairs."[93]

Studies of defense policies during the 1950s often pointed to a pattern in which Congress had some say-so over the size of the armed forces and the amount of money to be spent on weapon systems, but had little influence over strategic decisions about the deployment and use of those forces. A more recent study by Arnold Kanter shows that Congress does play an active role in determining eventual decisions about procurement and research, development, testing, and evaluation of weapon systems.[94] But, in the case of both strategic defense policies and foreign affairs, congressmen must generally make decisions based only on the information given to them by the executive branch. "Unless the administration volunteers the information, Congress is pretty helpless. We lack the expert staff to do the effective cross-examination needed to get the facts," is the way one representative put it. Other congressmen express similar complaints:

> The terrifying thing is that what we are talking about is the ability of Congress to make decisions on the basis of information furnished by the executive, and the indications are, on relatively superficial study, that in the field of defense we don't have an effective decision making apparatus in the executive. The basic decision is never made by Congress. We may choose between "A" or "B" missile systems, but we never get all the facts to determine whether the choice should then be made between "A" or "B". Perhaps the choice should be "C" or "D."[95]

> There's no real hot line to let you know what is really going on. Sure, if you sat down in Mac Bundy's basement all the time, you'd know as much as he does. But information is lacking. What do you do when they say the Dominican Republic is being taken over by Communists? I looked at the 58 names, too, but they meant nothing to me.[96]

241

The executive branch's control over information required for any effective decision-making gives it a great edge over Congress in these areas. And it is not the sort of imbalance that can be righted by simply expanding congressional staffs and information systems. For as long as the primary source of foreign policy and defense intelligence is located in the executive branch, the legislature can never hope to play a major role in the determination of such policies.

As in the case of pressure groups, we have found that the relative influence on policy exerted by the executive varies with the type of policy under consideration. The extent of executive influence goes from relatively minor influence of the president and control by subgovernments which we found in distributive policy areas to virtual domination by the president and the executive branch which we find in redistributive and foreign policies. We come back, then, to the basic premise stated at the beginning of this chapter: that different policies are handled in different ways by the American political system, and further, that broad statements about Congress being the tool of pressure groups or the president in formulating policies are misleading. Sometimes, these outside groups are found to have a great deal of influence over policy, while at other times their impact is minor.

NOTES

1. American Institute of Public Opinion, June 1944 survey reported in H. Cantril, ed., *Public Opinion, 1935-46* (Princeton University Press, 1951), p. 931. For a good discussion of this focus on legislative process rather than policy, see Donald R. Matthews, "Seminal Research Projects Revisited: The APSA Committee on Congress and the APSA Study of Congress," paper delivered at the 66th Annual Meeting of the American Political Science Association, 1970, pp. 10 and 12.

2. Roger Davidson, David Kovenock, and Michael O'Leary, *Congress in Crisis: Politics and Congressional Reform* (Wadsworth, 1966), pp. 56–57.

3. Robert L. Peabody, "Research on Congress: A Coming of Age," in Peabody and Ralph K. Huitt, *Congress: Two Decades of Analysis* (Harper & Row, 1969) pp. 68–69.

4. Matthews, "Seminal Research Projects Revisited," p. 20. Robert

Peabody also discusses the need for more policy-oriented research in his essay, "Research on Congress: A Coming of Age," pp. 72–73.

5. Stephen K. Bailey, *Congress Makes a Law* (Vintage, 1964); Daniel M. Berman, *A Bill Becomes a Law,* (Macmillan, 1966); John C. Donovan, *The Politics of Poverty* (Pegasus, 1967); Eugene Eidenburg and Roy D. Morey, *An Act of Congress* (W. W. Norton, 1969).

6. The respective quotes are from: Bailey, *Congress Makes a Law*, p. x; Berman, *A Bill Becomes a Law*, p. vii; and Eidenburg and Morey, *An Act of Congress*, p. x.

7. Theodore Lowi, "American Business, Public Policy, Case Studies, and Political Theory," *World Politics*, Vol. 16, no. 4 (July 1964), pp. 677–715.

8. Lowi, "American Business, Public Policy, Case Studies, and Political Theory," pp. 689–690.

9. See, for instance, the essays in Austin Ranney, ed., *Political Science and Public Policy* (Markham, 1968), especially pp. 41–52 and 151–175.

10. See Grant McConnell, *Private Power and American Democracy* (Vintage, 1966), pp. 11ff for a discussion of the *New York World* articles and their effect. The Report of the Association of the Bar of the City of New York's Special Committee on Congressional Ethics, *Congress and the Public Trust* (Atheneum, 1971), pp. 80 ff. discusses Phillips's earlier work.

11. "Mark J. Green, James M. Fallows, and David R. Zwick, *Who Runs Congress?* (Bantam, 1972), p. 32.

12. Drew Pearson and Jack Anderson, *The Case Against Congress* (Pocket Books, 1969), pp. 299–300. Copyright © 1968 by Drew Pearson and Jack Anderson.

13. Quoted in McConnell, *Private Power and American Democracy,* p. 14.

14. Donald R. Matthews, *U.S. Senators and Their World* (Vintage, 1960), p. 177.

15. Congressional Quarterly Service, *Legislators and the Lobbyists* (1968), p. 28. Under the 1946 Federal Regulation of Lobbying Act, organizations must register as lobbyists only if there is *direct* communication with a member of Congress. The language is sufficiently ambiguous that such organizations as the National Association of Manufacturers, the National Association of Home Builders, the National Rifle Association, and the U.S. Chamber of Commerce do not list expenditures. The Nader Congress Project estimated that there were 5,000 or more full time lobbyists

in Washington, or ten for each member of Congress. Green et al., *Who Runs Congress?* p. 30.

16. Matthews, *U.S. Senators and Their World*, p. 178.

17. Representative are Lester Milbraith, *The Washington Lobbyists* (Rand McNally, 1963) and Lewis Anthony Dexter, *How Organizations Are Represented in Washington* (Bobbs-Merrill, 1969).

18. Raymond Bauer, Ithiel de Sola Pool, and Lewis Anthony Dexter, *American Business and Public Policy* (Atherton, 1963), pp. 352–353. Matthews's discussion of the effects of lobbying uses the framework of reinforcement, activation, and conversion. The idea that most votes are decided by elections rather than lobbying is expressed by one lobbyist in *U.S. Senators and Their World*, p. 193:

> Ninety percent of what goes on here during a session is decided on the previous election day. The main drift of legislation is decided then: it is out of our control. There is simply no substitute for electing the right folks and defeating the wrong folks.
>   Our job is a little like that of a football coach. Our material is given. By carefully coaching we can sometimes improve the effectiveness of the material.

19. Gilbert Steiner and Samuel K. Gove, *Legislative Politics in Illinois* (University of Illinois Press, 1960), p. 77. Quoted in Murray Edelman, *The Symbolic Uses of Politics* (University of Illinois Press, 1964), p. 136.

20. Donald Matthews and James Stimson, "The Decision Making Approach to the Study of Legislative Behavior," paper delivered at the annual meeting of the American Political Science Association, New York, 1969; David Kovenock, "Influence in the U.S. House of Representatives: Some Preliminary Statistical Snapshots," paper delivered at annual meeting of the American Political Science Association, Chicago, 1967, p. 22.

21. Edwin M. Yoder, "Washington Report," *Harpers*, June 1970, p. 34.

22. Matthews, *U.S. Senators and Their World*, p. 179; and Lester Milbrath, *The Washington Lobbyists* (Rand McNally, 1963), p. 122.

23. Charles Clapp, *The Congressman: His Work as He Sees It* (Anchor, 1964), p. 203.

24. *Ibid.*, p. 204.

25. Pearson and Anderson, *The Case Against Congress*, pp. 95–96.

26. *Congress and the Public Trust*, pp. 50–51.

27. Matthews, *U.S. Senators and Their World*, p. 178.

28. Stanley Surrey, "The Congress and the Tax Lobbyist—How Special Tax Provisions Get Enacted," *Harvard Law Review,* May 1957, pp. 1155–1156.

29. E. E. Schattschneider, *The Semi-Sovereign People* (Holt, Rinehart & Winston, 1961).

30. Peter Bachrach and Morton Baratz, *Power and Poverty* (Oxford University Press, 1970), p. 44. Grant McConnell discusses attitudes toward government shared by business, labor, and agriculture in *Private Power and American Democracy,* pp. 89ff.

31. For an excellent history of the AMA fight against medicare see Richard Harris, *A Sacred Trust* (Pelican, 1969). Representative Aimé Forand tried to get behind the symbolic smokescreen of "socialized medicine" by asking for a definition of the term:

> DR. LARSON: Mr. Forand, I think it is very difficult to define "socialized medicine." I know of nothing in the record of our Association that would spell out what the Association thinks is socialized medicine.
>
> MR. FORAND: Dr. Allman (President of the AMA) labelled my bill "socialized medicine." I would like to know just what you mean by "socialized medicine."
>
> DR. LARSON: He was speaking as the president of the American Medical Association and as an individual sir. [*A Sacred Trust,* p. 81]

During these hearings the AMA seemed to make the mistake of using, in congressional hearings, political rhetoric designed for mass consumption. Edelman discusses how this backfires in *The Symbolic Uses of Politics,* pp. 123 ff. After the hearings a committee member said:

> They were invited to appear as expert witnesses, but they displayed no expertise at all. I know that I didn't care for their presentation, and a number of my colleagues didn't either. We knew there was something in the air—those millions of old people stirring out in our districts—and some of us were sure that sooner or later a bill like this was inevitable. And the members of the committee who didn't like the bill—by far the majority at the time—were looking to the AMA for some help, some way to defend their position back home. I'm afraid they didn't get anything except the usual hokum. [*A Sacred Trust,* pp. 81–82.]

32. The Taft-Hartley Act says that the National Labor Relations Board cannot use staff members for economic analysis, that the hearing examiner cannot make recommendations in representa-

tion cases, and that the trial examiner in unfair labor practices cannot be present when the board considers the case at which he presided. The promanagement implications of these procedures is noted by Edelman:

> Such provisions quite explicitly bar the board from paying overt attention to certain types of data or points of view, particularly facts and values growing out of observation of what occurred, or allegedly occurred, in the plant. The board is thus encouraged to behave less like an investigating administrative agency and more like a court, confining its attention chiefly to past interpretations of the law. Such ignoring of actual behavior in the plant is practically certain to mean overlooking much of the evidence that an employer charged with an unfair labor practice did things which indicate he has an anti-union bias. [*The Symbolic Uses of Politics,* p. 67.]

33. For an interesting discussion of the corporate bias in policies designed to stimulate economic growth see Kenneth Dolbeare and Murray Edelman, *American Politics: Policies, Power and Change* (D. C. Heath, 1971), pp. 147ff.

34. Andrew Scott and Margaret Hunt, *Congress and Lobbies: Image and Reality* (University of North Carolina Press, 1966), pp. 95–96.

35. Edelman, *The Symbolic Uses of Politics,* p. 60.; Grant McConnell also discusses how the "countervailing power" notion does not apply to union-management interaction in the steel industry:

> The most serious and illuminating example of this is the history of events in the steel industry since the end of World War II. This is a record of repeated contests between the industry, led by the United States Steel Corporation and the United Steel Workers. The outcome of these contests, with slight exceptions, has been a pattern of settlement in which the union has obtained higher wages and the industry has obtained prices sufficiently higher to cover not only the added costs of the wage increases but something additional. Perhaps the most startling feature of this history is that the effects of collaboration between labor and industry have been achieved in the face of genuinely sharp and even bitter hostility between the two sides. [*Private Power and American Democracy,* p. 251.]

36. Pearson and Anderson, *The Case Against Congress,* p. 338. See also, A. Lee Fritschler, *Smoking and Politics* (Appleton-Century-Crofts, 1969).

37. William Cary, "Pressure Groups and the Revenue Code: A Requiem in Honor of the Departing Uniformity of the Tax Laws," *Harvard Law Review*, March 1955, p. 778. A study of testimony before the House Committee on Banking and Currency on federal housing policy showed the same sort of biases in favor of representation of organized economic interests; see Jay S. Goodman, "Federal Policy and Urban Impact" (mimeograph, Wheaton College, 1971).

38. Philip Stern, "The Slow Quiet Murder of Tax Reform," *Harpers*, December 1963, p. 68.

39. For a more complete discussion of these points see Mancur Olson, Jr., *The Logic of Collective Action* (Harvard University Press, 1965).

40. A good discussion of relative interest group activity influence on different policies in the 1950s and 1960s is James Sundquist's in his *Politics and Policy* (The Brookings Institution, 1968), pp. 392ff.

41. Green et al., *Who Runs Congress?* p. 33.

42. Pearson and Anderson, *The Case Against Congress*, pp. 324–325.

43. Joseph Pechman, *Federal Tax Policy* (W. W. Norton, 1971), p. 43. John Manley's, *The Politics of Finance* (Little, Brown, 1970) provides an excellent description of the role of lobbyists' influence over tax legislation.

44. Pearson and Anderson, *The Case Against Congress*, p. 125.

45. Philip M. Stern, *The Great Treasury Raid* (New American Library, 1964), pp. 31–32.

46. *New York Times*, November 18, 1972, p. 20.

47. Nick Kotz, *Let Them Eat Promises* (Anchor, 1971), pp. 43 and 60. Also see Theodore Schultz, *Economic Crisis in World Agriculture* (University of Michigan Press, 1965) and Charles L. Schultz, *The Distribution of Farm Subsidies* (The Brookings Institution, 1971).

48. The statement is by a former committee staff member. Quoted in Green et al., *Who Runs Congress?* p. 40.

49. Lewis Anthony Dexter, "The Representative and His District," in Nelson Polsby and Robert Peabody, eds., *New Perspectives on the House of Representatives* (Rand McNally, 1969), p. 24.

50. Bauer, Pool, and Dexter, *American Business and Public Policy*, pp. 434–435.

51. Robert Peabody, Jeffrey Berry, William Frasure, and Jerry Goldman, *To Enact a Law* (Praeger, 1972), p. 60.

52. Sundquist, *Politics and Policy*, p. 392.

53. Green et al., *Who Runs Congress?* p. 36.

54. Eidenburg and Morey, *An Act of Congress*, p. 60.

55. David Truman discusses these differences between forming an "alliance" and engaging in logrolling in *The Governmental Process* (Alfred A. Knopf, 1962), pp. 362ff.

56. E. E. Schattschneider, *Politics, Pressure, and the Tariff* (Prentice-Hall, 1935).

57. Eidenburg and Morey, *An Act of Congress*, p. 222n.

58. Bailey, *Congress Makes a Law*, p. 236.

59. Sundquist, *Politics and Policy;* Donovan, *The Politics of Poverty;* and John Bibby and Roger Davidson, *On Capitol Hill* (Holt, Rinehart & Winston, 1967), pp. 219–251 are the major sources used for the poverty program discussion.

60. Bailey, *Congress Makes a Law*, pp. 75–76.

61. Berman, *A Bill Becomes a Law*, p. 114 and Sundquist, *Politics and Policy*, p. 268.

62. Bibby and Davidson, *On Capitol Hill*, pp. 239–240.

63. Quoted in Bailey, *Congress Makes a Law*, p. 141.

64. See Bailey, *Congress Makes a Law*, pp. 145, 134, and 130 for the respective citations.

65. Quoted in Berman, *A Bill Becomes a Law*, p. 53.

66. Sundquist, *Politics and Policy*, p. 266.

67. Green et al., *Who Runs Congress?* p. 94.

68. Arnold Kanter, "Congress and the Defense Budget: 1960–1970," *American Political Science Review*, Vol. 66, no. 1 (March 1972), p. 142.

69. The quotes, in order, are from Arthur Blaustein, "536 Characters in Search of a Legislative Program," *Harper's*, March 1969, p. 31; Samuel P. Huntington, "Congressional Responses to the Twentieth Century," in David Truman, ed., *The Congress and America's Future* (Prentice-Hall, 1965), p. 6; and C. Wright Mills, *The Power Elite* (Oxford University Press, 1956), p. 229.

70. Sundquist, *Politics and Policy*, p. 535; George E. Reedy, *The Twilight of the Presidency* (World, 1970), p. 130; and John F. Kennedy, quoted in Louis W. Koenig, *The Chief Executive* (Harcourt, Brace and World, 1964), p. 126.

71. Aaron Wildavsky, "The Two Presidencies," reprinted in his reader, *The Presidency* (Little, Brown, 1969), p. 230. Presidential

dominance in this area is also supported by James Robinson's findings in *Congress and Foreign Policy-Making* (Dorsey, 1967).

72. Samuel P. Huntington, *The Common Defense* (Columbia University Press, 1961), p. 124.

73. Quoted in Roger Hilsman, *The Politics of Policy Making in Defense and Foreign Affairs* (Harper & Row, 1971), p. 1.

74. Grant McConnell, *Private Power and American Democracy* (Vintage, 1966), p. 244. Other descriptions of these subgovernments may be found in Ernest S. Griffith, *The Impasse of Democracy* (Harrison-Hilton Books, 1939), p. 182; Douglass Cater, *Power in Washington* (Random House, 1964); and J. Leiper Freeman, *The Political Process* (Random House, 1965).

75. Cater, *Power in Washington,* pp. 17–18.

76. Theodore Lowi, *The End of Liberalism* (W.W. Norton, 1969), p. 112.

77. Quoted in Robert Sherrill, "Who Runs Congress?" *New York Times Magazine,* November 22, 1970, p. 85.

78. Sundquist, *Politics and Policy,* p. 490.

79. Eidenberg and Morey, *An Act of Congress,* p. 230.

80. Sundquist, *Politics and Policy,* p. 212.

81. Harris, *A Sacred Trust,* pp. 190–191.

82. Green et al., *Who Runs Congress?* pp. 114–115. For a description of this general pattern, see Louis Fisher, "The Politics of Impounded Funds" in Robert Golembiewski et al., *Public Administration* (Rand McNally, 1972), pp. 134–155; and Robert Goosetree, "The Power of the President to Impound Appropriated Funds," *American University Law Review,* January 1962, pp. 32–47.

83. James Turner, *The Chemical Feast* (Grossman, 1970), p. 52 and Chapter 3 generally.

84. Peter Grose, "Pentagon Slips Its Goodies to Its Friends," *New York Times,* April 5, 1970, Section 4, p. 2.

85. Both quotes are from Seymour Scher, "Conditions for Legislative Control," in Raymond Wolfinger, ed., *Readings on Congress* (Prentice-Hall, 1971), p. 410.

86. Wildavsky, "The Two Presidencies," p. 232.

87. *Ibid.,* p. 242.

88. Donovan, *The Politics of Poverty,* p. 37.

89. Bibby and Davidson, *On Capitol Hill,* pp. 220 and 238.

90. Sundquist, *Politics and Policy*, p. 493.

91. Rowland Evans and Robert Novak, *Lyndon B. Johnson: The Exercise of Power* (New American Library, 1966) pp. 378–379.

92. Don Riegle, *O Congress* (Doubleday, 1972), pp. 81–83.

93. Robinson, *Congress and Foreign Policy-Making*, pp. 173–174.

94. Kanter, "Congress and the Defense Budget: 1960–1970," pp. 129–143.

95. Quoted in Clapp, *The Congressman: His Work as He Sees It,* pp. 310 and 311.

96. Quoted in Richard Fenno, "Congressional Committees: A Comparative View," paper delivered at the 66th Annual Meeting of the American Political Science Association, Los Angeles, 1970, p. 20.

Index

Index

Index